The New York Times

PASSOVER
COOKBOOK

Also by *The New York Times*

Craig Claiborne's Favorites from The New York Times
by Craig Claiborne

The New New York Times **Cookbook**
by Craig Claiborne and Pierre Franey

The New York Times **Cookbook**
by Craig Claiborne

The New York Times **Heritage Cookbook**
by Jean Hewitt

The New York Times **International Cookbook**
by Craig Claiborne

The New York Times **Large Type Cookbook**
by Jean Hewitt

The New York Times **Menu Cookbook**
by Craig Claiborne

The New York Times **Natural Foods Cookbook**
by Jean Hewitt

The New York Times **Sixty-Minute Gourmet**
by Pierre Franey

The New York Times

PASSOVER

more than 200 holiday recipes from top chefs and writers

COOKBOOK

EDITED BY LINDA AMSTER

William Morrow and Company, Inc. • New York

Library of Congress Cataloging-in-Publication Data

The New York Times Passover Cookbook : more than 200 holiday recipes
    from top chefs and writers / edited by Linda Amster.
        p.   cm.
    Includes bibliographical references and index.
    ISBN 0-688-15590-1
    1. Passover cookery.   I. Amster, Linda.   II. The New York Times.
    TX739.2.P37N48   1999
    641.5'676—dc21   98-41282
                                                                  CIP

Printed in the United States of America

First Edition

                6   7   8   9   10

BOOK DESIGN BY BONNI LEON-BERMAN

www.williammorrow.com

With love and gratitude to my parents
Abraham Meyerson, from Minsk,
and
Belle Shirley Levine, from Mississippi,
for imbuing our family with a Jewish heritage
that enriches, sustains and transcends the generations

CONTENTS

ACKNOWLEDGMENTS

My thanks and appreciation to the chefs, restaurateurs, cookbook authors and other fine cooks who gave me their time and their encouragement and who allowed me to include their recipes in this book.

Special thanks to Joan Nathan, not only for her illuminating Introduction about Passover ritual and cuisine, but for her advice on many aspects of the cookbook. She was unfailingly generous with her time and expertise. My gratitude also to Florence Fabricant of *The Times* for reading the recipes and offering suggestions that were essential to the shaping of the book.

I am indebted to Rabbi Shmuel Singer of the Union of Orthodox Jewish Congregations of America for his invaluable guidance about the ingredients in this book.

My deep appreciation to Rabbi Jeffery Wohlberg of Adas Israel Congregation in Washington, D.C., for his helpful comments. And immense gratitude and thanks to Judy Wohlberg for her indispensable suggestions about many of the recipes.

At William Morrow, my editor, Justin Schwartz, provided uniformity to recipes that came from scores of sources, to give them coherence as a book. Christy Stabin ably assisted in the production process, and Sonia Greenbaum's copyediting was an invaluable contribution to these pages. Sincerest appreciation and thanks to all of them.

Very special thanks to Jane Slotin, who was vital to the preparation of this book—downloading recipes, working with the manuscript, offering ideas about content and organization and acting as a sounding board and cheerleader. Her contributions were incalculable.

I am also grateful to Patricia Tobias for putting the recipes from clippings and other print sources into electronic form and for her suggestions and support. Also at *The Times*, my appreciation to Carlos Briceno and to Dennis Laurie for their assistance.

Words cannot express how very thankful I am for the many dear friends who were a constant source of encouragement and my special gratitude to Judy Knipe, Ann Bramson and Sydney Miner, who also generously shared the knowledge they have gained from their experiences as cookbook editors.

My deep appreciation and thanks to Mitchel Levitas, Editorial Director of Book

Development at *The Times*, who took the idea I had presented to him and turned it into a reality, shepherding it through every stage. For all his efforts and for his confidence in the book and in me, I am extremely grateful.

Finally and especially, most loving thanks to Mort Sheinman who, more than anyone can imagine, made this book possible. His consummate editing, astute advice and abiding support are reflected on every page.

PREFACE

Passover has always been a holiday that evokes cherished memories for me, from the family around a small table when I was a child, to the larger gathering of friends, family—and, sometimes, even strangers—at my own Seders. There is always enormous satisfaction in sharing not only the yearly rituals that bind generations, but also the foods cooked especially for the holiday. In my parents' home, the menu rarely strayed from the traditional. The gefilte fish, the chicken soup with matzoh balls, the roast chicken, the tsimmes, the potato kugel and the sponge cake were as much a part of Passover as the Four Questions—and almost as unvarying.

But as the years passed and my range of experience broadened, new dishes slowly became a part of my Passover repertoire—many of them clipped from the food pages of *The New York Times* and passed from friend to friend. As those clippings became food-stained or brittle or misplaced, the idea of this cookbook began to take shape. It would be a compilation of the best Passover recipes that have appeared in *The Times* over the years. Going through articles dating back decades, I found a bountiful trove of holiday dishes that included the traditional food of my childhood as well as more current innovative fare.

Passover food coverage in *The Times* has evolved from an occasional recipe tucked away on the "women's pages"—instructions for a familiar favorite like gefilte fish (spelled "gefulte" in a 1953 article)—to today's major features that highlight diverse and sophisticated variations of Passover cuisine. The change in coverage began in the 1970s, thanks largely to Craig Claiborne, then the newspaper's renowned food editor, whose in-depth profiles of Jewish homemakers included recipes for several of their holiday specialties. For example, his 1974 interview with Mrs. Baruch Zeger, a splendid cook and the mother of novelist Erich Segal, featured some of her favorite Seder recipes. Judging from readers' responses, they were extremely popular, and when Craig Claiborne reprinted them in a book, he proclaimed her chocolate cake "indeed exceptional."

Since then, *The Times*'s coverage of Passover food has expanded greatly. Originally it focused on the traditional dishes served at Ashkenazic Seders in the New York metropolitan area. But a more inclusive coverage has introduced readers to the diverse cuisines of Seders held in other parts of the world: by Ashkenazim in France and other European nations, by Sephardim in Italy, Greece and other Mediterranean countries and by Jews from Yemen, Turkey, Iran and other parts of the Middle East. And while the recipes in early Passover articles were almost exclusively those of accomplished home cooks—usually for traditional dishes like gefilte fish and sponge cake—more recent articles also feature the original recipes of celebrated chefs, restaurateurs and cookbook authors. Combining new ingredients as well as time-tested ones, they provide fresh and contemporary versions of traditional holiday fare. For example, Wolfgang Puck's gefilte fish is served in cabbage leaves—a novel variation of the traditional meat-stuffed cabbage served in many Jewish households. And Paul Prudhomme's recipe for veal roast with mango sauce, which he created for a dinner in Jerusalem to mark the city's three thousandth anniversary, brilliantly combines a familiar cut of meat with unexpected ingredients for a dish that is as delectable as it is original. Chef Prudhomme says he considers this a very special recipe, one for which he has strong "sentimental" feelings because of the occasion for which he was asked to create it.

Some Passover recipes that appeared in *The Times* were omitted in this book to avoid duplication. Many of the recipes for haroseth published over the years, for example, were too similar to one another to justify including them. Occasionally, a recipe was excluded because it violated the laws of kashrut—for example, combining dairy and meat, which is forbidden.

To augment the recipes that appeared in the newspaper, there is a selection of imaginative dishes that complement and enhance the Passover table, reprinted from cookbooks by three of *The Times*'s past and present food critics and columnists, Craig Claiborne, Mimi Sheraton and Molly O'Neill.

The only foods that are *hametz*—universally forbidden by biblical law at Passover—are fermented or leavened wheat, rye, oats, spelt and barley, and their related products. After that, the rules are defined by each community: Jews who observe Ashkenazic rabbinical tradition will not eat any grains, including corn and rice, or any legumes and many seeds during Passover. Depending on the local traditions, Sephardic Jews and Middle Eastern Jews may or may not exclude some or all of these foods from their Passover menus and may use ingredients in their Passover dishes that observant Jews in other communities will not eat during the holiday. Some recipes in this book contain the following ingredients, which fall into this category: allspice, chili powder, cloves, cumin, ground coriander, fennel, nutmeg, orange blossom water, rose water, sesame seeds, turmeric, crystallized ginger, glacéed kumquats and dried cranberries.

To further complicate matters, the list of foods that are labeled kosher for Passover continues to change as the Union of Orthodox Jewish Congregations bestows certification on more products. So, a dessert that calls for confectioners' sugar is now permissible—if the sugar has been made without cornstarch and bears the kosher-for-Passover designation—whereas a few years ago that ingredient would have been unthinkable in a kosher Passover recipe.

Given such complexities, some recipes in this book may be acceptable to one community of Jews, but not to another. Although I have consulted a number of religious authorities to ensure that the ingredients are permissible at Passover to one or more communities, it is the ultimate responsibility of the reader to ascertain if a particular recipe meets the Passover dietary standards that he or she observes.

Because of the long time span over which these recipes were originally published, and because they come from so many different sources, there are a few inconsistencies in terminology, but they are minor and should pose no problem in preparation of the dishes. For convenience, the instructions of some older recipes, calling for manual chopping, slicing and pureeing, have been replaced with updated techniques using the food processor.

Similarly, the professional or personal identifications of many contributors have changed since their recipes were first published in *The Times*. I have updated the information wherever I could, but when that was not possible, I have continued to identify them as they were in the original article.

To aid the reader, all recipes are labeled Meat, Dairy and/or Pareve (acceptable with either meat or dairy dishes). Those with more than one designation contain either an optional dairy ingredient (such as butter) or an optional meat ingredient (such as chicken broth) that may be omitted to change the category of the dish.

Many aspects of Passover have remained constant through the centuries. The symbolism of the food on the Seder plate has not changed since the Exodus from Egypt, for example. Other characteristics of the holiday, however—the emergence of the role of women in the Seder ritual and the increasing diversity of the food—continue to evolve. Such transitions are reflected in four essays—three of them written for this book—that personalize the Passover experience. In her Introduction, Joan Nathan, a noted authority on Jewish cuisine, explains the Seder ritual, dietary laws and other aspects of Passover in the context of how her family observes the holiday; Ruth Reichl, *The Times*'s current restaurant critic, movingly recounts the way she unexpectedly came to appreciate the significance of the Seder—which in the past she had always found interminable—in a Charleston, South Carolina, garden; Molly O'Neill, who writes the food column for the paper's Sunday *Magazine*, presents a warm and revealing account of lessons that she, the Christian wife of a Jewish husband, has learned as she incorporates the Seder tradition into her life; and Mimi Sheraton, in the chapter reprinted from her memoir, *From My Mother's Kitchen,* lovingly reminiscences about the Passovers of her childhood in her family's observant home.

As each of those essays makes abundantly clear, individual feelings about Passover and its rituals can vary widely. So, too, can the foods with which the holiday is celebrated, as readers will see in the following pages.

For those whose tastes run to the traditional, there is a broad selection of recipes that go back countless generations. For those who are comfortable trying new variations of enduring dishes, there are modern versions with new and exciting combinations of ingredients.

Finally, for everyone, there is a wish for a *zissen Pesach*, "a sweet Passover," with good food, with loved ones and with the joy of peace.

—LINDA AMSTER

INTRODUCTION
OBSERVING PASSOVER

By JOAN NATHAN

Ask me about the highlight of my family's year, and the Passover Seder invariably comes to mind. We plan for it months ahead. How many people can we invite this year? Do we have fifty guests already? Do we move the living room to the dining room to accommodate the guests? Who is going to play Moses in our children's play between the main course and the dessert? We talk about the Haggadah—the narrative of the story of the flight from Egypt that describes how the Seder should be conducted. The whole family thinks spring cleaning: readying the house from top to bottom for this ancient festival where the Book of Exodus 12:15 tells us that "the first day ye shall put away leaven out of your houses; for whosoever eateth leavened bread from the first day until the seventh day, that soul shall be cut off from Israel." Jews in America interpret removing the *hametz*, the leaven or ferment, in many different ways. I start cleaning my house just after Purim. I leave the kitchen for last and let my twelve-year-old, David, check all boxed and canned goods to determine which are not kosher for Passover.

Unlike the ancient Israelites who, according to the Book of Exodus, had a simple meal of roast lamb, unleavened bread and bitter herbs, we prepare a complicated, symbolic meal and gather friends and family from afar.

When I plan the Seder menu, I often daydream about the ancient Israelites, who could not go to a grocery store to buy their flour. I imagine them trying to use up their flour before Passover in anticipation of the new wheat they would harvest from the spring crops. My mind paints a picture of Seders in the desert, where the Hebrews gathered the tender new spring greens (a bitter green that today the Arabs call *marora*). I can almost see them placing their flatbread—dough made of flour and water stretched on a disk—over an open fire, then eating this "matzoh" before dawn. "And they shall eat the flesh in that night, roast with fire, and unleavened bread; with bitter herbs they shall eat it" (Exodus 12:8). Today, although we sit comfortably in our dining rooms, eat from fine porcelain and create numerous courses for our celebration, Passover retains its ancient power as a festival of redemption from slavery and as a reminder of the laws handed down from Mount Sinai. It also celebrates the renewal of the home in harmony with nature, as spring renews the world.

For the past fifteen years or so, my husband and I have held Seders in our own home. I have also attended Russian Seders in Israel; French Seders in Paris; Moroccan, Iraqi and Iranian Seders in the United States, and, of course, the Seder of Holocaust survivors from Poland, where my in-laws were born. Each of them recalls the common Jewish heritage of failure and triumph, suffering and joy during this holiday of redemption.

Celebrated to commemorate the Exodus of the Jews from Egypt and their subsequent escape to the Wilderness, the first two nights of Passover provide Jews with the opportunity to teach their children about the Egyptian captivity, the miraculous survival of the Jews as God "passed over" their homes when He slew the firstborn of the Egyptians, and the flight of the Jews from Egypt into the land of Israel. Jews call the holiday Pesach, which comes from "passing over."

Passover, like many holidays, is layered. Two other names for the festival are Hag-Hamazot (Feast of the Unleavened Bread) and Hag-Haaviv (Spring Festival), a time of new grass, new lambs and growth in general in the desert.

The word *Seder*, or "order," refers to the rules that govern every aspect of the meal and its accompanying ritual. In Israel, Passover originally was celebrated as a pilgrimage festival to the Temple in Jerusalem. Josephus, the Roman Jewish historian who lived in the first century c.e. (Common Era), relates that hundreds of thousands of Jews brought lambs to be sacrificed in commemoration of the sacrifice eaten the night before the Exodus. The Dead Sea Scrolls tell us that the lamb had to be one year old.

According to Josephus, the Passover Seder moved to the home about twenty years after the destruction of the Second Temple in 70 c.e., when the Jews were banished from Jerusalem and forbidden to observe their religion. They fled once again and settled in Europe, the Middle East and North Africa. A family ritual around the table replaced the festival held by pilgrims at the Temple in Jerusalem.

Every civilization encountered by the Jews in their Diaspora (dispersion) has left its mark on the customs and food of the Seders. In Greco-Roman times, participants reclined on soft sofas, and it was in this period that wine, known since ancient times, became part of the ritual. Most likely the wine was not the sweet wine that Americans sip at their Seder while their children are given grape juice. Wine varied geographically. Some Jews made wine from raisins; others from varietal grapes. What makes the wine kosher is that a Sabbath-observant Jew makes it from the start of the process.

In Eastern Europe, Jews generally eat matzoh balls in their soup, while Sephardim—Jews from Spain and Portugal who later moved to Greece, the Levant and England—often put broken pieces of matzoh in their egg-lemon soup. Some Jews from the Middle East prepare fava bean dishes for Passover, while those from Eastern Europe reject any dish made of beans. Passover cakes made by the Sephardim often include almonds and oranges; those from Eastern Europe are more likely to be made with walnuts and apples. Horseradish is the bitter herb favored by the Eastern Europeans, while the Sephardim and Jews from the Middle East often choose hearts of romaine. The ingredients of the haroseth (clay), a nut and fruit paste made to commemorate the mortar used by the Israelites in Egypt to build the pyramids, vary as well. Different combinations of raisins, nuts, dates, apples, pears, figs, pomegranates, spices, and vinegar or wine are prepared by Jews from different countries. Lamb is eaten by the Sephardim, but roast lamb is avoided by most Eastern European Jews until the Temple of Jerusalem is rebuilt. Fish, which is often baked with fragrant spices and fresh vegetables, appears on Polish Jewish menus as gefilte fish, and as sweet-and-sour carp for Jews who hail from Alsace or southern Germany.

However different the specific foods served, the story as well as the structure of the meal is always the same, and the Passover table is as beautiful as the family can make it. It is compared to an altar in the Temple and set with the finest white cloths, china, glassware, silver and candlesticks. One of my best memories of Passover Seders is the beautiful table set by my own mother with a profusion of spring flowers in the center. Traditional families have separate sets of dishes, cutlery and cooking utensils for Passover. These are kept carefully packed away the rest of the year. In my own home, with my mammoth Seder, it has become a ritual for a friend, who has shared the holiday with us for over fifteen years, to help set the tables. First, we fit the tables together to form a grand "C" around the living room. Then we cover the tables with white cloths and stuff bright napkins into the wineglasses, arrange vases of spring flowers picked from the garden (I use tiny vases so that the guests can see each other), place copies of the Haggadah (literally, "the telling of the story of the Exodus") around, and make the seating arrangements with the place cards the children have decorated. I recently learned that there are over 3,000 versions of the Haggadah! From the basement I take out a box of Haggadot past (ones my children decorated in nursery school) to scatter around the room. I also bring out the matzoh cover embroidered by my mother-in-law, my father's Bar Mitzvah cup (we use it as the cup for Elijah the Prophet, who is a harbinger both of freedom and the Messiah), and my grandmother's brass candlesticks. She brought them with her on her journey to America from Cracow, Poland, in the great migration of Eastern European Jews at the turn of the century.

Two of the central elements of the Seder, besides the recounting of the tale of the Exodus of the Jews from Egypt to the children present, are the eating of the matzoh and the drinking of four cups of wine poured during the service for each person. Each cup symbolizes one of the four divine promises of redemption found in the Scripture in connection with Israel's liberation from Egypt. "I will bring you out . . . I will deliver you . . . I will redeem you . . . I will take you to me" (Exodus 6:6–7). The fifth cup of wine is poured for the prophet Elijah. It represents a fifth divine promise that follows the above four; "I will bring you to the Promised Land" (Exodus 6:8). The four cups of wine signify that the Seder night is protected from evil; the fifth cup, Elijah's cup, signifies the continued safety of the community. At some stage of the Seder service, the door is opened so Elijah may appear as a messenger of God to announce the arrival of the Messiah. One of my favorite childhood memories is of watching for the wine in Elijah's cup to go down.

Many feminists today have also introduced the cup of Miriam, in honor of Moses' sister. She played a central role in the lives of Moses and the Jewish people, especially ensuring that they had water in the desert. Miriam's cup is, therefore, filled with water.

At our table, to the right of my husband, Allan, who leads the ceremony, are placed a bottle of sweet wine; a bottle of the good varietal kosher wines from California, Israel or Europe; three matzohs wrapped in a cover, and the Seder tray or plate, which holds the five symbolic foods described during the service. Many of these foods are imbued with multiple meanings derived from the hope and abundance of spring, coupled with new meanings imposed upon them by Jewish history. They thus appear paradoxical, and mirror the Jews' moral position as faithful worshipers, worthy of God's love and aid, and their historical position as perpetual exiles and wanderers. Pain and exile are wedded to hope, deliverance and change.

The foods on the plate are the *zeroa*, or roasted lamb shank bone; *karpas* (parsley, chervil, celery, or potatoes); *betzah* (a roasted egg); *maror* (a bitter herb; generally chicory, cress or horseradish); and *haroseth* (a paste made of nuts and fruits, wine or vinegar).

THE ZEROA, or "forearm," represents the Paschal lamb that in ancient times was sacrificed in the Temple of Jerusalem. The word "forearm" refers to the outstretched arm of God when He delivered the Israelites from Egypt. Zeroa has another, perhaps darker, meaning: it symbolizes the miracle that spared the Jews when God passed over the Jewish houses and slew the firstborn of the Egyptians. To identify themselves to God, the Israelites were told to smear the blood of a lamb on the doorposts of their houses so that the Angel of Death would pass them by.

KARPAS, generally spring greens—but sometimes potatoes in houses of Jews from Poland and Russia, as a reminder of the lack of greens in Eastern Europe in early spring— are dipped into salt water. As the symbol of the covenant between God and His priests, salt is believed to purify what it touches, to ward off evil. Here it also serves to recall the tears shed by the Israelites, who were forced to labor as slaves for the Egyptians, and the compassion the Jews should feel for the Egyptians slain by the Angel of Death. Paradoxically, the greens—here associated with death and oppression—are the symbol of rebirth in springtime. Thus they offer hope for the future along with remembrance of a bitter past.

BETZAH, the roasted egg, is a symbol of the destroyed Temple in Jerusalem, as well as the festival sacrifices. But once again, because the egg is also a symbol of rebirth, its presence is a reminder of a future promise as well as a past tragedy. In my house I hard-boil the egg, dry it, then place a lighted match underneath it to singe it.

MAROR, bitter herbs such as horseradish or the heart of romaine, recall the bitterness of slavery in Egypt. Once again these young greens, reminders of what grows in the desert only in the months of March and April, are harbingers of spring and renewal.

HAROSETH, or clay, is usually a mixture of fruit, nuts, wine or vinegar. It represents the mortar the Jews used to build the pyramids in Egypt. To me, more than any other food, haroseth represents the Diaspora of the Jewish people. These dipping pastes, not part of the original Seder, probably came into the service during the Greco-Roman period. Iraqi Jews make theirs from slow-cooked dates turned into molasses; the Egyptians, from nuts, raisins and dates. Venetians include pine nuts and chestnuts in theirs, and the majority of Eastern European Jews use a recipe with nuts, apples, sweet wine and cinnamon. As Jews traveled throughout the world, they changed the haroseth recipe, depending upon what foods were available to them. In the United States, where we have the luxury of so many ingredients and so many recipes, I try to include at least three types of haroseth at my Seder—and, to my children's chagrin, I describe the journey of these dishes each year.

Though the Seder plate describes the ritual, the most important food on the table is matzoh. Made without yeast and quickly baked, matzoh is the unleavened bread of affliction eaten under the pharaohs' rule. It reminds us that the Jews fleeing Egypt had no time to leaven their bread and bake it properly. The three pieces of matzoh are placed in separate folds of a tripartite cloth or napkin, symbolizing the three classes of Jews: the Kohanim, or priests; the Levites, or warriors; and the Israelites, the rest of the population. Matzoh is eaten at the very beginning of the Seder, right after karpas (parsley or celery dipped in salted water). It is also the last thing taken at the end of the meal.

Also at the beginning of the Seder, the central matzoh is broken in half and the larger half—called the *afikomen* (Greek for dessert)—is hidden. After dinner is over, everyone goes to look for the afikomen.

Every year before the Seder, my husband purchases a small gift for each child attending, with one larger gift for the winner of the search. He hides the afikomen, and at the end of the Seder, the children scramble throughout the house looking for it. The anticipation of finding the hidden afikomen and winning the prize helps keep the children alert during the Seder meal.

In ancient times a woman in childbirth would bite into this matzoh for good luck. During the Middle Ages, Jews used it as an amulet, hanging it in the house or carrying a piece in a pouch or wallet. Venetian Jews continue this custom today.

The first food eaten is a symbolic sandwich of matzoh and the bitter herbs, which have been dipped in or spread with the haroseth and shaken dry. The sage Hillel insisted that such a combination be eaten in order to fulfill the commandment to eat bitter herbs and unleavened bread together. Through this dramatic act, like so many others at the Seder meal, each family is connected to the significant story of the Passover and symbolically relives its history.

The matzoh used in modern Sederim is generally crisp, square and delicate. It is quite different from the thick, rough, circular matzoh made by the ancient Israelites. Some Jews still make the handmade *shmurah*, "watched" or "guarded," matzoh. Closer to that which the ancient Israelites ate, shmurah matzoh differs from the commercial products both in its texture and appearance, and in the fact that the wheat is "watched" or "guarded" from the moment of its harvesting to ensure that it comes into no contact with water. Contaminants in such water might cause the flour to expand, and therefore rise. Leavened flour is prohibited during Passover. Machine-made matzoh is also "watched" from the moment it is brought into the mill for grinding. The mills reserved to grind the Passover flour are carefully cleaned. Workers, versed in the traditional rules, operate the machines while reciting, "For the sake of the mitzvah" (traditional obligation). Whether made by hand or machine, the matzohs require water; and the water, mixed with flour to make the dough, must sit for twenty-four hours with no foreign elements allowed to contaminate it. The flour is then set aside, carefully protected from contamination and held until the time comes to make Passover products.

The entire process—from the first step of mixing flour and water, through the piercing of holes and baking—must take no more than eighteen minutes from start to finish. Extending the time could cause the bread to rise, making it no longer fit for Passover. For this reason, matzoh dough is kneaded only on one side. The specification of eighteen minutes, like so many other rules, has more than one meaning. In Hebrew, the number 18 also represents *chai*, the symbol for life.

The night before the first Seder, pieces of bread are hidden in every room in the house. *Bedikat Hametz*, the search for leavening and for any wheat or crumbs left from the past year, is the final act of housecleaning for Passover the following year.

The search for leaven is a bit like a game and helps, once again, to focus the children's attention on the coming festival. Some people use a candle and a feathery brush for the search. When all the hametz is gathered together, it is removed from the house. The next day, the head of the household recites a blessing over it. He declares the house purified and burns the hametz.

Although all Jews regard matzoh as central to their Passover cuisine, in America today only the very traditional follow all the biblical injunctions literally. Some, for example, will not eat any matzohs made with eggs or additives of any kind, nor will they turn matzohs into matzoh balls or matzoh kugels or tortes because of the possibility that the additional ingredients might cause fermentation. They also refrain from cooking matzohs with other ingredients.

The injunction against leavening is joined to a prohibition against the consumption of all grains except that of wheat made into matzoh. Thus, regular flour is prohibited, and most observant American Jews never eat rice, corn, peas, lentils, chick-peas and dried beans on Passover.

The Sephardim eat most vegetables, and many serve rice at their Seders. Although rice is a grain, when dampened with water or any fluid, it rots rather than ferments. That technically would put rice beyond the prohibition. Nevertheless, Ashkenazi Jews forbid these grains and the vegetables listed above because they traditionally believe that allowing such foods might create confusion.

The existence of so much variation in custom suggests that, despite the considerable constraints of Passover, there is and always has been room for interpretation and change within the specified rules and forms of the Passover ritual. In recent years, for example, feminists have conducted their own women's Seders. At some Seders non-Jews are often invited to take part, and participants often present writings of their own, or they may read passages from other relevant literary works on slavery or redemption. At our Seder my husband asks people to talk about their own year, and what examples of slavery or freedom have passed in the world.

One of our most cherished family traditions is played out between the main course and the dessert. All the children present reenact the story of the Exodus from Egypt. My three joined the cast as soon as they learned to talk! The actors range in age from four to twenty-four, as even returning college students participate in this entertainment ritual.

This ability to allow changes within the structure keeps the Seder energized and fresh. It has also produced an innovative and tasty cuisine as Jews found new foods, new combinations and new ways of cooking to enrich their festival. As the recipes in this book demonstrate, each family has its own culinary traditions and its own way of conducting the meal. Some enact the entire ritual and the meal goes on for hours; others enjoy a shorter version. Many families have Seders on both nights of the holidays, a custom derived as Jews moved farther away from the land of Israel. Wanting to be correct on the date of the Seder and not fail to perform it at the specified time, many Jews took to celebrating on two nights. Some repeat the same menu; others with more time or resources prepare two different meals. Here, again, flexibility has transformed what was once an economic choice into a tradition that blends memory, history and family.

In our family I prepare one Seder for the first night, and we go to a friend's Seder for the second night. My Seder menu is usually the same: hard-boiled eggs dipped in salt water, my mother-in-law's homemade Polish-style gefilte fish with horseradish, her chicken soup with matzoh balls, my mother's brisket or turkey with matzoh, mushroom stuffing, asparagus and a vegetable kugel. There is a panoply of desserts, including a flourless chocolate torte or roll, a lemon almond torte, and *chremslach* with prunes, a hand-me-down recipe from my father's family in Germany. Through the years these recipes from both our backgrounds have created our own family traditions for our children. During the rest of the week we experiment with new or other traditional ethnic Jewish Passover recipes. We hope that the recipes provided in this book will not only enhance your own Seder but will help link you to the past, as well as to introduce some exciting new dishes to create your own Passover traditions.

HAROSETH

Haroseth symbolizes the mortar used by Israelite slaves in Egypt, but its taste evokes the sweetness of freedom. Ashkenazic haroseth, made with apples, nuts, seasonings and sweet wine, is universal for Jews of eastern European origin. But Sephardic and Mizrachi haroseth recipes vary greatly according to the country of origin—and sometimes the town or family. Halek, the Iraqi version, is one of the oldest and most time-consuming haroseth recipes. Dating back at least to the Babylonian exile in 579 B.C.E., this date jam, like those from grapes, pomegranates and bee honey, was a sweetener in the ancient world. It is still served today in various forms by Iraqi, Syrian, Burmese and Indian Jews. Yemenites may include cloves and pepper. Venetians add chestnuts and pine nuts, and those in the Dutch West Indies add coconut. At many American Seders, more than one version of the sweet blend of fruit and nuts is served as a delicious way to evoke the Diaspora.

Leftover haroseth makes a wonderful chicken stuffing, or a marvelous fruit topping for pot roast.

MIMI SHERATON'S ASHKENAZIC HAROSETH pareve

(FROM *FROM MY MOTHER'S KITCHEN*)

Renowned food authority Mimi Sheraton, formerly *The Times*'s restaurant critic, serves this classic American version of the apple-nut haroseth of Eastern European origin.

> 3 medium apples (1 pound) preferably McIntosh or Northern Spy
> ½ cup chopped walnuts
> ¼ to ½ teaspoon powdered ginger
> ¼ to ½ teaspoon powdered cinnamon
> 1½ tablespoons sugar to taste
> 3 tablespoons red Concord grape wine

1. Peel, core and chop the apples moderately coarse. In a bowl, toss with the chopped walnuts. Mix in the ginger, cinnamon, and sugar to taste.

2. Stir in 2 tablespoons red wine and adjust the seasoning. This should ripen in the refrigerator, covered, for at least 6 hours before it is served and is even better if it stands for 24 hours. Before serving, stir in the remaining 1 tablespoon wine.

makes about 1½ cups

MS

NATHAN FAMILY'S
HAROSETH BALLS pareve
(FROM *JEWISH COOKING IN AMERICA*)

Joan Nathan, whose cookbooks and public television series have popularized Jewish cooking in America, is an expert in Jewish culinary history. Her Passover recipes for *The Times* often include background about the origins of the dishes—as does this one, from the family of Emily Solis Nathan (no relation to her), whose lineage can be traced back to the Spanish and Portuguese Jews who arrived in Dutch New Amsterdam in the 1650s. This version of haroseth resembles the one described in the first kosher cookbook published in the United States, *The Jewish Cookery Book*, written in 1871 by Esther Jacobs Levy, as a "mixture made of chopped apples and raisins, and almonds rolled in cinnamon balls."

> 3 cups raisins
> 2 cups blanched almonds
> ½ apple, peeled, cored and quartered
> ½ teaspoon cinnamon, or to taste

   1. Grind the raisins and 1½ cups of the almonds together in a meat grinder (see Note). Put in a bowl.
   2. Grate the apple into the raisins and almonds and add the cinnamon. Mix well to combine.
   3. Using your hands, press the mixture into 1-inch balls. Using the remaining almonds, press one into each haroseth ball. There will be haroseth left over.

NOTE: Although members of the Nathan family never use a food processor for their haroseth, it is a little easier than the meat grinder: coarsely grind the raisins, 1½ cups almonds, apple and cinnamon as in Steps 1 and 2, using quick pulses so as not to overprocess.

   makes about 6 dozen haroseth balls

JN

RODEN FAMILY'S
EGYPTIAN HAROSETH pareve

(FROM *THE BOOK OF JEWISH FOOD*)

Claudia Roden, who was born into a giant extended family in Cairo that had for generations worked with ancient trade routes from the Iberian Peninsula to Asia, specializes in cookbooks about Sephardic and Middle Eastern cuisines. Her haroseth, an heirloom recipe from her mother, has a jamlike texture.

1 cup (½ pound) tightly packed, pitted dates
1½ cups (½ pound) tightly packed raisins
¾ cup sweet red wine
½ cup chopped walnuts for garnish

1. Finely chop dates and raisins. Put them into a heavy-bottomed pot with enough water to cover and leave them to soak overnight.

2. The following day, bring them to a boil in the same water. Simmer over very low heat, stirring occasionally with a wooden spoon to prevent the fruit from burning, and squashing it to a smooth, thick paste against the sides of the pan. Continue cooking and stirring until all liquid is dissolved, 10 to 15 minutes. Set aside to cool.

3. Remove to a serving bowl. Stir in the wine and garnish with walnuts just before serving.

makes 3 cups

LS

HAROSETH EDDA pareve
(FROM *THE CLASSIC CUISINE OF THE ITALIAN JEWS*)

Edda Servi Machlin, the daughter and granddaughter of rabbis, can trace her lineage in Italy back nine generations. An authority on the cuisine of her heritage, this haroseth reflects her Italian roots.

½ pound pitted dates
½ pound walnut meats
3 large apples, cored and peeled
1 large unpeeled seedless orange, washed very well and quartered
2 large bananas, peeled
½ cup sweet Malaga wine
½ teaspoon cinnamon
⅛ teaspoon ground cloves
1 tablespoon fresh lemon juice
Matzoh meal as needed

1. Chop the dates, walnuts, apples and orange very fine using a food processor. Transfer to a bowl.

2. Mash the bananas and add to the fruit and nut mixture. Add the wine, cinnamon, cloves and lemon juice, and mix well.

3. Add matzoh meal as needed to make a mortarlike paste.

makes 12 servings

MB

ANNE ROSENZWEIG'S HAROSETH pareve

Anne Rosenzweig, one of New York City's outstanding restaurateurs, created a version of haroseth that she says reminds her "not only of slavery and freedom in Egypt, but also of spring in the United States. That's why I added rhubarb."

1 cup sugar
1 cup water
1 cup diced rhubarb (see Note)
1 cup Riesling or other off-dry white wine
1 cup toasted pecans (see Note)
1 Granny Smith apple, peeled, cored and diced
1 cup diced jícama
1 teaspoon cinnamon
1 pinch cayenne pepper

1. In a saucepan, bring the sugar and water to a boil. Reduce the heat and simmer, uncovered, for 5 minutes. Stir in the rhubarb, and simmer for 1 or 2 minutes until soft but still crunchy. Drain and cool.

2. In another saucepan, cook the wine over high heat until it is reduced to ¼ cup. In a food processor, combine the reduced wine, pecans, apple, jícama, cinnamon, cayenne pepper and rhubarb, and pulse 2 or 3 times. Remove to bowl. If desired, add a little more sugar.

NOTE: When buying rhubarb, look for firm, shiny stalks. Take care to trim off any leaves because they contain high concentrations of oxalic acid, which can be toxic. Do not remove the strings from the stalks because they hold most of the color and will dissolve during cooking.

NOTE: To toast nuts, preheat oven to 450°F. Place nuts on a cookie sheet on the middle rack and toast for 4 to 5 minutes. Shake pan occasionally and watch nuts to make sure they don't burn. Remove nuts from oven and allow to cool for about 10 minutes.

makes 8 to 10 servings

JN

IRMA CARDOZO'S HAROSETH pareve

Irma Cardozo, whose husband, Abraham Lopes Cardozo, was the former minister of the Sephardic congregation in Surinam, cherishes this recipe. The coconut, dried fruit and cherry preserves are common in Surinam, where generations of her family have lived since 1492.

10 ounces sweetened grated coconut
7 ounces almonds, ground
3 cups water, approximately
8 ounces mixed dried fruits, preferably pitted prunes and dried apples, coarsely chopped
8 ounces raisins
7 ounces dried apricots, coarsely chopped
8 ounces dried pears, coarsely chopped
2 to 3 teaspoons cinnamon
12 ounces cherry preserves
⅔ cup Malaga wine or other sweet wine

1. In a large, heavy pot, combine all the ingredients except the jam and wine, add water to cover. Simmer over low heat until the mixture begins to thicken, stirring occasionally with a wooden spoon.

2. Add additional water as the mixture thickens to prevent it from drying out or sticking to the pot. Continue stirring.

3. After about 45 minutes, stir in the cherry preserves. Cook approximately 15 minutes longer until the coconut has softened and the mixture is extremely thick. Let stand and cool. Stir in the wine. The mixture should be moist and thick.

4. Refrigerate until serving. After the haroseth has been refrigerated, it often needs additional wine to remoisten it. Serve at room temperature.

makes 5 cups

MB

LARRY BAIN'S GRANDMOTHER'S HAROSETH pareve

Some of San Francisco's fine chefs began celebrating Passover together when chef-restaurateurs Larry Bain and his wife, Catherine Pantsios, moved to San Francisco from New York City and invited other Jewish chefs there to celebrate the Seder. Among them were Joyce Goldstein and Barbara Tropp, whose Seder recipes also appear in this book. This is an adaptation of the haroseth his grandmother served.

½ pound walnuts
¼ pound dried apricots
¼ pound dried pitted prunes
¼ pound pitted dates
3 whole apples, peeled, cored and quartered
1 large unpeeled seedless orange, washed and quartered
½ cup sweet Passover red wine
2 tablespoons brandy
½ teaspoon cinnamon
⅛ teaspoon ground cloves
⅛ teaspoon nutmeg
1 tablespoon fresh lime juice
2 tablespoons matzoh meal, or as needed

1. Using the steel blade of a food processor or other chopper, chop very fine, but not to a paste, the walnuts, apricots, prunes, dates, apples and orange. This may be done in batches, if necessary.

2. In a bowl, combine the chopped fruits and nuts with the wine, brandy, cinnamon, cloves, nutmeg and lime juice. If necessary, add matzoh meal to make a mortarlike consistency.

makes 6 cups

JN

YEMENITE HAROSETH pareve

Ruth Messinger, the Manhattan borough president, serves this Yemenite haroseth, which has a touch of cayenne pepper.

24 dried figs
24 pitted dates
½ cup sesame seeds
4 teaspoons honey
2 teaspoons ground ginger
½ teaspoon ground coriander
¼ teaspoon cayenne pepper, or more to taste

1. In food processor, grind the figs and dates to a sticky paste.
2. Place in a bowl and mix in the rest of the ingredients. Cover and store refrigerated for up to 2 weeks. Serve at room temperature.

makes 2½ cups

MB

GEFILTE FISH AND HORSERADISH

classic, variations, alternatives

For many Jews with Eastern European roots, Passover without gefilte fish is like Hanukkah without latkes. And gefilte fish without horseradish is like latkes without applesauce or sour cream.

Gefilte means "stuffed," and originally, gefilte fish was a kind of fish mousse cooked in the fish skin. As with many recipes that are handed down generation after generation, there is no consensus on how it should taste. Some like it sweet, others don't. However, it is traditionally made with freshwater fish—whitefish, pike and carp are most often used—the kinds of fish that were most readily available in Eastern Europe. Whitefish makes the mixture softer; carp adds flavor and richness but darkens the color of the mixture. For variation, other fish, like salmon, are also suitable.

When preparing gefilte fish, be sure the mixture is well seasoned. But never taste the raw mixture of freshwater fish; it must be cooked to destroy any parasites that are present. Poach a teaspoonful in a little stock or water, let it cool briefly, and then taste. Gefilte fish is best made a day in advance. Although chilling it thoroughly improves the texture, it should not be served ice cold.

For variations on tradition, try a gefilte fish terrine or a soufflé or loaf. For something different, consider Barry Wine's matzoh-meal crepes filled with gefilte fish, and Wolfgang Puck's gefilte fish–stuffed cabbage leaves. And for a fishless gefilte fish, you can make a mock version of veal and chicken.

If you prefer something else, there are numerous delicious fish alternatives to gefilte fish: pickled smoked salmon, salmon pâté, trout roulades with whitefish mousse, carp in parsley sauce. Some of these appetizers make excellent lunch courses when served in larger portions.

horseradish

As for the horseradish, this traditional accompaniment can be freshly grated or store-bought, white or reddened with beet. A word of caution about preparation: homemade horseradish is a much more forceful seasoning than the bottled variety. It requires careful preparation because the fumes released during the grating process may be nearly overpowering. If you are making it at home, cut the root into small cubes and grate them in a food processor, using the knife blade and an on-off pulse motion. The lid should be removed slowly, with your face averted from the machine. To avoid being overcome by the fumes, you might also want to place a damp towel over your nose and mouth. Allow the freshly grated horseradish to sit in the processor 30 minutes before using. Then remove to a bowl and add as much vinegar as the horseradish will absorb. Add a pinch of salt and, if desired, a pinch of sugar. Fresh horseradish in vinegar will keep only a couple of weeks, tightly covered and refrigerated. The flavor will become mellower if it is refrigerated for a day or two.

For a variation on the traditional horseradish theme, try serving your gefilte fish with beet tartare, or with a beet-horseradish aspic.

CLASSIC GEFILTE FISH pareve

Homemade gefilte fish is the pride of many Jewish cooks—particularly those of Eastern European heritage. This version is from food columnist Florence Fabricant, whose authoritative articles and recipes are an essential part of *The Times*'s Dining section.

> 3 pounds fish fillets, preferably 1 pound each, such as whitefish, pike and carp, cut in
>   1-inch squares
> 1 cup finely chopped onion
> 2 cloves garlic, minced
> 2 tablespoons minced parsley
> ⅓ cup matzoh meal
> Juice of 1 lemon
> ½ cup dry white wine or water
> 2 large eggs, lightly beaten
> 2 large egg whites, lightly beaten
> 2 teaspoons kosher salt, or to taste
> 1½ teaspoons freshly ground black pepper
> 1 quart Fish Stock (page 82)
> 2 carrots, peeled and sliced
> Prepared horseradish

1. In a food processor, grind the fish, but not too finely. This should be done in two batches, about 24 pulses each. In a bowl, mix the fish with the onion, garlic, parsley, matzoh meal, lemon juice, wine or water, and eggs and egg whites. Season with salt and pepper. Do not underseason. The best way to check the seasonings is to poach a small amount of the mixture in simmering water and taste.

2. In a large pan, bring the stock to a simmer.

3. Keeping your hands wet with cold water, form the fish mixture into oval patties about 3 inches long. Slip as many as will fit comfortably into the pan, and poach for 30 minutes. Remove and drain, and continue poaching the rest. When all the fish is cooked, transfer it to a bowl or serving dish. Add the carrot slices to the stock and simmer 10 minutes. Remove them with a slotted spoon and scatter them over the fish. Refrigerate.

4. Boil down the cooking liquid until it is reduced to about 3 cups. Strain through a fine strainer. Spoon some over the cooled fish. Refrigerate the rest. It should jell. Skim the fat off the surface.

5. Serve the fish cold with horseradish and jellied broth on the side.

makes 24 pieces, about 12 servings

FF

VERA ROSENNE'S GEFILTE FISH pareve

The gefilte fish served by Vera Rosenne, who was born in Romania and whose husband, Meir, was Israel's ambassador to the United States, is bound together by ground almonds instead of matzoh meal. The almonds are used in part because some Jewish customs hold that wet matzoh rises, like leavened bread. Because the taste is delicate, you may wish to serve it without horse-radish or with an herb- or horseradish-flavored mayonnaise.

1 medium onion, coarsely chopped
2 tablespoons unsalted pareve margarine
1 pound carp fillet
1 pound whitefish fillet
Salt and freshly ground white pepper
4 large eggs
1½ cups finely ground blanched almonds
12 cups strained Fish Stock (see Note below and page 82)
Carrot slices, steamed or cooked in boiling water, for garnish
Parsley for garnish
Prepared red horseradish for serving

1. In a skillet, sauté the onion in the margarine until soft. Combine the onion with the carp and whitefish and chop finely with steel blade in food processor (or chop by hand). Put the mixture in a bowl and season with salt and pepper to taste.

2. Add the eggs and mix well to blend. Blend in the almonds.

3. With wet hands, shape the fish mixture into ovals, using 2 tablespoons for each. Place the ovals in a pot of lightly boiling fish stock, cover and cook at a slow boil for about 30 minutes. Remove the fish balls from the bouillon and arrange on a serving dish. Strain the bouillon through a fine strainer over the fish and refrigerate. The bouillon will jell.

4. To serve, arrange one or two cooked carrot slices on each piece of gefilte fish, decorate with parsley and serve red horseradish on the side.

NOTE: If you are using a standard recipe for fish stock, you might add more carrots and onions, and tomato, zucchini, celery, parsley, bay leaf and leek, for additional flavor.

makes approximately 16 pieces, about 8 servings

MS

BARBARA KAFKA'S MICROWAVE GEFILTE FISH pareve
(FROM *THE MICROWAVE GOURMET*)

Barbara Kafka, an expert on microwave cookery, devised this method of preparing gefilte fish, which takes half the time of the traditional method. Refrigerate for at least 24 hours before serving.

fish stock
3 pounds fish heads, skin and bones, from the fish you are using and other
    similar fish, rinsed well and gills removed, cut in small pieces
1 medium carrot (about ½ pound), trimmed, peeled and quartered
1 medium onion, peeled and quartered
½ rib of celery, strung and quartered
1 bay leaf
4 cups water
1½ tablespoons kosher salt
3 medium carrots, trimmed, peeled and sliced crosswise, ⅛ inch thick

fish mixture
½ pound whitefish fillets, skinned
½ pound carp fillets, skinned
½ pound pike fillets, skinned
2 medium onions, peeled and quartered
3 large eggs
¾ cup matzoh meal
¾ cup cold water
1 teaspoon kosher salt
Large pinch freshly ground black pepper
1 teaspoon (½ envelope) unflavored gelatin, if necessary
Red and white prepared horseradish (optional)

1. To make the stock, place all the ingredients for the stock except the carrot slices in a 2-quart glass bowl. Cover tightly with microwave plastic wrap and prick the plastic to release steam. Cook at 100 percent power in a high-power microwave oven for 30 minutes. Remove from the oven and uncover.

2. Add sliced carrots. Cover tightly with microwave plastic wrap. Cook at 100 percent for 10 minutes. Remove from oven and set aside.

3. To prepare the fish mixture, place the fillets and onions in the workbowl of a food processor. Process until smooth. Add remaining ingredients except gelatin and horseradish and process just until combined. With damp hands, shape mixture into 12 plump ovals, 3½ inches by 2 inches.

4. Arrange the fish in a spoke around the edge of a 14-inch by 11-inch oval dish. Spoon carrot slices into center of dish and pour broth over all. Cover tightly with microwave plastic wrap, leaving a small vent in one corner. Cook at 100 percent for 12 minutes.

5. Place a small plate in the freezer (to test gel of fish stock).

6. Remove fish from oven. Uncover and turn each piece over. Let fish cool in the broth for 30 minutes.

7. Test the jelly by pouring a spoonful of broth onto the cold plate. Place the plate in the freezer for 1 minute. Broth should be firm. If it is not, place cooled broth in a bowl and sprinkle gelatin on top. Let stand for 2 minutes. Stir well and repeat test with chilled plate. If broth is still not firm, add rest of envelope of gelatin.

8. Place gefilte fish in the smallest deep container that can hold it in one layer. Cover with broth. Refrigerate overnight.

9. Serve gefilte fish chilled, with some of the jelled broth and carrots. Pass horseradish in a separate bowl, if desired.

makes 12 servings

BK

SALMON GEFILTE FISH pareve

Fresh and smoked salmon give this gefilte fish a distinctive color. The incorporation of horseradish in the recipe adds to the originality of the dish. Serve with parsley-flavored mayonnaise.

⅓ cup water
3 tablespoons olive oil
⅓ cup matzoh cake meal
2 large eggs
1½ teaspoons kosher salt
1 medium onion, finely chopped
1 carrot, peeled and finely chopped
2 leeks, white part only, well rinsed and finely chopped
1¼ pounds salmon fillet, diced
¼ pound smoked salmon, diced
Juice of 1 lemon
2 tablespoons prepared white horseradish
8 cups Fish Stock (page 82), or water, or a combination of water and white wine
¾ cup mayonnaise seasoned with ¼ cup minced parsley

1. Bring the water and 2 tablespoons of the oil to a boil in a small saucepan. Remove from the heat and add the cake meal. Whisk until smooth. Return to the heat and cook, stirring, for about 1 minute. Remove from the heat, and beat in the eggs one at a time. Add ½ teaspoon salt, and set aside.

2. Heat the remaining tablespoon of oil in a skillet over low heat. Add the onion, carrot and leeks, and sauté until tender but not brown.

3. Place the vegetables and fresh and smoked salmon in a food processor, and process until finely ground. Add the egg mixture, and process until smooth. Stir in the lemon juice and horseradish. Season with salt.

4. In a large saucepan, bring the fish stock, water, or water and wine to a simmer—the liquid should be about 2½ inches deep. With wet fingers or 2 tablespoons dipped in cold water, form the fish mixture into ovals. Slip the ovals into the simmering liquid, and poach for 20 minutes. Drain, and refrigerate until cold.

5. Serve with the parsley mayonnaise.

makes 8 servings

FF

GEFILTE FISH SOUFFLÉ dairy

This soufflé, using store-bought gefilte fish, has a pâté consistency and makes a tasty spread for matzohs when cold.

2 tablespoons margarine
¼ cup finely chopped mushrooms
¼ cup potato starch
1½ cups milk
4 large eggs, separated
One 15½-ounce jar unsalted gefilte fish
½ teaspoon salt (optional)
¼ teaspoon freshly ground black pepper (optional)

1. Preheat the oven to 350°F. Grease a 5-cup soufflé dish with margarine.

2. In a saucepan, melt the margarine. Sauté the mushrooms until wilted.

3. In a bowl, blend the potato starch with the milk. Gradually add the milk mixture to the saucepan, and cook over low heat, stirring constantly, until the sauce bubbles and thickens. Remove from the heat and cool slightly.

4. Beat in the egg yolks. In a bowl, mash the strained fish until very smooth and fold into the sauce.

5. In a bowl, beat the egg whites until stiff but not dry, and fold into the fish mixture. Season with salt and pepper to taste. Pour into the greased soufflé dish.

6. Bake 40 to 50 minutes, or until a cake tester inserted in center comes out clean. Serve immediately.

makes 4 to 6 servings

JH

ELLYN GOODRICH'S ALASKAN HALIBUT AND SALMON GEFILTE FISH TERRINE pareve

This recipe is from Ellyn Goodrich, one of the 5,000 Jews who live in Alaska (the "Chosen Frozen," as they call themselves). The fish is baked in a bundt pan and unmolded, for a festive look.

1 tablespoon pareve margarine
2 pounds halibut fillets, skinned and boned
1 pound salmon fillets, skinned and boned
3 tablespoons vegetable oil
4 medium Spanish onions, diced
4 large eggs
2 cups cold water
6 tablespoons matzoh meal
1 tablespoon salt, or to taste
2 teaspoons freshly ground white pepper
2 tablespoons sugar
1 tablespoon fresh lemon juice
2 tablespoons snipped dill, plus more for garnish
2 large carrots, peeled
Parsley, for garnish
Prepared red horseradish for serving

1. Preheat the oven to 325°F. Grease a 12-cup bundt pan with the margarine.

2. Cut the fish into large chunks, and place in the bowl of a food processor. Pulse about 20 times; do not puree, but grind fine. Place in the bowl of an electric mixer.

3. Heat the oil in a large frying pan, and sauté the onions over medium-low heat until soft and transparent. Let cool.

4. To the fish mixture, add the onions, eggs, 2 cups of cold water, matzoh meal, salt, white pepper, sugar and lemon juice. Beat in the electric mixer at medium speed, using a paddle attachment, for about 10 minutes. Add the dill, and grate in the carrots; mix well.

5. Pour the mixture into the greased bundt pan. Smooth the top with a spatula, and cover with foil. Place in a larger pan filled with water which is almost boiling and comes at least halfway up the sides of the bundt pan.

6. Bake in the oven for 1 hour, or until the center is solid. Cool for 5 minutes, or until mold is cool to the touch. Run a knife around the edges. Place a flat serving plate on top, and

then flip over, inverting mold onto the plate. If the mold does not come out easily, give the plate a shake. You should feel or hear it give.

7. Refrigerate for several hours or overnight. Slice as you would a torte, and serve as an appetizer. Garnish with the parsley and remaining dill, and serve with red horseradish.

makes 20 servings

JN

GEFILTE FISH–VEGETABLE TERRINE pareve

This gefilte fish mixture is baked as a terrine with a ribbon of bright vegetables running across each slice. A mild herb- or horseradish-laced mayonnaise is a wonderful accompanying condiment.

1 bunch leeks, white part only, cleaned and sliced
¾ pound carrots, peeled and sliced
3 tablespoons chopped parsley
Salt and freshly ground black pepper
1 tablespoon fresh lemon juice
Pinch of nutmeg
2 tablespoons matzoh meal
½ cup Fish Stock (page 82)
2 medium onions
1½ pounds whitefish fillets in 1-inch dice
½ pound pike fillets in 1-inch dice
½ pound carp fillets in 1-inch dice
2 large eggs
¾ cup mayonnaise seasoned with ¼ cup minced fresh herbs or with ¼ cup prepared
    white horseradish

1. Place leeks in a saucepan, cover with water and simmer until tender, about 25 minutes. Meanwhile, place the carrots in a separate saucepan, cover with water and simmer until tender, about 25 minutes. Drain the vegetables.

2. Puree leeks in a food processor along with 1 tablespoon parsley, and season with salt and pepper to taste. Set aside. Without washing the food processor, puree carrots and season them with lemon juice, salt, pepper and nutmeg and set aside.

3. Place the matzoh meal in a bowl, mix with the fish stock and set aside.

4. Without washing the food processor, add the onions and process until finely chopped. Add the fish and process until smoothly pureed. Add the softened matzoh meal, eggs and remaining parsley and process until well blended. Season with salt (about 1 teaspoon) and liberally with pepper. To taste for seasoning, poach a small amount of the mixture in simmering water, then cool briefly.

5. Preheat the oven to 350°F. Lightly oil a 6-cup loaf pan or ring mold.

6. Spread half the fish mixture in the pan, making a depression in the middle that extends to within about ½ inch of the sides. Spread half the leek mixture in the depression; spread the carrot puree over leeks and top with rest of leeks. Smooth in the remaining fish. Rap the pan several times on countertop to eliminate air holes. Place wax paper or parchment paper on top of the terrine.

7. Set the pan in a larger pan at least 2 inches deep and place in oven. Add 1 to 1½ inches of boiling water to the outside pan. Bake 50 minutes.

8. Remove from the oven and let cool. Remove the fish loaf from pan and place on a serving dish. Cover with plastic wrap and refrigerate at least 6 hours to chill completely. Serve in slices with herbed mayonnaise or horseradish-flavored mayonnaise on the side.

makes 12 servings

FF

MARIAN BURROS'S GEFILTE FISH LOAF pareve

Marian Burros, a food writer for *The New York Times* who specializes in creating dishes for healthy dining, devised this version of gefilte fish. Instead of a mixture of whitefish, pike and carp, it is made only with whitefish, which is high in omega-3 fatty acids, believed to be helpful in preventing heart disease.

6 medium carrots, peeled
2 pounds whitefish fillets
2 medium onions, coarsely chopped
1 medium carrot, grated
¼ cup matzoh meal
1 teaspoon peanut oil
2 teaspoons sugar
¼ teaspoon salt
Freshly ground white pepper
½ teaspoon nutmeg
1 large egg
2 large egg whites
½ cup cold water
Horseradish for garnish

1. Preheat the oven to 350°F.
2. Steam the carrots until slightly softened, 5 to 7 minutes.
3. In a food processor, process the fish to a paste.
4. In a bowl, combine the onions with the fish, grated carrot, matzoh meal, oil, sugar, salt, pepper, nutmeg, egg and whites and cold water; mix well.
5. Place ¼ of the fish mixture in a nonstick 9- by 5- by 3-inch loaf pan; arrange 2 whole partly cooked carrots lengthwise on top of the mixture; top with another ¼ of the mixture; arrange 2 more carrots on top; repeat with another ¼ of the mixture and remaining carrots, and cover with the remaining mixture.
6. Bake for 1 hour. Remove from the oven and cool in the pan. Then turn out, cover and refrigerate until chilled. Serve with horseradish.

makes 6 to 8 servings

MB

MIMI SHERATON'S KALECHLA meat

Mock Gefilte Fish

(FROM *FROM MY MOTHER'S KITCHEN*)

In Mimi Sheraton's family, this was called "fake gefilte fish" because it is made with chicken and veal. It is almost indistinguishable from the original. The only difference is a slightly drier, meatier texture.

1 pound lean, boneless shoulder of veal
2 pounds boneless, skinless chicken breast
4 large onions, peeled
2 teaspoons salt
1 teaspoon freshly ground white pepper
2 extra-large eggs
¼ cup club soda or seltzer
2 to 3 tablespoons matzoh meal, or as needed
Chicken backs, necks, bones or wing tips if available, about ¼ pound in all
1 large stalk celery, with leaves
2 carrots, peeled and sliced in ½-inch rounds
4 cups water, approximately
Pinch of salt
Horseradish for garnish

1. Remove all membranes and cartilage from the veal and chicken so they will not jam in the grinder. Cut 1 onion in large chunks.

2. Grind both meats and the onion chunks through the fine blade of a meat grinder. (A food processor will make the mixture too fine.)

3. Add the salt, pepper, eggs and soda to the ground meat mixture. Add enough matzoh meal to bind slightly. The mixture should resemble a thick, cooked oatmeal porridge.

4. Slice the remaining onions and place them, the chicken parts, the celery and carrots in a 2½- to 3-quart enameled pot that is more or less in the shape of a Dutch oven. Add just enough water to come to level of onions—about 4 cups. Add a pinch of salt to the water and bring to a boil.

5. Shape the *kalechla* in ovals with wet palms or with 2 wet tablespoons, using about 1 heaping tablespoonful of the mix per portion. Each oval should be about the size of a small lemon. Gently place in the boiling water. Reduce to a simmer, half-cover the pot and simmer gently until thoroughly cooked, 1 to 1½ hours. Taste the broth during cooking and add salt and pepper if needed.

continued

6. Let the *kalechla* cool in the broth. When cool, remove to a deep dish. Pick out the carrots and arrange around the *kalechla*.

7. Strain the cooking liquid into a bowl, forcing through all of the cooked onion slices, but discarding the chicken pieces and celery. Pour this onion-thickened broth over the *kalechla* and let chill at least 12 hours before serving. This broth will not really jell unless some bones are used in its preparation.

8. Serve 1 or 2 *kalechla* as an appetizer, with sauce and grated horseradish on the side.

makes about 12 *kalechla*

MS

WOLFGANG PUCK'S GEFILTE FISH pareve
(ADAPTED FROM *ADVENTURES IN THE KITCHEN*)

When famed Los Angeles chef Wolfgang Puck prepares gefilte fish for a Seder at Spago, the first of his successful California restaurants, he can be expected to add an original touch. In this recipe, he wraps tarragon-flavored fish dumplings in cabbage leaves before poaching them, and serves them with a garnish of julienned leek and carrots and freshly grated horseradish.

½ cup matzoh meal
5 cups Fish Stock (page 82)
2 heads green cabbage
1 tablespoon vegetable oil
1 medium onion, finely chopped
1 pound whitefish fillets
½ pound pike fillets
½ pound carp fillets
Salt and freshly ground black pepper
½ cup parsley, minced
2 tablespoons minced fresh tarragon
3 large eggs, separated
2 carrots, peeled and cut in julienne style
1 leek, white part only, cut in julienne style
1½ tablespoons white vinegar
Freshly grated horseradish mixed with a little vinegar for serving

1. Place the matzoh meal in a bowl, mix with 1 cup fish stock and set aside.

2. Place the cabbages in a large pot of simmering water. As leaves soften, take the heads of cabbage out of the water and carefully remove the leaves. You will need about 15 large unbroken leaves or twice that many smaller leaves, which can be put together overlapping to make a large leaf. Rinse softened leaves under cold running water, dry and cut away any large central ribs.

3. Heat oil in a small skillet, and sauté the onion over medium-low heat until translucent. Remove from the heat.

4. Cube the fish, season with salt and pepper and process, using a pulse mechanism, in a food processor. The fish should have some texture. Alternatively, the fish can be ground in a meat grinder or ordered ground from the fish market.

continued

5. In a bowl, mix the fish with the cooked onion, parsley and tarragon. Season with pepper. In another bowl, lightly beat the egg yolks and mix into the fish. Then add the matzoh meal mixture.

6. In another bowl, beat the egg whites until frothy, then fold into the fish mixture. To taste the mixture for seasoning, poach a small amount in simmering water, then allow to cool briefly.

7. Place 2 heaping tablespoons of the fish mixture in a cabbage leaf or leaves, and roll to enclose the fish mixture completely, making a package. Repeat until all of the fish mixture is used.

8. Place the cabbage rolls, seam side down, in a large saucepan, and scatter the carrots and leek over them. Mix remaining 4 cups of stock with the vinegar, and pour over the cabbage rolls. Bring to a simmer. Cover, reduce the heat and simmer 10 minutes. Let cool completely in the stock. Remove the fish rolls from the stock and refrigerate until 30 minutes before serving. Serve with fresh horseradish.

makes 15 servings

FF

BARRY WINE'S GEFILTE FISH BEGGAR'S PURSES pareve

For his Seder, four-star chef Barry Wine created a dish of matzoh meal crepes filled with gefilte fish and grated horseradish root. It is an adaptation of Beggar's Caviar Purses, the crepes filled with dollops of beluga caviar and crème fraîche and tied up with strands of chives, a signature dish at The Quilted Giraffe, his famed Manhattan restaurant, now closed. The best way to eat these crepes is with the hand, popping the entire purse into the mouth at once.

matzoh crepes

    1½ cups matzoh cake meal
    12 large eggs
    2 cups water
    ½ teaspoon salt
    ¼ cup peanut oil
    1 tablespoon pareve unsalted margarine, melted

gefilte fish

    ¾ pound whitefish fillets, plus rib cage from the fish
    ¾ pound pike fillets, plus rib cage from the fish
    1 carrot, peeled
    1 celery rib
    1 onion
    2 tablespoons chopped parsley
    1 lemon, sliced
    2 sticks cinnamon
    Kosher salt and freshly ground pepper
    6½ cups water
    Pinch of nutmeg
    2 tablespoons pareve unsalted margarine
    ¼ cup matzoh meal
    2 shallots
    2 large eggs, separated
    ½ cup grated fresh horseradish
    36 long chive strands

1. To make the crepes, in a bowl, combine the matzoh cake meal, eggs, water and salt. Let rest for at least 30 minutes at a temperature slightly above room temperature.

continued

2. Right before using the crepe batter, add the peanut oil and strain. The consistency should be that of heavy cream. If, after making your first crepe, it is too thick, add more water.

3. Use a well-seasoned 5- or 6-inch crepe or Teflon-coated pan over medium heat. If necessary, use a paper towel lightly dipped in melted margarine to grease the pan. Pour just enough batter into the pan to lightly coat the bottom, pouring back any excess into the uncooked batter. Cook the crepe until browned on one side. Lift with a small spatula and flip the crepe over to cook for 15 seconds more. Remove from the pan and repeat. The recipe makes about 36 crepes.

4. Trim the crepes to 5 inches. Wrap in plastic wrap as soon as completed to avoid their drying out.

5. To make the gefilte fish, first make a stock. In a pot, combine the fish bones without the head and skin with the carrot, celery, onion, parsley, lemon, cinnamon and salt and pepper to taste. Add 6 cups of the water and simmer, uncovered, for about 30 minutes. (By omitting the heads and skin and adding the lemon and cinnamon, the fish will taste—and the house smell—better.) Strain the stock, reserving the onion and carrot.

6. Meanwhile, combine the remaining ½ cup of water, nutmeg, margarine, and ½ teaspoon salt in a saucepan. Bring to a boil.

7. Add the matzoh meal. Stir until dry, about 1 minute, remove from the heat and let cool.

8. Taking care that the fish stays very cold, grind the fish fillets and the shallots in a food processor until smooth, but slightly textured, using the on-off pulse to a count of 10. You do not want a mush.

9. Take half the reserved carrot and onion from the stock and chop to make a fine yet textured dice.

10. In a bowl, fold the egg yolks into the fish mixture. Fold in the carrot and onion.

11. Using your hand, combine the fish and the matzoh mixtures. Chill, covered.

12. Bring the strained fish stock to just under a boil.

13. In a bowl, whip the egg whites to stiff peaks. Fold into the fish and matzoh mixture.

14. With a small scoop, make ¾-inch balls. Put about 10 fish balls at a time into the hot stock and poach gently for 5 minutes. Drain and cool.

15. Lay out the crepes, 12 at a time. Put a scant teaspoon of grated horseradish root in the center of the crepe. Place the gefilte fish on top of the horseradish.

16. Carefully pleat the crepe up around the fish. About ½ inch from the top, tie with the chive strands, which have been dipped in hot tap water to soften. Cut off excess chive. Repeat with remaining gefilte fish and crepes.

17. Cover with plastic wrap, refrigerate and remove from the refrigerator before serving. This dish can be made a day or two in advance. If desired, add additional horseradish for dipping.

makes 12 servings of 3 purses per person

JN

JOYCE GOLDSTEIN'S PICKLED SALMON pareve

(FROM *BACK TO SQUARE ONE*)

The original recipe for pickled salmon called for smoked salmon, the only kind once available to the Jews of Eastern Europe. It required soaking for days to remove the salt before pickling. In her contemporary version, San Francisco chef and food consultant Joyce Goldstein significantly reduces the preparation time by substituting fresh salmon.

2 cups white vinegar
1½ cups water
6 tablespoons sugar
2 tablespoons kosher salt
2 pounds salmon fillet, skin and bones removed
2 tablespoons mixed pickling spices
6 bay leaves
2 white or yellow onions, sliced ¼ inch thick

1. Bring the vinegar, water, sugar and salt to a boil. Let this mixture cool completely.
2. Cut the salmon into pieces that are approximately 1 by 2 inches.
3. In a ceramic crock, glass bowl or plastic container, place a layer of salmon pieces, then a sprinkling of pickling spices and bay leaves, a layer of onions, then salmon, spices and onions—continuing until you have used it all. Pour the cooled marinade over the fish. Cover the container and refrigerate for 3 to 4 days.
4. Serve the salmon chilled, but not ice cold, along with the marinated onions.

NOTE: The salmon will keep 3 to 4 days after the pickling is finished.

makes 10 to 12 servings

JN

CRAIG CLAIBORNE'S SALMON PÂTÉ dairy

Craig Claiborne, *The Times*'s legendary food expert, raised awareness and appreciation of fine dining with his articles, recipes and critiques. His salmon pâté is a fine addition to the holiday table. It is particularly good if made with the leftover morsels of a poached whole salmon, the bits that cling around the main bones of the fish, near and in the head of the fish. These morsels are rich and gelatinous.

2 cups cooked, boneless, skinless salmon
¼ to ½ cup heavy cream
2 tablespoons lemon juice, or to taste
1 tablespoon chopped fresh dill, plus more for garnish (optional)
Salt and freshly ground pepper to taste
Matzoh

1. Place the fish in the container of a food processor or blender. Add about ¼ cup of cream and blend. Gradually add more cream until desired consistency is reached, taking care the mixture does not become too liquid. Stop the blending at intervals and scrape down the sides of the container with a plastic spatula. When properly blended, the mass should be mousselike, holding its shape when picked up with the spatula.

2. Spoon and scrape the mixture into a bowl and add the lemon juice, dill, salt and pepper. Spoon the pâté into a serving dish, such as a small soufflé mold. Cover and chill well, preferably overnight. Garnish, if desired, with chopped dill. Serve with matzoh.

makes 4 to 6 servings

CC

TROUT ROULADES WITH WHITEFISH MOUSSE pareve

In this recipe, fillets of brook trout are wrapped around a whitefish mousse mixture, tied with a string of scallion, and poached in the oven in wine and fish stock. The dish may also be served as a main course.

2 leeks, white part only, cleaned and chopped
1 tablespoon vegetable oil
4 scallions with long, fresh-looking leaves
1 tablespoon chopped fresh basil
½ pound whitefish fillets
1 large egg
1 tablespoon fresh lemon juice
Salt and freshly ground black pepper
4 whole brook trout, boned, skinned and cut into 8 fillets
1 cup Fish Stock (page 82)
½ cup dry white wine
¾ cup mayonnaise seasoned with ¼ cup minced fresh herbs

1. Preheat oven to 350°F.
2. Sauté half the leeks in the oil until tender but not brown. Set aside.
3. Coarsely chop white part of scallions, reserving leaves, then process with sauteed leek and the basil in a food processor until finely chopped. Add whitefish and process until finely pureed. Add egg and lemon juice and process until smooth. Season with salt and pepper. Taste for seasoning by poaching a small amount in simmering water, then allowing to cool briefly.
4. Place a trout fillet on a plate or work surface with the side that had the skin up, and season lightly with salt and pepper. Place a heaping tablespoon of whitefish mixture at the wide end. Roll trout fillet over the mousse, stand it up and smooth the mousse on top. Tie a scallion leaf around fillet (this is only decoration; the fillet will remain tightly wound around mousse without it). If scallion leaves are too stiff to tie, dip briefly in hot water to wilt. Repeat with 7 remaining trout fillets.
5. Place fish rolls standing up in a glass or enamel baking dish. Scatter remaining leek around them, then add the fish stock and wine. Cover top with a piece of wax paper or parchment paper, place in oven and bake 30 minutes. Cool, then refrigerate. Serve the chilled fish rolls with herbed mayonnaise.

makes 8 first-course servings or 4 main-course servings

FF

ANDREE ABRAMOFF'S FISH DUMPLINGS IN TURMERIC SAUCE pareve

Belehat Arouss

Andree Abramoff created this dish from the traditional Egyptian menu of her childhood in Cairo. She serves it and other Sephardic specialties for which she is known at Café Crocodile, her Manhattan restaurant. Unlike gefilte fish, these fishballs are deep-fried, then simmered in a turmeric-tomato sauce.

2 pounds cod or tilefish fillets
1 small onion, quartered
3 cloves garlic, sliced
2 teaspoons ground cumin
$\frac{1}{8}$ teaspoon cayenne pepper
1 large egg
Salt and freshly ground pepper
1 cup matzoh meal
Oil for deep-frying
4 cups fish stock or water
1 tablespoon fresh lemon juice
$\frac{1}{2}$ teaspoon turmeric
3 tablespoons tomato paste
Sprigs of flat-leaf parsley, for garnish

1. Cut the fish into 1-inch pieces. Place in food processor and add the onion, garlic, cumin, cayenne pepper, egg, and salt and pepper to taste. Process until smooth. Add the matzoh meal and process until incorporated.

2. Shape the fish mixture into plump ovals about 3 inches long.

3. Heat the oil for deep-frying to 375° F in a deep fryer, saucepan or wok. Fry the fish mixture until golden brown. Drain on paper towels.

4. Bring the stock or water to boil in 1 or 2 large saucepans, and add the lemon juice, turmeric and tomato paste. Bring to a slow simmer over low heat. Place the drained fish rolls in a single layer into the simmering broth and cook slowly, uncovered. Simmer until the broth has reduced and thickened, about 40 minutes. Garnish with parsley and serve warm.

makes 8 servings

FF

STEWED FISH À LA JUIVE pareve

Carpe à la Juive

This is possibly the first recipe for a Jewish dish to appear in the pages of *The Times*. Published in a Household Hints column in 1879, it instructed readers on the preparation of carp, a then unfamiliar fish. This recipe is still contemporary, for *Carpe à la Juive* is a holiday classic—particularly among Jews of Alsatian heritage, who serve it at Seder in place of gefilte fish.

½ cup chopped parsley
3 small onions, sliced in rounds
2 cups water
1 teaspoon freshly ground white pepper
½ teaspoon grated nutmeg
1 tablespoon matzoh meal
1 sprig saffron
Juice of 3 lemons
One 3-pound carp, pike or salmon, cut into 1-inch steaks (reserve head and tail)
3 egg yolks

1. In a large pot over high heat, bring parsley, onions and water to a boil, then reduce the heat to medium and simmer until tender, about 5 minutes. Add the white pepper, nutmeg, matzoh meal, saffron and lemon juice.

2. Put all the fish pieces (the head and tail, as well as the steaks) into the water, adding more water to cover, if necessary. Cover and poach over medium heat for 10 to 15 minutes or until the fish is cooked. Remove the steaks to a platter, arranging them in the original form of the fish. Leave the head and tail in the broth and cook over medium-high heat until the broth is reduced by half, about 15 minutes. Adjust the seasoning and strain broth into a bowl, reserving the head, tail and parsley mixture. Return the broth to the pot, add the 3 yolks, whisking well, bring just to a boil, and remove from the heat. Bring to room temperature.

3. Add the head and tail to the steaks, re-forming the entire shape of the fish. Cover with the onions and the parsley and some of the reduced broth. Cover and refrigerate overnight, with the remaining broth refrigerated separately. Serve the fish at room temperature with any remaining broth poured over it or in a separate bowl.

NOTE: For a variation, substitute 2 cloves minced garlic, 2 teaspoons grated fresh ginger, salt to taste and, if desired, 1 cup sliced mushrooms for the nutmeg, saffron and lemon juice in Step 1. Omit the egg yolks.

makes 6 servings   JN

GRAVLAX pareve

This is delicious served either with Horseradish Sauce with Walnuts (page 37) or with Beet Tartare (page 38).

One 3½- to 4-pound center cut of salmon, filleted but with skin left intact
3 tablespoons peppercorns, preferably white
5 tablespoons sugar
3 tablespoons kosher salt
2 to 3 bunches (about ¼ pound) fresh dill sprigs

1. Carefully run your fingers over the boned surface of the fillet. Use a pair of pliers or tweezers to pull out and remove any bones that may remain. Discard the bones.

2. Put the peppercorns on a flat surface and crush them coarsely with a mallet or the bottom of a clean skillet. Or crush them in a mortar. Put the pepper in a small bowl and add the sugar and salt.

3. Cut the salmon fillet in half crosswise and place the 2 halves, skin side down, in one layer. Sprinkle evenly with the salt mixture.

4. Make a generous layer of dill sprigs over the bottom of a flat dish large enough to hold 1 salmon fillet compactly. Place 1 fillet, skin side down, on the dill. Cover with a generous amount of dill. Place the other salmon piece, skin side up, over the layer of dill. Cover with remaining dill and cover closely with plastic wrap.

5. Place a smaller flat dish on top of the salmon and add weights, about 10 pounds. Refrigerate for 48 hours.

6. Every 12 hours, remove the weights, the top dish and the plastic wrap from the salmon. Carefully turn the "sandwich." Always cover the dish with plastic wrap, the plate and weights.

7. When ready to serve, scrape away all the dill and pat the salmon halves dry. Carve each piece on the diagonal into thin slices, cutting away the skin.

makes 12 or more servings

CC

FRESH HORSERADISH pareve

For mellower flavor, cover horseradish tightly with plastic wrap and refrigerate for a day or two.

    1 pound fresh horseradish root
    ⅔ cup white vinegar
    4 to 6 tablespoons dry white wine
    2 teaspoons sugar
    Salt to taste

    1. Peel the horseradish root and cut into small pieces. Process finely in food processor (you may have to do this in batches).
    2. In a bowl, mix the ground horseradish root with the vinegar, wine, sugar, and salt to taste. The fresher the mixture, the hotter it will be.

    makes 2½ cups

MB

HORSERADISH SAUCE WITH WALNUTS dairy

A splendid sauce for Gravlax (page 36) or for poached or smoked fish

    1 cup sour cream
    ¼ cup heavy cream
    ½ cup grated horseradish, preferably freshly grated
    4 ounces walnuts
    1 tablespoon sugar
    Salt to taste

    1. In a mixing bowl, combine the sour cream, heavy cream and horseradish.
    2. Process the walnuts in a food processor until fine, but do not blend to a paste. Add the walnuts to the sauce along with the sugar and salt. Stir to blend well. Refrigerate and serve cold with smoked fish or with cold or lukewarm poached fish.

    makes about 2 cups

CC

JEAN-GEORGES VONGERICHTEN'S BEET TARTARE pareve

(FROM JEAN-GEORGES: COOKING AT HOME WITH A FOUR-STAR CHEF)

This simple beet tartare, adapted from a recipe by the chef and co-owner of four-star restaurant Jean Georges in New York, is a delicious change of pace from bottled red horseradish to serve with gefilte fish. Unlike horseradish, it tastes wonderful even without the fish, and it won't make your eyes water. The beet tartare is also excellent as a salad, on a bed of arugula.

6 medium beets
1 shallot, finely chopped
2 tablespoons finely chopped vinegar pickles (cornichons)
1 tablespoon mayonnaise
1 teaspoon prepared horseradish, plain or beet
2 tablespoons minced parsley
1 teaspoon red wine vinegar
Salt and freshly ground black pepper to taste

1. Preheat oven to 350°F.
2. Stem and quarter the beets, place in a roasting pan and roast with the skin for 2 hours. When they are cool, peel them and chop coarsely in a food processor.
3. In a mixing bowl, mix the beets with the remaining ingredients.
4. Form into small mounds and serve at room temperature.

makes 6 to 10 servings

FF

MARION SINER GORDON'S
BEET AND HORSERADISH ASPIC pareve

This molded gelatin salad is a novel and tasty variation on the standard prepared red horseradish.

1 package lemon-flavored vegetable gelatin
2 cups boiling beet juice or strained borscht
2 bunches beets, stems removed, boiled until tender, peeled and finely diced
One 4-ounce jar white or red horseradish

1. Dissolve the gelatin in the boiling beet juice or borscht. Chill. When it begins to set, add the diced beets and horseradish. Mix well.

2. Pour the mixture into an oiled 1½-quart ring mold or into individual molds. Cover and refrigerate until set. Unmold.

makes 8 servings

CC

epiphany in a charleston garden

By RUTH REICHL

"This year," my mother always said, "we're going to light the Hanukkah candles."

I think she really meant it. But somehow she could never find the menorah. I know we had one, because it would usually surface when we were putting up the Christmas tree, hidden among the colorful bulbs, candy canes and bubbling water lights. "There it is," Mom would say as she pulled it out. "Next year we are definitely going to light it."

But we never did.

We never celebrated Seder in our house either. We lacked not only the Haggadahs, but also the older male to lead the ceremony. My father, a devout atheist, would not have dreamed of doing so. Some years we were invited to Seder at other people's houses, but my memories of those are fuzzy. What I mostly recall is this: hurrying through the ceremony, the grown-ups drinking more wine than required and singing "Dayenu." I also remember that nobody ever, ever wanted to continue the ceremony after dinner was done. Mostly, I think, we didn't.

But religious epiphanies occur when you are least expecting them. Mine took place a few years ago in a Charleston garden. We had gone, two northern families, children in tow, to spend spring vacation in the sun. When we got to the airport, I asked my friends why their suitcases were so heavy. "Oh," they replied casually, "they're full of Haggadahs."

John and Diana, it turned out, took Seder seriously, and they had arranged to celebrate at the home of a Charleston friend. "It will be wonderful," John exulted. "He is not Jewish and he's never been to a Seder. He is inviting some other friends, who will also be experiencing it for the first time. This will be really meaningful."

"Oh, great," I thought. "Not only do we have to suffer through Seder, but now we have to explain its meaning as well." I eschewed suntan lotion, hoping sunburn would excuse me from the ceremony.

My strategy did not work, and at twilight on the first night of Passover I found myself on a lovely old Charleston street. The house was surrounded by a fence; the gate swung open and we found ourselves in a lush garden filled with blooming amaryllis and violets and torch ginger. Set right in the middle of all this vegetation was a table, covered with old silver, candles and antique plates. In the middle of each plate was *The New Union Haggadah* with drawings by Leonard Baskin.

The guests began to arrive. In the spirit of the day, each carried a special offering. "Our son is engaged to a Jewish woman," explained one man, setting a basket of home-baked matzohs on the table, "and I've been trying to learn Jewish cooking. I thought it would bring me closer to her." He had also made a special Sephardic haroseth. Faced with such generosity of spirit, my grumpiness faded away.

It was, in any case, impossible not to surrender to the magic of the setting. The light was fading as we took our seats, and we could hear the low hum of bees throbbing in the azaleas. Birds chirped cheerfully above us, and a neighborhood dog came nosing in, looking hungrily at the lamb bone on the Pesach plate. We opened our Haggadahs. As John began to read, "'Now in the presence of loved ones and friends we gather,'" I realized that it was going to be an entirely different event from any I had experienced before.

His tone was solemn; he meant it when he said, "'Living our story that is told for all peoples whose shining conclusion is yet to unfold.'" I began to understand, for the first time, that this was a festival of freedom.

We drank the first cup of wine, and I looked around at the flowers in the garden. "'Flowers appear on the earth,'" intoned John. "'The time of winging is here. . . . '" A shiver went down my back. We were in the South, and the ghosts of all the slaves who ever lived were whispering around us, drawn to the table as we dipped the greens in salt water. I tasted its bitterness; I understood the tears.

John broke the matzoh and said, "'Let all who are hungry come and eat. Let all who are in want share the hope of Passover.'" His words went up, into the night air, over the wall. As he continued, "'Now we are all still bondsmen,'" I recognized the special meaning of the Seder. Self-conscious in the knowledge of being surrounded by people who did not know the ceremony, I was suddenly filled with pride. I inhaled the significance of the words and tried, truly, to imagine myself as a slave and to experience the joy of liberation. Is there any other religion whose central ceremony requires identification with the oppressed?

We made Hillel sandwiches with the matzoh and lovingly made haroseth. We piled on the horseradish, and someone said, slightly giddily, "Hotter than barbecue," and we all ate some more. It was delicious.

Then the youngest child asked the first question, and it was more than words to me. Yes, I thought, this night really is different from all other nights. We ate the maror, saying together, "'Today, wherever slavery remains, Jews taste its bitterness.'" I drank the second cup of wine, with wonder and gratitude. Here, in our sheltered garden, we had come together in the realization that none of us can be free until everybody is.

Eating the feast, we told family stories about celebrations in other places. The ceremony had joined us, somehow, and when one woman told hilarious tales of her eccentric aunt, she had become the aunt of us all. The meal ended, but no one suggested skipping the end of the ceremony. We wanted the journey to continue.

The children found the afikomen, hidden under the torch ginger. We shared it, and then we started the traditional answer and response that goes like this:

Leader: "'On the festival of matzoh, inspire us to goodness.'"
Group: "'On this Day of Liberation, make us a blessing.'"

We drank more wine. We opened the door for Elijah. We were very happy.

I may never have another Seder in a Charleston garden. But I will certainly never let another Seder go by without celebrating in some way. I've still never cooked a Seder myself. But when I do, I plan to put my mother's menorah on the table. I know its light will shed a special glow.

APPETIZERS

chopped liver and other starters

Chopped liver is one of the most traditional Jewish appetizers—at Passover or any other time of year—and in many Jewish families, recipes are treated as heirlooms, treasured from generation to generation.

Some purists insist that the flavor and texture of chopped liver are not right unless the ingredients are chopped in a wooden bowl with a half-moon chopping knife. Many cooks today, however, prefer the convenience of a food processor and claim the results are indistinguishable from the hand-chopped version.

Whatever method you choose, what gives chopped liver its distinctive taste is chicken fat, or schmaltz. Pull the globs of fat away from the chicken and freeze them until you have a cup or more. Then render them for use in cooking (see recipe, page 48). For maximum flavor, bring the chopped liver to room temperature before serving and, if desired, garnish with a sprinkling of grated egg yolk.

The classic chopped-liver recipe that follows can be modified to reduce cholesterol. And a version of chopped liver made without meat, which tastes deceptively like the real thing when flavored with schmaltz, becomes a true vegetarian "chopped liver" when butter is substituted for the chicken fat.

Vegetable salads are also a good way to begin a Passover meal. For a traditional starter, there is an eggplant salad. Carrot salads from chefs Alice Waters and Wolfgang Puck are exceptional—hers with parsley and garlic, his with chard and Middle Eastern seasonings. For a novel combination, there is chef Barry Wine's Vegetable-Matzoh "Salad," good enough to serve at any time of the year.

CHOPPED LIVER—
CLASSIC OR LOW FAT meat

For a healthier version, this may be made with reduced fat and with egg whites only.

¼ cup raw chicken fat (optional)
2 cups finely sliced onions
1 pound chicken livers (see Note)
½ tablespoon vegetable oil (optional)
2 large hard-cooked eggs, quartered, or 3 hard-cooked egg whites
Kosher salt and freshly ground black pepper

1. If desired, place the chicken fat and ⅛ cup of the onions in a small nonstick saucepan or skillet. Cook very slowly over low heat, stirring from time to time, until the fat is completely liquefied and the onions and resulting cracklings from the fat are golden brown.

2. Remove from heat and strain fat into a small crock, pressing as much fat as possible from the onions and cracklings. Reserve the browned onions and cracklings.

3. Place 3 tablespoons of the rendered fat in a large, heavy skillet and sauté the remaining onions over medium-low heat until golden brown. Remove the onions from the pan, draining as much fat as possible back into the pan. As an alternate method, sweat the onions without fat by cooking them slowly in a tightly covered nonstick skillet with a little salt. When the onions are soft, remove the cover, increase the heat and allow them to become lightly browned.

4. Trim the chicken livers of any connective tissue or membranes and pat dry with paper towels. If you are observing kashrut, broil the livers lightly and quickly (see Note) and proceed to Step 5. Otherwise, sauté them over medium heat in the pan used for the onions, adding another tablespoon of chicken fat, or if no chicken fat is used, adding ½ tablespoon vegetable oil. Cook the livers until they are lightly browned and no longer pink in the middle. Remove from the heat.

5. Combine the livers, all the sautéed onions and hard-cooked eggs or egg whites, plus the cracklings, if desired, in a wooden bowl and chop them together by hand. The mixture can also be ground in a meat grinder, using a medium blade. Alternately, the mixture can be chopped in a food processor, using a plastic blade. To do this, first cut the livers and eggs or egg whites into uniform ½-inch pieces. Then mix them with the onions and cracklings, if desired, in the bowl of the food processor and pulse briefly about 5 times until the mixture has a uniform, medium-coarse texture. Do not make it smooth.

continued

6. Season the chopped liver to taste with salt and pepper and, if desired, with additional chicken fat. Place the chopped liver in a bowl or serving dish and cover it tightly with plastic wrap. Refrigerate if it is not being served within 2 to 3 hours, but allow it to come to room temperature before serving.

NOTE: According to kashrut, liver must be broiled over a fire before it is cooked so that the fire will draw out all the blood. Beef liver must be cut open and placed cut side down over a fire; chicken liver may be broiled whole. The liver is washed and lightly salted, then broiled with a forked utensil over a grate so that the blood is consumed by fire or drained off, and then washed 3 times so that the blood is rinsed off. After this koshering process is completed, the liver may be sautéed.

makes 8 to 12 servings

FF

RENDERED CHICKEN FAT meat
Schmaltz

Pull the globs of fat away from the chickens you buy and freeze these until you have ½ cup or more. Then render the fat to use in cooking. If desired, brown slices of garlic or sliced or chopped onion in the fat while it is rendering for additional flavor.

½ cup raw chicken fat
Pinch of kosher salt

1. Place the chicken fat and salt in a small, heavy saucepan.
2. Cook very slowly over low heat, stirring from time to time, until the fat is completely liquefied and the cracklings are golden brown.
3. Strain the fat into a jar or crock, cover and refrigerate. Reserve the cracklings—crisp, fried bits that are left after fat is rendered—to use in making chopped liver or as a garnish for salads or mashed potatoes.

makes ½ cup

FF

QUICK CHICKEN LIVER PÂTÉ meat

A refined version of basic chopped liver.

½ pound chicken livers
Chicken stock to cover
2 large hard-cooked eggs
½ cup chopped onions
2 tablespoons chicken fat or pareve margarine
Salt and freshly ground pepper to taste
Cognac (optional)

1. Simmer the livers in the chicken stock until done, 8 to 10 minutes. Drain. If you are observing kashrut, broil the livers lightly and quickly (see Note, page 48) and proceed to Step 2.

2. Grind the livers with the eggs, using the medium blade of a food chopper, or puree in a food processor, using a little chicken stock.

3. Brown the onions lightly in the fat and blend all the ingredients to make a paste. Season with salt and pepper. If desired, season further with a dash of Cognac. Serve with matzoh.

makes about 1 cup

CC

CHOPPED MUSHROOMS, EGGS AND ONIONS dairy/meat/pareve

Vegetarian Chopped Liver

(FROM *FROM MY MOTHER'S KITCHEN*)

Schmaltz imparts a traditional "chopped liver" flavor to this appetizer salad, but vegetarians will find it equally delicious when made with either butter or margarine. Like chopped liver, this dish can be served on individual plates garnished with lettuce and black olives or spread on matzohs.

2 tablespoons butter, margarine or Rendered Chicken Fat (page 48)
1 tablespoon minced onion
4 medium mushrooms, cleaned and coarsely chopped
4 eggs, hard cooked and coarsely chopped
Salt and freshly ground white pepper to taste

1. Heat the butter, margarine or fat in a small skillet over moderate heat, and when hot and bubbly add the onion. Sauté until it begins to wilt. Add the mushrooms and continue to sauté, stirring frequently, until the mushroom liquid evaporates and they begin to soften, 5 to 7 minutes. Do not brown the mushrooms or onion.

2. Turn the mixture onto a chopping board or into a wooden bowl. Add the coarsely chopped eggs and continue to mix by chopping until evenly combined. Be sure to scrape in all the fat and any liquid left from the sautéing. Season to taste. Chill several hours before serving.

makes about ¾ cup

MS

SOUR CREAM AND MUSHROOM DIP dairy

(FROM *JEWISH COOKING IN AMERICA*)

4 tablespoons salted butter
2 medium onions, diced
1 pound white mushrooms, coarsely chopped
Salt and freshly ground white pepper to taste
1 cup sour cream
2 tablespoons coarsely snipped fresh dill
Paprika to taste

1. Melt 2 tablespoons of the butter in a frying pan over medium heat and sauté the onions until golden. Set aside.

2. Place the remaining butter in the pan and add the mushrooms. Sauté about 10 minutes, stirring occasionally until the moisture evaporates.

3. Combine the onions and mushrooms in a serving bowl. Season with salt and pepper. Bring to room temperature. Fold in the sour cream and sprinkle with fresh dill and paprika. Serve as a dip with fresh vegetables or as a spread with matzoh.

makes 3 cups

JN

FLORENCE AARON'S SALMON AND EGG SALAD pareve

A favorite recipe of Florence Aaron, a fine cook whose late husband, Sam Aaron, was a founder of Sherry-Lehmann Wine and Spirits in Manhattan, one of the world's best-known retail wine shops. The dish is best if made a day in advance so the flavors have more time to combine.

10 hard-cooked eggs
¼ to ½ pound thickly sliced fine-quality smoked salmon
1 cup thinly sliced red onion rings
½ cup chopped fresh dill
⅔ cup olive oil
4 tablespoons red wine vinegar
Salt and freshly ground black pepper

1. Peel and slice the eggs. Cut salmon into 1-inch pieces.

2. Arrange the egg slices in a dish and cover with pieces of smoked salmon. Sprinkle with the onion rings and ¼ cup of the chopped dill.

3. Blend the olive oil and vinegar, and salt and pepper to taste and pour over the salad. Loosely cover with plastic wrap and let stand for 2 hours before serving. When ready to serve, sprinkle with the remaining chopped dill. Or refrigerate, covered, overnight and bring to room temperature before serving.

makes 6 to 8 servings

CC

HERRING SALAD WITH BEETS, POTATOES AND APPLES pareve

(FROM *JEWISH COOKING IN AMERICA*)

1 cup pickled herring
2 beets, peeled and boiled
4 medium potatoes, boiled and cooled
1 large Granny Smith apple, cored but not peeled
3 slices medium red onion
6 to 8 lettuce leaves (optional)
¼ cup vinaigrette dressing, or to taste
2 tablespoons chopped walnuts

1. Remove and discard any onion that might come with the herring and drain. Cut the herring, beets, potatoes and apple into ½-inch cubes. Dice the onion and combine with the herring, beets, potatoes and apple in a bowl.

2. Place portions of salad on lettuce leaves or plates. Add vinaigrette to taste and sprinkle with walnuts.

makes 4 to 6 servings

JN

SPA SLAW WITH LEMON AND ORANGE DRESSING pareve

Chef Joachim Splichal, of the Patina restaurant in Los Angeles, created this recipe for the Canyon Ranch spa in Tucson, Arizona.

1 ½ tablespoons lemon juice
1 tablespoon orange juice
½ teaspoon grated orange rind
½ teaspoon grated lemon rind
2 ½ teaspoons olive oil
1 tablespoon water
⅛ teaspoon cracked black pepper
⅛ teaspoon crushed red pepper flakes
⅛ teaspoon salt, plus more to taste
1 tablespoon thinly sliced scallion greens
4 cups shredded Napa cabbage
1 cup thinly sliced red bell pepper

1. In a bowl, whisk together all ingredients except the cabbage and bell pepper.
2. Toss the cabbage and bell pepper together in a medium bowl. Toss with dressing and serve.

makes 4 servings

MO

CABBAGE SALAD WITH GINGER DRESSING pareve

Onions and ginger make this a particularly tasty salad.

½ cup cold water
½ cup white vinegar
1 slice fresh ginger, crushed
3½ tablespoons sugar
1 tablespoon salt
1 large onion, cut into thin slices, about 2 cups loosely packed
5 cups cabbage, sliced as thinly as possible and loosely packed
1¼ cups carrot, shredded as finely as possible
2 cups thinly sliced, unpeeled cucumber

1. In a large salad bowl, combine the water, vinegar, ginger, sugar and salt. Add the onion, cabbage, carrot, and cucumber, and stir to blend thoroughly.

2. Refrigerate for at least 1 hour before serving.

makes 8 or more servings

CC

ALICE WATERS'S GRATED CARROTS WITH PARSLEY AND GARLIC pareve

A simple but delicious raw carrot salad from Alice Waters, the chef and owner of the famed Chez Panisse restaurant in Berkeley, California.

6 large carrots, peeled and grated
⅔ cup chopped parsley leaves
1 small clove garlic, minced
4 teaspoons red wine vinegar
¼ cup light olive oil or vegetable oil
¼ teaspoon salt, plus more to taste

1. Peel and grate the carrots up to 3 hours ahead. Put in a bowl and set aside.
2. When ready to serve, mix the grated carrots with the parsley.
3. Combine the garlic and vinegar in a separate bowl and whisk in the oil. Pour the vinaigrette over the carrots and toss well. Season with salt. Serve immediately.

makes 6 to 8 servings

MO

WOLFGANG PUCK'S
MOROCCAN CARROT SALAD pareve

Chef Puck uses Swiss chard and cumin to give this carrot salad its zing.

2 pounds carrots, peeled and cut across into ⅛-inch-thick slices
1½ pounds Swiss chard, washed and stemmed
2 tablespoons ground cumin
½ cup fresh lemon juice
2 tablespoons white wine vinegar
½ cup olive oil
1 tablespoon grated lemon zest
2 tablespoons minced garlic
2 tablespoons chopped fresh parsley
1 tablespoon sugar
Kosher salt and freshly ground black pepper

1. Bring 2 large pots of water to boil. Add the carrots to one and cook just until tender, about 8 minutes. Drain and set aside. Meanwhile, add the Swiss chard to the second pot of water and blanch for 5 minutes. Drain and immediately plunge into a bowl of cold water. Drain, press out all of the water, chop coarsely and set aside.

2. In a bowl, whisk together remaining ingredients except salt and pepper. Add the carrots and Swiss chard, and toss. Season to taste with salt and pepper. Cover and refrigerate at least 2 hours before serving.

makes 8 servings

MB

MARINATED EGGPLANT AND MUSHROOMS pareve

1 medium eggplant (about 1 pound), left unpeeled
½ cup red wine vinegar
1 clove garlic, mashed
Salt and freshly ground black pepper
12 raw button mushrooms
½ cup diced celery
1 teaspoon fresh rosemary
½ cup extra-virgin olive oil

1. Dice the eggplant into 1-inch cubes. Place in a saucepan, cover with water and simmer over medium heat 10 to 15 minutes. Drain thoroughly.

2. Combine the vinegar and garlic. Toss with the eggplant and season with salt and pepper. Fold in the mushrooms, celery and rosemary. Allow to marinate in the refrigerator overnight.

3. Just before serving, stir in the olive oil and check the seasonings.

makes 6 to 8 servings

FF

EGGPLANT SALAD _pareve_

(FROM _JEWISH COOKING IN AMERICA_)

3 pounds eggplant
1 red or yellow bell pepper, cored
2 medium onions
4 medium tomatoes or 2 cups canned plum tomatoes, drained
6 tablespoons olive oil
1 clove garlic, minced
1 teaspoon salt
½ teaspoon sugar
¼ teaspoon oregano
⅛ teaspoon freshly ground black pepper
2 tablespoons fresh lemon juice
Lettuce leaves for garnish
2 tablespoons chopped parsley
2 tablespoons pine nuts

1. Keeping the vegetables separate, slice the eggplants lengthwise and then into ½-inch half-moon slices. Cut the bell pepper into julienne strips. Peel the onions and slice into thin rounds. If using fresh tomatoes, peel them, remove the seeds, core and cut into small chunks.

2. Place 3 tablespoons of the olive oil into a large skillet. Sauté the sliced onions and pepper strips over medium-low heat until they are just wilted, about 5 minutes. Add the garlic and the eggplant. Cover and cook, stirring occasionally, until the eggplant is done, about 10 minutes. Add the salt, sugar, oregano and pepper, and stir and cook about 2 minutes more.

3. Remove from the stove and gently stir in the tomatoes. Transfer the mixture to a large bowl. Mix in the remaining olive oil and the lemon juice. Chill at least 4 hours.

4. Serve on lettuce leaves, sprinkled with parsley and pine nuts.

makes 8 servings

JN

PARSLEY SALAD pareve

4 bunches flat-leaf parsley, leaves only
½ teaspoon salt
½ teaspoon freshly ground black pepper
2 tablespoons fresh lemon juice
⅓ cup olive oil
1 red onion, cut in wafer-thin slices
1 tomato, diced

1. Rinse, spin-dry and refrigerate the parsley.
2. Place the salt and pepper in a salad bowl. Add the lemon juice. Slowly whisk in the olive oil.
3. When the vinaigrette is thick and stable, add the onion and the tomato and toss. Add the parsley, toss gently and serve.

makes 6 servings

MO

QUICK PARSLEY PESTO pareve

In this variation on the traditional pesto sauce, parsley substitutes for basil. It is excellent as a dressing for romaine lettuce and with grilled or poached fish or chicken.

2 cloves garlic
1½ tablespoons pine nuts
⅓ cup, packed, Italian parsley leaves (about ½ bunch)
⅓ cup olive oil
3 tablespoons balsamic vinegar
Salt and freshly ground black pepper

1. Turn on a food processor fitted with its steel blade. With the machine running, drop the garlic and nuts through the feed tube and process until finely chopped. Then stuff the parsley leaves through the feed tube and continue to process until finely chopped. Turn the machine off and scrape the ingredients down from the sides of the container.

2. Turn the machine on again and slowly drizzle in the olive oil, then the vinegar. Transfer this mixture from the food processor to a small bowl and season to taste with salt and pepper.

makes 1 cup

FF

CLAUDIA RODEN'S PEPPERS STUFFED WITH CHEESE dairy

Pipiruchkas Reyenadas de Keso

(ADAPTED FROM *THE BOOK OF JEWISH FOOD*)

6 red or yellow bell peppers
2 tablespoons vegetable oil
2 cloves garlic, minced
1 pound tomatoes, peeled and chopped, or a 12- or 14-ounce can stewed plum tomatoes
Salt and freshly ground black pepper
1 teaspoon sugar
¾ pound mozzarella cheese, cut into 6 slices

1. Preheat the oven to 500°F. Place the peppers on a baking sheet and roast for 1 hour. Place in a brown paper bag, seal and let rest for 15 minutes. Use a sharp knife to cut out the cores, then remove the skins, ribs and seeds, leaving the peppers as intact as possible.

2. Place the oil in a skillet over high heat and sauté the garlic until golden, about 1 minute. Add the fresh or canned tomatoes, crushing them between your fingers while allowing as few seeds as possible into the sauce. Season with salt and pepper to taste, add the sugar and simmer for 20 minutes, stirring occasionally.

3. Lower the oven temperature to 350°F. Slip a slice of cheese inside each pepper, place in a baking dish, cover with tomato sauce and bake for 20 minutes. Serve very hot.

makes 6 servings

MO

ROMAINE AND WALNUT SALAD pareve

(FROM *THE PLEASURE OF YOUR COMPANY*)

5 large shallots, unpeeled
2 teaspoons olive oil
3 tablespoons white wine vinegar
6 tablespoons walnut oil
¾ teaspoon kosher salt
Freshly ground black pepper
1½ heads romaine lettuce, cored, rinsed, dried, and coarsely chopped
¾ cup walnuts, toasted and coarsely chopped (see Note, page 6)

1. Preheat the oven to 350°F.

2. Place the shallots in a small casserole with a lid and drizzle with the olive oil. Cover and bake until very soft, about 1½ hours. Let cool.

3. Slip the shallots from their skins and use a knife to chop into paste. Place in a bowl and whisk in the vinegar. Slowly whisk in the walnut oil. Season with salt and pepper to taste.

4. Just before serving, combine the romaine and walnuts in a large bowl. Toss with the vinaigrette.

makes 8 servings

MO

WATERCRESS AND FENNEL SALAD pareve

2 bunches watercress, well-rinsed and dried
1 large fennel bulb
4 scallions
¼ cup white wine vinegar
⅓ cup extra-virgin olive oil
Salt and freshly ground black pepper

1. Remove most of the stems from the watercress and place the leaves in a salad bowl. Trim the stalks and leaves from the fennel and slice the bulb, including the core, very thin. Add to the bowl. Trim the scallions, chop and add to the bowl.

2. Mix the vinegar and olive oil. Pour over the ingredients in the salad bowl and toss. Season to taste with salt and pepper.

makes 6 servings

FF

VEGETABLE-MATZOH "SALAD"

pareve/meat

(ADAPTED FROM BARRY WINE)

This novel dish is a simple and delicious accompaniment to brisket or roast chicken.

10 matzoh squares
¼ cup chicken fat or margarine
1 red bell pepper, diced fine
1 cucumber, diced fine
2 to 3 teaspoons capers (optional)
1 bunch chives, chopped fine
Salt and freshly ground black pepper

1. Preheat the oven to 300°F.

2. Run a rolling pin over the matzohs to break them up into small pieces (no larger than ¼ inch).

3. Cook over medium-high heat in a dry sauté pan or toast in a 300°F oven for 10 minutes. Transfer to a bowl.

4. Heat the chicken fat or margarine in a saucepan over medium heat, and add the red pepper and cucumber. Cook for 1 minute. Turn off the heat, and add the capers, if desired, and chives.

5. Toss in a mixing bowl with the toasted matzohs. Add salt and pepper to taste. Serve immediately.

makes 8 servings

JN

MARGARETEN FAMILY'S PASSOVER VEGETABLE TERRINE pareve

Several recipes in this book, like this one, are the cherished heirlooms of the Margareten family, whose matzoh company, Horowitz-Margareten, has been in existence for more than a hundred years. The vegetables in this aspic can be layered or not, as you like. Either way it adds a festive-looking note to the Passover table.

2 tablespoons plain gelatin
½ cup lemon juice
1 tablespoon grated lemon peel
3 tablespoons sugar
1 medium onion, grated
1½ cups chopped celery
1 cup peeled, seeded cucumber, chopped
½ cup chopped scallions
2 tablespoons minced fresh dill
2 tablespoons minced parsley
2 tablespoons finely chopped watercress
1 cup grated or finely julienned carrot
¼ cup sliced or chopped radishes
½ cup chopped green bell pepper
½ cup chopped red bell pepper
⅔ cup mayonnaise
Salt and freshly ground black pepper
Sprigs of watercress for garnish

1. Dissolve the gelatin in ¼ cup cold water in a large bowl, preferably metal. Add 2 cups boiling water and stir until the gelatin is completely dissolved. Stir in the lemon juice, lemon peel, sugar and onion. Refrigerate for about 30 minutes, or until it begins to thicken.

2. Mix the vegetables all together in a bowl or, to make a layered terrine, combine the celery, cucumber, scallions, dill, parsley and watercress in one bowl and the carrot, radishes and peppers in another.

3. When the gelatin mixture has begun to thicken, remove it from the refrigerator and stir until smooth. Mix the mayonnaise with a few tablespoons of the gelatin mixture, then fold the mayonnaise into the rest of the mixture, stirring until smooth. Season to taste with salt and pepper.

4. Lightly oil a 6-cup mold. Either mix all the vegetables with the gelatin mixture and pour into the mold or, if you have separated the vegetables into two groups, mix the celery group with about two-thirds of the gelatin mixture and the carrot group with the rest. Spoon half the celery combination into the mold, add the carrot mixture and top with the remaining celery mixture.

5. Chill several hours until firmly set. Unmold onto a platter, garnish with watercress and serve.

makes 8 to 10 servings

FF

ALL MANNER OF SOUPS AND MATZOH BALLS

Though not prescribed in the Haggadah, chicken soup is an essential part of the Seder meal for many Jews, especially those of Ashkenazi heritage.

The secret of chicken soup is the bird—the older and fatter, the richer the broth. Bring the soup slowly to a simmer and skim it frequently. Be sure to bring it to room temperature before refrigeration, to prevent possible souring. Once refrigerated, the fat will congeal and is easily removed.

Although a relatively late entry into Jewish cuisine, matzoh balls have become as familiar a part of Passover as the chicken soup with which they are usually served (page 71). They can be made in any number of innovative ways—stuffed with beef, or flavored with fresh ginger and nutmeg, or with marrow replacing schmaltz or even a low-fat, low-salt version.

Root vegetables are components of another favorite soup—borscht. The heavy version, made with beef and cabbage, is served piping hot at meat meals, while the classic cold beet borscht garnished with sour cream is often the prelude to a dairy meal. Other dairy soups combine milk with fresh vegetables that evoke the spring season.

Vegetable broths, which are pareve, are satisfying in themselves, but can also be used as poaching liquid or as the basis for heartier soups with the addition of other ingredients.

When garnishing soup with dill, chop it coarsely. Finely chopped dill will feel gritty in the mouth.

matzoh balls

classic and variations

Light or heavy, plain or filled, matzoh balls did not enter the Jewish gastronomic vocabulary until well after the Jews' expulsion from Spain in the fifteenth century. Sephardic and Oriental Jews had never eaten them. Instead, at the Seder meal, Greek Jews broke up pieces of matzoh in an egg-lemon soup, while North African Jews preferred to add fresh vegetables to soup.

Ultra-Orthodox Jews still refuse to eat matzoh balls during Passover because they believe that if matzoh or matzoh meal touches water it will rise, going against the biblical injunction against eating leavened food. Instead, they eat noodles made from potato starch and eggs.

To prepare firm, dense matzoh balls, add a high proportion of matzoh meal to the mixture, and cook for 20 minutes or less. To prepare light matzoh balls, increase the number of eggs, and simmer the matzoh balls 30 minutes or longer. The lightest versions usually call for stiffly beaten egg whites folded into the mixture.

For a change of pace, try matzoh balls stuffed with ground beef, or matzoh balls flavored with marrow instead of schmaltz.

NATHAN FAMILY'S CHICKEN SOUP meat

(FROM *THE JEWISH HOLIDAY KITCHEN*)

Emily Solis Nathan serves this rich and satisfying soup with Marrow Balls, which are another of her family's heirloom recipes (page 81). Be sure to bring hot chicken soup to room temperature before refrigerating it, to prevent it from acquiring a sour taste.

4 quarts tepid water
1 large cut-up chicken, preferably stewing or large roaster
2 whole onions, peeled
4 parsnips, peeled
2 stalks celery with leaves
1 rutabaga, peeled
1 large turnip, peeled
1 kohlrabi, quartered (optional)
6 carrots, peeled (slice 2 into matchlike sticks)
6 tablespoons chopped parsley
6 tablespoons fresh dill
Salt and freshly ground black pepper
1 whole zucchini, sliced into matchlike sticks
Marrow Balls (page 81)

1. In a large saucepan, bring the water and the chicken to a boil. Skim off any residue that accumulates. Add the onions, parsnips, celery, rutabaga, turnip, kohlrabi (if using), the 4 whole carrots, 4 tablespoons of the parsley, 4 tablespoons of the fresh dill, and salt and pepper to taste. Cover and simmer over low heat for 2½ hours.

2. Strain the soup; remove the meat, celery and onion and discard or use for other purposes. When the soup has cooled slightly, remove the remaining vegetables, slice them into thin strips and return to saucepan.

3. Bring to room temperature. Refrigerate the strained soup until the fat congeals on the surface, about 3 hours or overnight. Skim off the fat.

4. Add the zucchini and the remaining carrots. Add the marrow balls and cook as in Step 3 of the marrow ball recipe. Serve warm, garnished with the remaining parsley and dill.

makes 12 servings

JN

BARBARA KAFKA'S MICROWAVE CHICKEN SOUP meat

(FROM *THE MICROWAVE GOURMET*)

Microwaving reduces the cooking time to 40 minutes. Conventional cooking would take 3 to 4 hours.

4 pounds chicken bones, cut in 2-inch pieces
2 small carrots, peeled and cut in chunks
1 small onion, peeled and cut in chunks
1 small turnip, peeled and cut in chunks
1 rib celery, cut in chunks
1 leek, white part only, trimmed, washed and cut in chunks
½ small parsnip, peeled and cut in chunks
1 clove garlic, smashed and peeled
Stems from 1 bunch parsley (about 1 ounce)
8 cups water
½ cup loosely packed dill sprigs, chopped
2 teaspoons kosher salt

1. Place all the ingredients except the dill and salt in a 5-quart microwave-safe casserole with a tightly fitting lid. Cook in the microwave, covered, at 100 percent power in a high-power oven for 40 minutes.

2. Remove from microwave and uncover. Strain through a fine sieve.

3. Add the dill and salt before serving. This soup can be used to poach matzoh balls or for matzoh ball soup.

NOTE: Most rabbis agree the microwave oven is a kosher way of cooking, and can be made to conform to the special requirements of Passover just as an ordinary oven can. If you wish to do so but are uncertain about how, consult a rabbi.

makes 8 servings

BK

MIMI SHERATON'S KNAIDLACH meat

Matzoh Balls

(FROM *FROM MY MOTHER'S KITCHEN*)

If you have any of these delectable matzoh balls left over, cook and then refrigerate them. Sliced and fried, they make a breakfast treat the next morning.

> 3 large eggs
> ¼ cup plus 2 tablespoons cold water
> 3 heaping tablespoons rendered, solidified chicken fat
> ½ teaspoon salt
> Pinch of freshly ground white pepper
> ⅔ to ¾ cup matzoh meal
> Hot chicken soup for serving
> Unsalted butter or pareve margarine for frying (optional, see Note)

1. In a bowl, beat the eggs lightly with the water. Add the chicken fat and stir until the fat is dissolved. Add salt and pepper.

2. Gradually stir in the matzoh meal, 2 tablespoons at a time, processing slowly as it thickens so not too much is added. The mixture should be as thick as light mashed potatoes, and just a little soft and spongy. Chill for 5 to 7 hours.

3. Half an hour before serving time, bring 2½ to 3 quarts of water to boil. Salt the water, as for pasta.

4. With wet hands or 2 tablespoons dipped in cold water intermittently, shape balls about 1 to 1½ inches in diameter. Drop gently into the boiling water, cover the pot loosely and let boil at a moderately brisk pace for about 25 minutes.

5. When one ball tests done (cut it open and see if it is light colored and cooked all the way through), remove all carefully with a slotted spoon. Serve in hot chicken soup.

NOTE: To make fried matzoh balls, chill the cooked balls overnight. In the morning, cut into slices between ¼ and ½ inch thick and fry them either in hot chicken fat or pareve margarine, if observing kashrut, or in hot butter in a skillet over low heat, turning so both sides become golden brown and the insides are thoroughly heated.

makes 10 to 12 large matzoh balls

MS

MATZOH BALLS WITH FRESH GINGER AND NUTMEG meat

(FROM *THE JEWISH HOLIDAY KITCHEN*)

4 large eggs, slightly beaten
2 tablespoons melted chicken fat or pareve margarine
1 cup matzoh meal
1 teaspoon grated fresh ginger
½ teaspoon nutmeg
2 tablespoons chopped parsley
1 teaspoon salt, or to taste
6 tablespoons chicken soup
4 quarts salted water

1. In a medium bowl, beat together the eggs and the fat. Stir in the matzoh meal, ginger, nutmeg, parsley and salt. Add the chicken soup. Refrigerate for 1 hour or more, to permit the meal to absorb the liquids.

2. In a 6-quart pot with a lid, bring the salted water to a boil. Reduce the heat and simmer. Form the matzoh dough into balls about 1½ inches in diameter. Drop them into the water. Cover the pot and cook, at a simmer, for 20 minutes for hard matzoh balls, or 30 to 40 minutes for soft. Place in chicken soup and serve.

makes 20 matzoh balls

JN

CAROL WOLK'S PRIZE-WINNING MATZOH BALLS meat

This recipe won the grand prize in 1988 at the first Matzoh Bowl, a contest held by the Stage Delicatessen in Manhattan. If you're sensitive to salt, you may want to reduce the quantity to 1 tablespoon or less.

    8 cups plus 1 tablespoon chicken broth
    1¼ cups matzoh meal
    5 large eggs
    1½ tablespoons salt
    1 tablespoon vodka
    2 tablespoons club soda
    ¼ cup vegetable oil

1. Place the 8 cups chicken broth in a deep pot over medium heat. Meanwhile, in a mixing bowl, combine the matzoh meal and eggs. Add the salt, vodka, club soda, remaining 1 tablespoon chicken broth and vegetable oil. Mix well. Put in the freezer for 45 minutes.

2. Use 2 tablespoons to form matzoh balls that are about 2 inches in diameter. When the broth is hot but not yet boiling, use a slotted spoon to place each ball into the soup. Cover the pot, cook for 40 minutes and serve.

makes 18 large matzoh balls

MO

LOW-FAT, LOW-SALT MATZOH BALLS meat

For the health conscious, here is a low-fat, low-salt version of the traditional matzoh ball recipe, made without egg yolks or chicken fat.

½ cup matzoh meal
4 egg whites, slightly beaten
2 tablespoons vegetable oil
2 tablespoons water
¼ teaspoon salt
3 cups chicken soup, approximately

1. In a bowl, combine all the ingredients except the chicken soup, and place in refrigerator for 20 minutes.
2. Shape into 10 balls.
3. In a covered pot, boil the matzoh balls in hot chicken soup to cover for 20 minutes.

NOTE: This may be made ahead and reheated in chicken soup.

makes 10 matzoh balls

MB

MATZOH DUMPLINGS meat
Matzeknepfle

Matzeknepfle, matzoh dumplings, are also called *schmalz-knepflichs* because they can be made with goose fat. Often served floating in a beef bouillon, they also frequently accompany *pot-au-feu* (boiled beef) for Passover in Alsace.

2 matzohs
1 medium onion, peeled and diced
1 tablespoon goose or chicken fat, or cooking oil, plus fat or oil for greasing hands
Salt and freshly ground pepper
½ teaspoon ground ginger
1 large egg
1 tablespoon matzoh meal
6 cups beef broth

1. Soak the matzohs in water to cover until soft. Then squeeze dry.

2. In a frying pan, sauté the onion with the fat or oil over medium heat. When the onions are transparent after about 5 minutes, add the matzoh and mix until smooth but not dry. Add the salt and pepper to taste, ginger, egg and matzoh meal. Remove from the heat and let stand 1 hour.

3. Put the beef broth in a large pot and bring to a simmer. Grease hands with fat or oil and form the mixture into balls the size of a large walnut. Add to the simmering beef broth and poach, covered, for 20 minutes (or fry in goose fat). Serve with *pot-au-feu* (Weyl Family's Boiled Beef with Horseradish, page 180) or any similar meat dish.

makes 11 to 12 dumplings

JN

SYLVIA SHELL BUB'S SOUTH AFRICAN–LITHUANIAN STUFFED KNEYDLAKH meat

Matzoh Balls
(FROM *THE JEWISH HOLIDAY KITCHEN*)

A specialty of Mrs. Bub's, whose family emigrated from Lithuania to South Africa before coming to the United States. With their meat stuffing spiked with cinnamon, these matzoh balls are a hearty and unusual addition to chicken soup or beef broth.

for the meat filling
¼ pound ground beef
1 tablespoon vegetable oil
2 large egg yolks
2 tablespoons softened chicken fat
2 tablespoons matzoh meal, approximately
Pinch of salt
¼ teaspoon cinnamon

for the matzoh balls
2 large eggs
2 cups water
10 teaspoons chicken fat, plus fat for greasing pan
1¼ cups matzoh meal, approximately
1 teaspoon salt, or to taste
3 quarts salted water
2 teaspoons cinnamon

1. To prepare the filling, in a skillet, sauté the meat in the oil over medium heat until browned, breaking it up with a fork as it cooks. Drain and cool. In a bowl, combine with the egg yolks, chicken fat, matzoh meal, salt and cinnamon. Refrigerate for at least 1 hour.

2. Meanwhile, prepare the matzoh balls. In a bowl, beat the eggs well. Add the water and 6 teaspoons of the chicken fat and mix well. Add enough matzoh meal and salt to make a soft dough. Refrigerate for at least 1 hour.

3. Divide the matzoh meal mixture into 8 to 10 balls of equal size. Flatten the dumplings and place 1 teaspoon of meat filling in the center of each. Enclose the filling, pinch the edges and form into balls.

continued

4. In a large pot, bring the salted water to a rapid boil. Add the matzoh balls, cover, reduce heat and simmer for 20 minutes.

5. Preheat the oven to 400°F. Drain the matzoh balls and place in a pan greased with chicken fat, cover with the remaining 4 teaspoons chicken fat and sprinkle with the remaining cinnamon. Bake for 15 to 20 minutes, or until slightly browned. Serve each matzoh ball in a soup bowl with chicken soup ladled over it.

makes 8 to 10 matzoh balls

JN

EMILY SOLIS NATHAN'S MARROW BALLS meat

(FROM *THE JEWISH HOLIDAY KITCHEN*)

These airy dumplings made with beef marrow, instead of the chicken fat used in matzoh balls, are always served at Nathan family Seders. Their inclusion could be a nod to the Dutch, German and Alsatian tradition of marrow ball soup. Serve with Nathan Family's Chicken Soup (page 72).

¼ cup marrow (from about 1½ pounds beef marrow bones, see Note)
3 large eggs, well beaten
1 teaspoon salt, or to taste
Dash of nutmeg
1 tablespoon chopped parsley
½ cup matzoh meal
Chicken broth

1. In a bowl, cream the marrow with a fork until perfectly smooth. Mix in the eggs, salt, nutmeg and parsley. Mix in enough matzoh meal to make a soft dough. Cover the bowl with plastic wrap and set aside for several hours in the refrigerator.

2. Using your hands, roll the dough into balls the size of a quarter. Meanwhile, in a large pot, bring the chicken broth to a simmer. Fill a separate saucepan with water and bring it to a boil. Drop one marrow ball into the water; if it doesn't hold together, add more matzoh meal to the dough.

3. Test again. When the test ball holds together, drop the remaining balls into the simmering soup and cook until light and cooked through, 10 to 15 minutes.

NOTE: To remove the marrow, place the bones on a paper towel or plate in a microwave for 40 seconds. Scrape out the marrow with a spoon or a table knife.

makes about 20 marrow balls

JN

FISH STOCK pareve

3 pounds fish bones and heads
8 cups water (approximately)
1 large carrot, peeled
1 large onion, peeled and quartered
3 bay leaves
1 teaspoon white peppercorns
Kosher salt to taste

1. Place the fish bones and heads in a stockpot. Cover with cold water and bring to a boil. Boil about 5 minutes, skimming constantly. Lower the heat to a simmer.

2. Add the carrot, onion, bay leaves and peppercorns and simmer very gently for about 1½ hours, adding additional water as needed to keep the ingredients covered. Strain through a very fine strainer. Season with salt.

makes 1 quart, approximately

FF

BEEF BROTH meat

Marrow may be removed from the bones after cooking and spread on matzohs or used for Marrow Balls.

1 pound beef shinbones, with meat on bones
2 pounds marrow bones
5 quarts water
2 cloves garlic, quartered
1 large onion, quartered
3 carrots, peeled and halved
3 stalks celery, cut in half
1 bay leaf
1 tablespoon salt
6 black peppercorns
Chopped parsley or dill (optional)

1. Place all the ingredients except the parsley or dill in a 10-quart stockpot. Bring to a boil and immediately reduce heat to a simmer. Skim off any scum that rises to the top.

2. Simmer for 1½ to 2 hours, stirring occasionally. Make sure that the bones are not scorching on the bottom of the pot.

3. Strain the broth and discard the vegetables.

4. Refrigerate the broth uncovered until the fat congeals. Remove and discard the fat.

5. Garnish with chopped parsley or dill, if desired.

makes about 4 quarts

CC

CECILE RATNER'S RUSSIAN CABBAGE SOUP meat
(ADAPTED FROM *THE NEW YORK COOKBOOK*)

Molly O'Neill is known for the innovative recipes that are showcased in her food column for *The Times's Sunday Magazine*, but she also has an appreciation of more traditional fare like this hearty soup given to Mrs. Ratner by her mother-in-law. Citric acid, an Ashkenazi flavoring, imparts a distinctive sour tang to any dish in which it is used.

1 head green cabbage, shredded
2 onions, thinly sliced
1 tart apple, peeled, cored and thinly sliced
1 cup tomato sauce
2½ pounds beef flanken
2 beef soup bones (about 1½ pounds)
1 tablespoon salt
¼ teaspoon freshly ground white pepper
½ teaspoon paprika
11 cups cold water
¼ teaspoon sour salt (also called citric acid)

1. In a stockpot, combine the cabbage, onions, apple, tomato sauce, beef, beef bones, salt, pepper, paprika and 10 cups cold water. Bring to a boil over medium heat, reduce the heat, cover and simmer for 1 hour, skimming occasionally.

2. Add an additional 1 cup cold water and the sour salt. Simmer, uncovered, for 30 minutes.

3. Remove the soup bones and skim off the fat. Adjust the seasonings. Serve hot.

makes 6 to 8 servings

MO

MIMI SHERATON'S COLD BEET BORSCHT pareve/dairy

(FROM *FROM MY MOTHER'S KITCHEN*)

4 large fresh raw beets (see Variation)
Juice of 2 lemons
5 cups water
Pinch of salt (optional)
Pinch of sour salt (also called citric acid) (optional)
4 large egg yolks
Pinch of sugar, if needed
Salt and freshly ground white pepper to taste
Boiled potatoes, garnish (optional)
Sour cream, garnish (optional)

1. Wash and peel the beets and grate on the coarse side of the grater. Place in a saucepan with the lemon juice, 5 cups of water, and, if desired, salt and sour salt. Bring to a boil, reduce the heat, cover and simmer until beets are tender, about 30 minutes. Remove from the heat.

2. In a bowl, beat the egg yolks with a fork until they are thin and watery. Slowly ladle some of the hot borscht into the eggs, beating constantly. When about half the soup has been added, pour the egg mixture back into the pot with the remaining soup, again pouring slowly and beating constantly.

3. When all the egg mixture has been added, pour the soup back and forth between the pot and a bowl or pitcher about 10 or 15 times until the mixture is smooth, airy and creamy. Add more lemon juice to produce a winey effect; add a tiny pinch of sugar, salt and white pepper as needed. Pour back and forth several more times. Chill thoroughly.

4. Garnish each serving with a boiled potato. Sour cream is another traditional garnish for this soup, unless it is being served at a meal that includes meat and rules of kashrut are being observed.

VARIATION: Canned beets can also be used for this soup, with excellent if slightly less flavorful results. Use whole beets, even though you will grate them, as they have more taste and better color. For the above recipe use a 1-pound can of whole beets and grate them. Cook for 10 minutes in a combination of their own canning liquid plus 1½ cans of water to make a total of about 5 cups of liquid. Proceed with the recipe as described above.

makes 1 to 1½ quarts

MS

BARBARA KAFKA'S VEGETARIAN BORSCHT pareve/dairy

(FROM *SOUP, A WAY OF LIFE*)

Dried and fresh mushrooms add a subtle flavor to this delicious borscht.

1 ounce dried mushrooms, preferably porcini
2 tablespoons vegetable oil
½ pound white mushrooms, wiped clean and sliced ¼ inch thick
1 large onion, cut into ¼-inch slices
10 small or 7 to 8 medium beets, peeled, quartered and cut across into ¼-inch slices; if
       the beet greens look nice, use half, and cut across in narrow strips
2 medium carrots, peeled and cut across into ¼-inch rounds
1 medium parsnip, peeled and cut across into ¼-inch rounds
1 very small or ½ medium celery root, peeled and cut into ½-inch cubes
3 medium baking potatoes, peeled and cut into ½-inch cubes
½ small white cabbage, shredded
3 large cloves garlic, smashed and very finely chopped
3 tablespoons tomato paste
1 medium bunch dill, coarsely chopped
¼ cup sugar
½ cup cider vinegar
2 tablespoons kosher salt
Freshly ground black pepper

for garnish
    Coarsely chopped dill
    Sour cream (optional)

1. Soak the dried mushrooms in 1 cup warm water for 15 minutes. Drain and squeeze out the excess liquid. Strain all the soaking liquid through a coffee filter or cloth. Reserve the liquid (there should be slightly less than 1 cup) and the mushrooms separately.

2. In a tall, narrow stockpot, warm the oil over medium heat. Stir in the fresh mushrooms, and cook, stirring occasionally, for 4 minutes. Stir in the onion, and cook, stirring occasionally, for 8 minutes.

3. Add the beets, carrots, parsnip, celery root, 8 cups water and the mushroom soaking liquid. Bring to a boil. Lower the heat, and simmer for 5 minutes. Stir in the potatoes, cabbage, garlic and, if using, the beet greens. Dissolve the tomato paste in ½ cup of the liquid, and stir

back into the soup. Return to a boil. Lower heat, and simmer for 5 minutes. Stir in the soaked dried mushrooms, and simmer for 5 minutes, or until all the vegetables are tender.

4. Remove from the heat. Stir in the dill, sugar, vinegar, salt and pepper to taste. Pass around bowls of the chopped dill and, if desired, sour cream for garnish.

makes 8 servings

BK

ASPARAGUS SOUP WITH DILL pareve

A splendid springtime soup.

¾ cup chopped onion
2 tablespoons olive oil
1 pound medium-thick asparagus, chopped
1½ stalks celery, chopped
1 baking potato, peeled and chopped
4 cups vegetable stock or water
1 cup dry white wine
¼ cup chopped fresh dill
Salt and freshly ground black pepper
Dill sprigs for garnish

1. Place the onion in a heavy 3-quart saucepan. Stir in the oil, cover tightly and cook over low heat until the onion is soft but not brown, about 10 minutes.

2. Stir in the asparagus, celery and potato, cook for about a minute, then add the stock, wine and dill. Simmer, partly covered, about 30 minutes, until the vegetables are very tender.

3. Allow the mixture to cool briefly, then puree in a blender or a food processor. You may have to do this in two batches. Run the soup through a sieve into a clean saucepan.

4. To serve, reheat the soup and season it to taste with salt and pepper. Spoon it into 6 warm soup plates. Float a few sprigs of dill on each as a garnish.

makes 6 servings

FF

LEON ALCALAI'S CUCUMBER-YOGURT SOUP WITH FRESH DILL dairy

This is an adaptation of a recipe that Leon Alcalai, an Israeli restaurateur and television chef, inherited from his Bulgarian grandmother.

32 ounces plain low-fat yogurt
2 large seedless cucumbers, peeled and coarsely grated (3 cups)
1 clove garlic, minced
2 tablespoons olive oil
1 tablespoon chopped fresh dill
2½ teaspoons kosher salt, plus more to taste
2 cups water

1. Place the yogurt in a paper-towel–lined sieve and let drain over a bowl in the refrigerator, several hours or overnight.

2. In a bowl, stir together the cucumbers, garlic, olive oil, dill and salt. Place the drained yogurt in a large bowl and gradually whisk in the water until very smooth. Stir in the cucumber mixture.

3. Refrigerate the soup until very cold, at least 3 hours. If needed, thin with a little more water. Taste and add more salt, if necessary. Ladle into bowls and serve.

makes 4 servings

MO

CHARLIE TROTTER'S CARROT CONSOMMÉ pareve

Chef Trotter, owner of the acclaimed Chicago restaurant that bears his name, adds ginger to this broth to tang the carrots' sweetness.

    4 pounds carrots
    1 large white onion, unpeeled
    2 whole cloves
    2 inches fresh ginger, split in half lengthwise
    2 ribs celery
    2 bay leaves
    5 black peppercorns
    2 sprigs thyme
    3 quarts water

1. Combine all the ingredients in a large pot with 3 quarts of water. Bring the soup to a simmer over medium-high heat, then reduce the heat to a slow simmer for 3 hours.

2. Remove from the heat and cool for 1 hour. Strain carefully through a fine mesh strainer.

3. Discard the vegetables and reserve the broth. Season to taste with salt and pepper.

NOTE: For a thicker soup, puree some of the strained vegetables with the broth.

    makes 2 quarts

MO

TERESA THOMPSON'S MUSHROOM CONSOMMÉ meat

(FROM *THE NEW YORK COOKBOOK*)

Throughout the year, Teresa Thompson, of New York City, wraps leftover mushroom stems and chicken scraps and saves them in her freezer to make this deep-flavored, woodsy broth.

3 pounds mushrooms or mushroom stems (domestic and/or wild mushrooms), cleaned, trimmed and quartered
½ pound fresh white mushrooms, cleaned, trimmed and quartered
5 pounds chicken scraps, including backs, necks, and gizzards (no livers)
1 white onion, coarsely chopped
2 carrots, peeled and coarsely chopped
1 rib celery, chopped
12 black peppercorns
¼ teaspoon whole allspice berries
2 bay leaves
½ bunch fresh parsley, rinsed
½ teaspoon dried thyme
½ teaspoon salt
Vodka (see Note) (optional)

1. Combine all the ingredients except the vodka in a large stockpot. Cover with 2 to 3 gallons of cold water and slowly bring to a boil. Reduce the heat and simmer very slowly for at least 6 hours, skimming frequently. The broth can simmer for up to 24 hours. It should reduce by half and turn black.

2. Strain the broth, discarding the solids. Adjust the seasonings with additional salt or pepper to taste. Serve the mushroom consommé in a cup.

NOTE: Teresa Thompson sometimes splashes each cup with vodka and serves it to guests as an aperitif.

makes 8 to 12 servings

MO

ROASTED VEGETABLE BROTH pareve
(FROM *A WELL-SEASONED APPETITE*)

Roasting the vegetables before simmering gives the broth a faintly smoky taste as well as a caramelized note. By simply adding some chopped vegetables, potatoes or leftover meats, you can turn out a meal in a bowl in a matter of minutes. The broth can also be used for braising chicken or beef, or for flavoring fish. It will keep in the refrigerator for up to 1 week or can be frozen for up to 2 months.

1 teaspoon vegetable oil
8 large carrots, peeled and cut into large pieces
2 large onions, peeled and quartered
2 turnips, halved
1 clove garlic, peeled
3 quarts plus 1 cup water
1 clove
1 sprig fresh thyme
1 teaspoon grated fresh ginger

1. Preheat the oven to 400°F. Lightly oil a baking pan or cast-iron skillet and line it with the carrots, onions, turnips and garlic. Roast, turning frequently, for 45 minutes to an hour to caramelize well. Remove from oven.

2. Place the vegetables in a soup pot. Add 1 cup of cold water to the roasting pan, scrape well with a wooden spoon and drain what remains into the soup pot.

3. Add 3 quarts of water to the vegetables, as well as the clove and thyme. Simmer for 2 hours. Remove from heat.

4. Add the ginger. Allow the broth to sit for 1 hour and strain. Discard the vegetables.

makes 2 cups

MO

LITTLE SPRING SOUP dairy

This cold soup, served with hot potatoes on the side, is nutritious and very filling. For best flavor, be sure that the vegetables are thoroughly chilled before adding them to the milk.

1 bunch radishes, cut wafer thin and chilled
2 green onions, sliced wafer thin and chilled completely
½ bunch peppery greens, such as watercress or arugula, minced and chilled
10 leaves lettuce, finely shredded and chilled completely
1 cup minced fresh dill
8 small new potatoes, peeled
2 cups whole milk
¾ teaspoon sour salt (also called citric acid)
1 tablespoon butter
Salt and freshly ground black pepper

1. In a bowl, combine the well-chilled radishes, onions, greens and lettuce with half of the dill; return to the refrigerator.

2. Boil the potatoes in lightly salted water until tender. Meanwhile, place the milk in a nonreactive bowl, whisk in the sour salt and refrigerate for 10 minutes.

3. Combine the cold vegetables and the milk mixture, and return to the refrigerator. When the potatoes are tender, drain, toss them with the butter and remaining dill, and season to taste with salt and pepper. Serve the soup very cold with the hot potatoes on the side. Alternate eating the hot potato with the tart soup.

makes 4 servings

MO

WATERCRESS, POTATO AND SCALLION SOUP dairy

A delicious soup for a dairy meal.

1 tablespoon olive oil
5 scallions, finely chopped
1 large baking potato, peeled and cut in chunks
3 cups water
1 bunch watercress, coarsely chopped
¾ cup low-fat milk
Salt and freshly ground black pepper
¼ cup heavy cream, or more, to taste

1. Heat the oil in a 3-quart saucepan. Add all but one of the scallions and sauté over low heat until the scallions turn bright green.

2. Add the potato chunks and about 3 cups of water, enough to cover the potatoes. Bring to a boil and cook over medium heat until the potatoes are very tender, about 25 minutes. Stir in the watercress and remove from heat. Allow to cool about 10 minutes.

3. Puree the contents of the saucepan in a blender or food processor. Add the milk, puree again and season to taste with salt and pepper. Return to the saucepan and stir in the cream.

4. Reheat and serve, sprinkled with the remaining chopped scallion.

makes 3 to 4 servings

FF

FROM MATZOH AND EGGS...

The laws governing the baking of matzoh for Passover are so stringent that doing so at home is virtually impossible, but recipes are included here that might be attempted at other times of the year by Jews who observe kashrut. They include a classic recipe and an unusual variation with honey and pepper that dates from sixteenth-century Spain.

Plain matzoh forms the basis of holiday treats such as matzoh brei—plain or combined with asparagus—and matzoh pies, known as minas. And for variety, the squares can be seasoned with garlic or onion. Popovers, blintzes, pancakes—even "bagels"—are all made with matzoh meal, as is a superb "polenta," served at Manhattan's Union Square Cafe.

Eggs add variety to the Passover menu, transforming vegetables into showcase soufflés, flans, fritadas and puddings.

MATZOHS pareve

(ADAPTED FROM *FROM MY MOTHER'S KITCHEN*)

2 cups unbleached flour, more if needed (see Note)
½ to ¾ cup cold water, as needed

1. Preheat the oven to 500°F.

2. Place the flour on a board or in a wide mixing bowl and make a mound with a well in the center. Pour in ½ cup water and begin to stir in the flour gradually, using your fingertips or a fork. Add more water as needed until all the flour is mixed in and you have a soft, pliable dough that is just barely sticky.

3. Divide the dough in quarters. On a floured board, knead each portion of dough 8 or 10 times, working in a little flour if it is too sticky to be rolled. Clean the board of all dough scraps, reflour. With a floured rolling pin, roll the dough into a circle about 7 inches in diameter and a little less than ⅛ inch thick.

4. Pierce the surface all over with the tines of a fork, being sure you pierce through the bottom of the dough. This will keep the matzoh from buckling while it bakes.

5. If you have enough room in your oven or on your baking sheets, you can bake all the matzohs at once. In that case, roll out all the dough and do so. Otherwise bake them one or two at a time, but do not roll out the remaining dough until you are ready to bake it. Lift the pierced dough over a rolling pin and turn onto ungreased baking sheet or tiles. Bake for about 10 minutes.

6. When the matzoh curls, looks very dry and shows some golden-brown patches and edges, turn and bake the second side for 5 to 8 minutes, or until it too is golden brown. Some very dark edges are desirable, for they add a special flavor. Remove from the oven and cool on a rack.

NOTE: Matzoh cake meal may be substituted for the flour, though it does not roll out as well. Increase the water by one half and bake for 3 minutes longer.

makes 4 seven-inch matzohs

MS

freshening and seasoning matzohs

To freshen the flavor of matzohs, dampen them lightly on both sides by rubbing wet hands over them or running them under water. Bake in a 375°F oven for a few minutes until dry and crisp and faintly brown around the edges. Watch carefully so they do not burn. Coarse salt can be sprinkled on the top side of each after wetting and before baking.

Baked matzohs can also be seasoned with garlic or onion, in which case they are delicious with soup or cheese or with various canapé spreads. Rub one side of each matzoh with a cut onion or garlic clove. Dampen the matzoh slightly, sprinkle with salt and bake for 6 or 7 minutes at 375°F.

MS

ANGELINA DE LEON'S MATZOHS pareve

This recipe dates from the Spanish Inquisition. It survives because it was used as evidence in the trial of Angelina de Leon, to prove that she was a Jew. Honey and black pepper impart a sweet and spicy flavor.

4 cups white flour (see Note)
1 tablespoon freshly ground black pepper
4 large eggs, beaten
6 tablespoons honey
4 teaspoons olive oil
8 tablespoons water

1. Preheat the oven to 400°F.
2. In a large mixing bowl, combine the flour and pepper. Mix well.
3. Mix in the eggs, honey, olive oil and just enough water to make a very dry dough. Do not overmix.
4. Divide the dough into 12 equal portions, and shape into balls. On a lightly floured surface, roll each ball into a thin disk about 8 inches in diameter. Pierce all over with fork.
5. Bake on cookie sheets for 10 minutes, or until matzohs are puffed and begin to brown. Cool on racks.

NOTE: Matzoh cake meal may be substituted for the flour, though the dough does not roll out as well. Increase the water by one half and bake for 3 minutes longer.

makes 12 eight-inch matzohs

AB

PASSOVER POPOVERS pareve/dairy

An extremely popular Passover recipe.

2 large eggs
¼ cup water or milk
2 tablespoons vegetable oil
½ teaspoon salt
½ cup matzoh cake meal

1. Preheat oven to 450°F. Oil a standard muffin tin with 2½-inch cups.
2. In a bowl, beat together the eggs, water or milk, oil and salt. Add the matzoh cake meal, stirring with a fork until ingredients are well blended.
3. Pour 3 tablespoons of batter into each cup of the prepared muffin tin. Bake in the lower third of the oven 30 minutes until nicely browned and firm to the touch.

makes 12 popovers

FF

PASSOVER CRISPY STICKS pareve

(FROM *THE NEW YORK TIMES HERITAGE COOKBOOK*)

Serve with soup or as a snack.

    1 large egg
    ½ cup water
    1 teaspoon salt
    1 cup sifted matzoh meal
    1 cup vegetable oil
    1 teaspoon kosher salt

1. In a mixing bowl, using a beater, beat together the egg, water and salt. Gradually stir in the matzoh meal. Cover and chill at least 1 hour.

2. With lightly greased hands, pinch off a ½-inch nugget of dough and roll it out into a pencil shape between the palm of the hand and a clean flat surface to make a thin strip about 1½ inches long. Place on a flat plate. Repeat until all the dough is used.

3. Heat the oil in a heavy skillet and add the dough strands, a few at a time, and fry until golden. Drain sticks and shake in a paper bag containing the coarse salt.

makes 3 dozen

JH

HANNA GOODMAN'S PASSOVER "BAGELS" pareve/dairy
(ADAPTED FROM *JEWISH COOKING AROUND THE WORLD*)

These puffy golden rings are based on a *pâte à choux* made with matzoh meal instead of flour. Though they are completely unlike the heavier yeast and flour bagel, they perform much the same service during the Passover season. Made in peaked rounds, without the holes, they can be used as cream puff shells.

1 cup water
½ cup (1 stick) pareve margarine or butter
2 cups matzoh meal
1 tablespoon sugar
1½ teaspoons salt
6 large eggs

1. Bring water to a boil in a 2-quart saucepan and add the margarine or butter. When the margarine or butter has melted, remove from the heat and add the dry matzoh meal, sugar and salt all at once.

2. Beat rapidly over medium heat, using a wooden spoon, until the mixture forms a ball and leaves the sides of the pan. Remove from the heat.

3. Add the eggs, one at a time, beating each in thoroughly before adding the next.

4. Preheat the oven to 375°F. Grease a large baking sheet with margarine or butter.

5. Using 2 tablespoons dipped in cold water, drop 15 peaked rounds onto the baking sheet, placing them about 2 inches apart. Dip the handle tip of a wooden spoon in cold water, and with it make a round hole in the center of each bagel.

6. Bake for about 1 hour, or until puffed up and golden brown. Pierce a small hole in the side of each bagel to release steam so the bagel will not collapse. Store in a sealed container. Warm in the oven before serving.

makes 15 "bagels"

MS

MIMI SHERATON'S MATZOH BREI dairy
(FROM *FROM MY MOTHER'S KITCHEN*)

Many people consider matzoh brei one of Passover's special breakfast treats. The savory version is made with black pepper and is often served with cottage cheese. For a sweeter brei, you may wish to reduce or omit the black pepper and to sprinkle the matzoh brei with sugar or cinnamon sugar immediately after it is divided onto a heated platter or individual plates. Jam is also a good accompaniment to the sweeter brei.

8 matzoh squares
3 to 4 cups boiling water
4 extra-large eggs, lightly beaten
1 teaspoon salt, or to taste
¼ to ½ teaspoon freshly ground black pepper
½ cup (1 stick) unsalted butter
Cottage cheese, for garnish (optional)

1.   Break the matzohs into 1½- to 2-inch squares, or approximate-size pieces. Place in a large bowl, preferably with a handle, or in a large saucepan, so draining will be easy.

2.   Bring the water to a boil and pour over the matzohs. Drain immediately through a sieve or colander. It is not necessary to stir the matzoh pieces through the water, or to let them stand. They should be only very slightly moistened so they absorb egg, but should not become soggy. Drain very thoroughly and return to the bowl or saucepan.

3.   Add the beaten eggs, salt and pepper. Toss lightly with a fork until all of the matzoh pieces are well coated with egg and the seasonings are distributed evenly. Do not mix or stir vigorously as the matzohs should not be broken up any more than necessary. Matzohs are bland, so plenty of salt and pepper will be needed.

4.   Heat the butter until hot and bubbling (but not brown), in a heavy 10- to 12-inch skillet, preferably of black iron, over medium heat. Turn the matzoh mixture into the skillet and fry. When the underside begins to brown, turn in sections with a spatula. Keep turning until all sides are light golden brown. It is not necessary, or even desirable, to keep a pancake shape. A jumble of pieces, some golden brown contrasted with others that are slightly golden and tender, is ideal. Check seasoning once during frying and adjust as needed. Total frying time will be about 10 minutes. Serve on a heated platter or on individual plates, with cottage cheese on the side, if desired.

makes 4 servings

MS

ASPARAGUS MATZOH BREI dairy/pareve

Pairing matzoh brei with a spring vegetable is a perfect Passover combination.

½ pound medium asparagus
3 tablespoons butter or olive oil
1 cup thinly sliced onions
5 matzohs
6 large eggs, beaten
Salt and freshly ground black pepper
Freshly grated Swiss cheese (optional)

1. Snap the ends off the asparagus where they break naturally. Peel the spears. Cut the asparagus in 1-inch lengths.

2. Place the asparagus in a steamer basket or in a pot of simmering water, and steam or cook about 3 minutes until they are just tender and still bright green. Drain the asparagus, if necessary, and refresh under cold running water. Dry well.

3. Heat 1 tablespoon of the butter or oil in a large nonstick skillet over medium-low heat. Cook the onions until golden, about 6 minutes. Remove the onions from the pan and mix in a bowl with the asparagus.

4. Crumble the matzohs and soak them in a bowl of hot water about 30 seconds. Drain well and squeeze out as much water as possible. In a bowl, mix the eggs and matzohs together. Season with salt and pepper. Stir in the onions and asparagus.

5. Heat the remaining 2 tablespoons butter or oil in the skillet over medium-high heat. Add the matzoh mixture and cook several minutes until the mixture sets on the bottom and around the edges. Cover the skillet with a large plate and, holding both plate and skillet together, flip them over so the matzoh brei is cooked side up on the plate. Slide it back into the pan and cook the second side. Cut it in wedges and serve with a sprinkling of grated cheese, if desired.

makes 4 servings

FF

MIMI SHERATON'S MATZOH MEAL PANCAKES dairy

(FROM *FROM MY MOTHER'S KITCHEN*)

Although most recipes for this dish call for water to be added to egg yolks, results are more soufflélike and more lasting if water is omitted. This makes a delicious dessert or light main course for breakfast.

> 3 extra-large eggs, separated
> 2 tablespoons sugar
> 1 tablespoon fresh lemon juice
> Grated rind of ½ lemon
> Pinch of salt
> ½ cup plus 2 tablespoons matzoh meal
> Unsalted butter
> Sugar or cinnamon sugar for sprinkling

1. In a bowl, beat the egg yolks with 1 tablespoon sugar until very thick and almost white. Beat in the lemon juice and rind.

2. In another bowl, beat the egg whites with a pinch of salt and, as they get foamy, gradually beat in remaining 1 tablespoon of sugar. Beat until the whites stand in stiff but shiny peaks.

3. Stir 2 or 3 tablespoonfuls of beaten whites into the yolk mixture.

4. Using a rubber spatula, fold the remaining whites and the matzoh meal into the yolks, quickly, gently and thoroughly.

5. Lightly butter a skillet or griddle. Drop a rounded tablespoonful at a time onto the hot skillet. Fry slowly over moderate heat so the pancakes turn golden brown without having the butter burn. Turn to brown the second side. Total frying time should be 5 to 7 minutes for each batch. Serve immediately, sprinkling the tops of the pancakes with plain or cinnamon sugar.

NOTE: Because these pancakes deflate rapidly, it is a good idea to use two skillets for frying, so all can be served at once.

makes 12 to 14 pancakes; about 4 servings

MS

UNION SQUARE CAFE'S MATZOH MEAL POLENTA meat
(ADAPTED FROM *THE UNION SQUARE CAFE COOKBOOK*)

Michael Romano and Danny Meyer, of the Union Square Cafe, one of Manhattan's most acclaimed restaurants, collaborated to create a polenta made from matzoh meal instead of from cornmeal. At their restaurant, it is served with Sautéed Mushrooms (page 219), but it is extremely versatile. Try it with other toppings or with gravy from roast meats and poultry. Although not created specifically for Passover, this dish is one of the most original food ideas for the holiday.

Olive oil for coating pan
2¼ cups chicken stock
1 chicken bouillon cube
¼ teaspoon each minced fresh rosemary, sage and thyme
¾ cup matzoh meal, plus extra for coating the cakes
1 large egg
1 large egg yolk
Kosher salt and freshly ground black pepper
⅓ cup olive oil
Chopped parsley for garnish (optional)

1. Lightly oil an 8-inch cake pan or straight-sided tart pan.
2. In a 2-quart saucepan, bring to a boil the chicken stock, bouillon cube and herbs. Reduce the heat and simmer until the bouillon cube is completely dissolved, about 3 minutes.
3. Slowly pour the matzoh meal into the liquid with one hand while whisking constantly with the other. (Be sure to use a firm whisk.) Continue whisking until smooth and creamy. The mixture will become quite thick. Reduce the heat to low and cook for 5 minutes, stirring occasionally to prevent sticking.
4. In a bowl, beat the egg and egg yolk together; whisk the eggs into the matzoh polenta. Raise the heat slightly and return the mixture to a boil. Boil, whisking constantly, for 1 minute. Season with salt and pepper to taste and remove from the heat.
5. Pour the cooked matzoh polenta into the cake pan. With a spatula, spread the mixture evenly and smoothly. Cover, place in the refrigerator and chill thoroughly, at least 30 minutes and up to 24 hours.
6. Cut the polenta into pie-shaped wedges. In a large sauté pan, heat the olive oil over a moderate flame. Dredge the matzoh wedges in the extra matzoh meal and sauté on both sides until golden brown. Sprinkle with chopped parsley, if desired.

makes 4 to 6 servings

FF

PASSOVER CHEESE BLINTZES dairy

Serve with sour cream or jam.

for the batter

3 large eggs
¼ cup matzoh cake meal
1½ cups water
½ teaspoon salt
Unsalted butter

for the filling

1 pound cottage cheese
1 large egg
½ teaspoon salt
1 teaspoon sugar
Unsalted butter

1. To make the batter, in a bowl, beat together the eggs, matzoh cake meal and water to make a thin batter. Mix in salt.

2. Place a 6-inch skillet over medium heat and brush with butter. Pour about 3 table-spoons batter into the skillet, spreading as thinly as possible by tilting the pan to coat the bottom. Fry until brown and carefully turn out, browned side up, onto a towel. Repeat with the remaining batter.

3. To prepare the filling, in a bowl, combine the cottage cheese, egg, salt and sugar. Spread 1 tablespoon of mixture along one side of each blintz. Tuck in the ends and roll up like a jelly roll.

4. In the same skillet, brown the blintzes in butter, a few at a time, over medium heat and serve hot.

makes about 10 blintzes   JH

MRS. ARNOLD STEIN'S COTTAGE CHEESE CHREMSELE dairy

4 large eggs, separated
1 cup fine-curd cottage cheese
½ teaspoon salt
¼ cup matzoh meal
Unsalted butter

1. In a bowl, beat the egg yolks with the cottage cheese and salt. Stir in matzoh meal.
2. In another bowl, beat the egg whites until stiff. Fold into matzoh meal mixture.
3. Heat a well-greased skillet or griddle over medium-low heat. Form small pancakes, using 2 tablespoons of batter for each. Fry in the hot skillet until nicely browned, about 3 minutes on each side.

SERVING SUGGESTIONS: With jam or cinnamon sugar for breakfast; with fresh or canned fruit or sour cream and chives as a luncheon dish.

makes 8 four-inch pancakes

FF

CAROL FIELD'S ARTICHOKE, MATZOH AND SPINACH PIE pareve/meat
(ADAPTED FROM *CELEBRATING ITALY*)

Sephardim traditionally serve this type of matzoh pie, known as a mina, during Passover. Those made with meat are often served as part of the Seder meal or as a main course during the rest of the holiday. Vegetable minas, which are lighter, are excellent at brunch or lunch. This versatile recipe, in which meat is an optional ingredient, is delicious either way it is prepared.

12 matzoh squares
13 tablespoons olive oil, approximately, plus oil for greasing the pan
1 pound ground beef (optional)
Salt and freshly ground black pepper
1½ pounds onions, sliced thin
4 artichokes or two 8-ounce cans of artichoke hearts (see Note)
Juice of 1 lemon, plus ½ cup fresh lemon juice
6 cloves garlic, minced
¾ teaspoon minced rosemary
¾ teaspoon minced sage
2 pounds fresh spinach
1 peperoncino (dried red chile), seeded and minced
½ teaspoon freshly grated nutmeg
1 pound mushrooms, sliced
Margarine for greasing the pan
6 large eggs
1 cup beef or vegetable broth

1. Preheat the oven to 400°F.
2. Cover the unbroken matzohs with cold water, and let sit until soft (about 2 minutes). Drain very well on cloth or paper towels.
3. If using the ground beef, heat 1 tablespoon of the olive oil in a skillet, and sauté the beef, stirring until it is no longer red. Add salt and pepper to taste. Drain, and set aside.
4. In the same skillet, sauté the onions in 3 tablespoons of olive oil until golden. Drain, and set aside.
5. Clean the artichokes and remove the chokes and fibrous leaves. Put the artichokes in a pot, and add enough water to cover and the juice of 1 lemon to keep them from turning black.

Simmer for about 20 minutes. Drain, and allow the artichokes to cool. Quarter the artichokes, and in the skillet used for the onions, sauté them in 3 tablespoons of the olive oil with about ⅓ of the minced garlic, the rosemary and sage, and salt to taste. Drain, and set aside. If using canned artichoke hearts, cut in half and then sauté.

6. Wash and stem the spinach. Cook in a saucepan over medium heat for 4 to 5 minutes with only the water left on the leaves. Squeeze dry. In the same skillet, add 3 tablespoons of the olive oil, and sauté the spinach with about a third of the minced garlic, the peperoncino and nutmeg, and salt to taste. Drain, and set aside.

7. In the same skillet, sauté the mushrooms in the remaining 3 tablespoons of the olive oil, the remaining garlic and salt to taste.

8. Grease a 9- by 13-inch baking dish, and if using the ground beef, cover the bottom with the sautéed meat. Add a layer of 3 matzohs (it doesn't matter if they fall apart). Cover with the onions. Add successive layers, in this order: 3 matzohs, the artichokes, 3 matzohs, the spinach, 3 matzohs and, finally, the mushrooms.

9. Beat together the eggs and the remaining ½ cup lemon juice, and pour over the top of the dish. Add enough of the broth to moisten well.

10. Bake in the oven for about 30 minutes, or until the mixture is set and cooked through.

NOTE: If you can find them, tender baby artichokes will yield the best results. Double the number to 8, and cut the cooking time in half. Halve the artichokes, instead of quartering them. Almost all of a baby artichoke can be eaten except the fibrous tips of the leaves.

makes 8 servings

JN

CYNTHIA ZEGER'S CARROT SOUFFLÉ RING pareve

A treasured family recipe of Cynthia Zeger, whose son Erich Segal wrote *Love Story* and other novels. This is a delectable way to serve carrots.

> 3 cups ¼-inch-thick carrot slices
> 1 bay leaf
> 1 onion
> Salt
> Boiling water
> 3 tablespoons ground cinnamon
> 1 tablespoon ground ginger
> Freshly ground black pepper
> 5 large eggs, separated
> 1 cup sugar
> ½ cup matzoh meal
> 1 cup ground walnuts

1. Preheat the oven to 350°F.
2. Place the carrots in a saucepan. Add bay leaf, onion, salt and boiling water barely to cover. Bring to a boil, cover and simmer until the carrots are very tender, about 20 minutes.
3. Remove the onion and bay leaf, drain the carrots and mash thoroughly. Stir in the cinnamon, ginger, 1 teaspoon salt and pepper to taste.
4. In a bowl, beat the egg yolks with the sugar until very thick and lemon colored. Stir in the carrot mixture.
5. In another bowl, beat the egg whites until stiff but not dry, and fold into the carrot mixture alternately with the matzoh meal and nuts.
6. Turn into a greased 2½- to 3-quart ring mold or cake pan, and set in a pan of boiling water. Bake 40 minutes, or until set. Alternatively, a greased 10-inch springform pan can be used. Bake directly on the oven shelf with a pan of boiling water set beneath it on the bottom of the oven.

makes 12 servings

CC

CLAUDIA RODEN'S
TURKISH EGGPLANT FLAN dairy

Almodrote de Berengena
(ADAPTED FROM *THE BOOK OF JEWISH FOOD*)

4 pounds eggplant
9 ounces drained feta cheese
2 large eggs, lightly beaten
¼ cup matzoh meal
1 cup grated cheddar cheese
5 tablespoons vegetable oil, plus more for the baking dish

1. Preheat the oven to 500°F. Prick the eggplants repeatedly with a fork. Place on a baking sheet and bake, turning to prevent burning, for 45 minutes. Cool. Peel or scoop out the flesh into a colander. Drain and press out the juices, then chop the flesh with a knife and mash it with a fork.

2. Lower the oven temperature to 350°F. In a large bowl, mash the feta cheese. Add the eggs, matzoh meal, 5 tablespoons of the cheddar and 4 tablespoons of the oil. Beat well.

3. Add the mashed eggplant and mix. Pour the mixture into an oiled baking dish, drizzle 1 tablespoon of the oil over the mixture and sprinkle with the remaining cheddar cheese. Bake for 1 hour until lightly colored.

makes 8 servings

MO

ANGEL FAMILY'S
SPINACH PUDDING pareve/dairy

Fritada de Espinaca

(FROM *SEPHARDIC HOLIDAY COOKING*)

A traditional Sephardic dish served by Gilda Angel, an authority on Sephardic cooking and the wife of Rabbi Marc D. Angel of Congregation Shearith Israel, the Spanish and Portugese Synagogue in Manhattan. If this pudding is to be served at a dairy meal, two cups of cottage cheese—a very good addition as it makes for a creamy texture—or 1½ cups of grated cheddar cheese can also be stirred into the mixture.

    2 pounds fresh spinach
    4 matzohs
    7 large eggs
    1½ teaspoons salt
    ½ teaspoon freshly ground black pepper
    Vegetable oil for pan

1. Preheat the oven to 350°F.
2. Wash the spinach thoroughly in several changes of water until all sand is removed. Break off and discard the stems and chop the leaves finely.
3. Soak the matzohs in warm water to cover for 10 minutes, or until completely soft. Pick up small handfuls and squeeze out as much water as possible. In a bowl, combine the eggs, salt and pepper with the matzoh pulp. Stir in the spinach.
4. Pour the oil into 9- by 13-inch baking pan. You should have about ⅛-inch depth. Turn the pudding mixture into the pan and brush a little more oil over the top. Bake in middle of the oven for about 1 hour, or until high and puffy and thoroughly set. Cut in squares and serve immediately.

VARIATIONS: One or 2 tablespoons of grated onion and/or ½ teaspoon nutmeg can be added to the spinach mixture. Although Mrs. Angel does not do so, 2 tablespoons of oil can be stirred into the mixture to make it a little smoother and creamier. Butter may be substituted for oil if this is not to be served with meat.

    makes 8 to 10 servings

MS

ILANA AMINI'S SPINACH AND GREEN HERB PIE pareve

Kookoo Sabzi

The green color of this Persian specialty heralds verdant spring. The pie is delicious either hot or cold.

3 cups chopped spinach leaves
2 cups chopped parsley
¾ cup chopped dill
6 scallions, with white and green portions chopped
¼ cup chopped fresh cilantro (optional)
1 tablespoon vegetable oil
½ to ⅔ cup matzoh meal, or as needed
3 to 4 extra-large eggs, or as needed
1 teaspoon salt
½ teaspoon freshly ground white pepper

1. Preheat the oven to 350°F.
2. Combine the first 5 ingredients including the cilantro, if using, in a mixing bowl. Add the oil and ½ cup matzoh meal. Stir in 3 eggs. Mix well with wooden spoon. Consistency should be fairly thick but slightly runny; the mixture should drop in mass from tablespoon, and just a little liquid should be visible. Add an additional egg or matzoh meal, if needed, to attain that texture. Season with salt and pepper to taste.
3. Spread thin film of oil over bottom and sides of baking dish that measures about 8 by 11 by 1½ inches. Turn in the egg mixture and smooth top with back of spoon.
4. Bake for 25 to 35 minutes, or until the pie is completely set and slightly shrunken away from sides of dish.
5. Serve hot or cold.

makes 8 to 10 servings as a side dish

MS

CLAUDIA RODEN'S SPINACH FRITADA pareve
(ADAPTED FROM *THE BOOK OF JEWISH FOOD*)

This egg dish is cooked on the top of the stove and finished under the broiler. It resembles an Italian frittata. Be sure to use a skillet with a handle that will not be damaged under a broiler, or wrap the handle well with heavy-duty foil. Cut it into slices and serve it either hot or at room temperature.

1 pound fresh spinach, washed and trimmed
¼ cup light vegetable oil
6 large eggs
¼ cup matzoh meal
Salt and freshly ground black pepper to taste
Pinch of freshly grated nutmeg
2 whole scallions, finely chopped
3 tablespoons minced cilantro or parsley (optional)

1. Preheat the broiler.
2. In a large saucepan over medium heat, cook the spinach, covered, with 2 tablespoons of the oil until it collapses into a soft mass. Drain.
3. In a large bowl, beat the eggs lightly. Add the spinach, matzoh meal, seasonings, scallions and cilantro or parsley, if desired.
4. In a large, heavy-bottomed, ovenproof skillet over very gentle heat, heat remaining 2 tablespoons oil. Pour in the egg mixture and cook until the bottom of mixture is set. Then place skillet under the broiler until top of mixture is set and slightly browned.
5. Turn out of skillet and cut in slices like a cake. Eat hot or cold.

makes 4 to 6 slices

LS

MRS. ARNOLD STEIN'S VEGETABLE SOUFFLÉ meat

1½ cups sliced carrots
½ cup sliced celery
½ cup sliced onion
½ cup water
2½ teaspoons salt
1 scallion, chopped
1 tablespoon fresh dill
3 tablespoons vegetable oil
⅓ cup matzoh cake meal
½ cup chicken broth, approximately
3 large egg yolks
4 large egg whites

1. Combine the carrots, celery and onion with the water and 1 teaspoon salt in a saucepan. Simmer, covered, until tender, about 15 minutes. Drain, reserving the cooking liquid.

2. Preheat the oven to 375°F. Oil a 6-cup soufflé dish.

3. Puree the vegetables in blender or food mill along with the scallion and dill. Pour into a bowl.

4. Heat the oil in a saucepan over medium heat. Add the cake meal, stirring with a whisk, and cook for a minute or two. Add enough chicken broth to the reserved vegetable liquid to make 1 cup. Gradually add this stock to the cake meal mixture in the saucepan, stirring constantly. Simmer, stirring, several minutes until quite thick. Stir into the vegetable puree.

5. Add the egg yolks and 1 teaspoon salt to vegetable mixture.

6. In a bowl, beat the egg whites with ½ teaspoon salt until stiff. Fold into vegetable mixture. Pour into the prepared soufflé dish.

7. Bake in lower third of preheated oven about 40 minutes until puffed and brown. Serve at once.

makes 6 to 8 servings

JH

MAIN
DISH
FISH

Ashkenazi traditionally serve freshwater fish, since they were the only kind available in the inland countries of Eastern Europe, and their recipes also incorporate the vegetables that were at hand. Some Sephardim had access to saltwater fish, and their recipes convey the flavors of the Mediterranean. Recently, venturesome cooks have created fish recipes that are particularly appropriate for Passover. For example, scrod under horseradish meringue combines two holiday flavors in an original way. And rhubarb, used in several fish dishes, heralds the spring season.

WHOLE ROASTED FISH pareve

1 large whole striped bass or salmon, 5 to 8 pounds
2 tablespoons olive oil
Salt and freshly ground black pepper
1 large bunch fresh rosemary
Several large sprigs of fresh cilantro for garnish
1½ to 2 cups Romesco Sauce (recipe follows)

1. Preheat the oven to 500°F.

2. The fish should be cleaned and gutted but left whole. For flavor and dramatic presentation, the head should be left on the fish, but you may have to remove it if the fish will not fit in your oven with the head. You will need an oven at least 20 inches wide to accommodate a whole fish larger than 6 pounds. You will also need a very large pan to hold the fish. You can improvise one using a standard 17-inch baking sheet, wrapping it in several thickness of heavy-duty foil and extending the foil beyond the ends of the baking sheet to create a surface that will fit the fish. Turn up the edges of the foil to catch pan juices.

3. Rub the fish inside and out with the olive oil. Season the cavity of the fish with salt and pepper and stuff it with the rosemary.

4. Place the fish on the prepared pan, place it in the oven and roast it for 5 minutes per pound. Remove the fish from the oven and turn off the oven. Cover the fish loosely with a tent of foil and allow it to rest at least 15 minutes. It can rest for up to 1 hour and then be served at room temperature. Alternatively, after the resting period, the fish can be returned to the oven set at the lowest possible temperature (140° to 150°F) and kept warm without overcooking for up to 1 hour.

5. At serving time, transfer the fish to a platter and garnish with the fresh cilantro.

6. To serve, peel off the top layer of the skin of the fish. Then, using a large fork and a spatula, carefully lift sections of the fish off the bone. When all the exposed flesh has been removed from the bone, lift off the skeleton in one piece to expose the flesh underneath. Serve portions of it, lifting it off the skin, with Romesco Sauce on the side.

makes 6 to 10 servings

FF

ROMESCO SAUCE pareve

This sauce is a tasty complement to whole roasted fish or to baked, poached or grilled fish. For best flavor, serve it at room temperature.

½ cup chopped blanched almonds
4 tablespoons olive oil
½ cup finely chopped onion
4 cloves garlic, minced
2 large sweet red peppers, seeded and chopped
1 cup water
2 tablespoons red wine vinegar
1 ripe tomato, seeded and chopped
Salt to taste
Dried hot red pepper flakes to taste

1. Place a heavy skillet over medium-high heat, add the almonds and cook, stirring for a couple of minutes until they are toasted. Remove the almonds from the skillet. Place in a food processor, grind them fine and leave in the food processor.

2. Add the oil to the skillet and when it is hot, add the onion. Sauté until it is golden, then stir in the garlic. Add the peppers, water and vinegar, lower the heat and cook gently until the peppers are tender, about 15 minutes. Stir in the tomato and season the mixture with salt and hot red pepper. Remove from the heat.

3. Add the mixture to the almonds in the food processor and puree. Taste for seasoning; serve at room temperature.

makes 2 cups

FF

IVANA DI MARCO'S BAKED BASS meat

(ADAPTED FROM OSTERIO ROMANO, PHILADELPHIA)

Eight 8-ounce fillets of striped bass or black bass
Salt and freshly ground black pepper to taste
4 cups chicken broth
5 ribs celery, julienned
5 carrots, scraped and julienned
5 onions, thinly sliced
2 cups dry white wine

1. Preheat oven to 375°F.
2. Sprinkle the fish with salt and pepper. Place in a single layer in a large baking dish. Pour in the broth. Distribute the celery, carrots and onions over fish.
3. Bake 15 minutes. Add the wine and cook 15 minutes more, or until done.
4. Serve with vegetables on top, adding a few spoonfuls of broth to each serving.

makes 8 servings

GF

SEARED STRIPED BASS WITH ROASTED SHALLOT AND GARLIC PUREE AND CARAMELIZED LEEKS dairy

(FROM *A WELL-SEASONED APPETITE*)

the fish

1 teaspoon coarsely ground black pepper
1 teaspoon coarsely ground white pepper
1 teaspoon sugar
1 teaspoon finely chopped fresh rosemary
Six 6-ounce striped bass fillets (or any firm white fish from the bass or snapper family)
1 teaspoon unsalted butter
2 teaspoons olive oil

the puree

3 cloves garlic, unpeeled
12 whole shallots, unpeeled
2 teaspoons salt
1 teaspoon freshly ground black pepper
2 tablespoons olive oil
¼ cup heavy cream

the leeks

1 cup water
½ cup sugar
2 teaspoons grated lemon rind
1 cup thinly sliced leeks (white part only)

the vinaigrette

1 cup extra-virgin olive oil
½ cup white wine vinegar
4 shallots, finely chopped
1 teaspoon sugar
Salt and freshly ground black pepper to taste
1 tablespoon finely chopped chives

continued

1. For the fish, in a small bowl, combine the peppers, sugar and rosemary. Use a sharp knife to make crosshatch marks on the skin of each fish fillet. Rub the spice mixture into the skin and marinate for 1 hour.

2. Meanwhile, preheat the oven to 375°F. Place the garlic and shallots in a small baking dish. Sprinkle with salt, pepper and olive oil. Cover with aluminum foil and bake until soft, about 30 minutes. Let cool to room temperature. Peel the garlic and shallots and puree in a food processor with the heavy cream. Set aside.

3. While garlic mixture roasts, make the leeks. Combine the water, sugar and lemon rind in a medium saucepan. Cook over medium heat until the mixture turns a golden color. Have an oiled baking sheet ready. Stir the leeks into the caramel and immediately scrape onto the baking sheet. Cool. Separate the leeks and set aside.

4. To make the vinaigrette, place all the ingredients except the chives in a blender and blend until well combined. Stir in the chives and set aside.

5. Melt the butter in a large nonstick skillet over medium heat. Add the oil. When the pan is hot, add the fish, skin side down, and cook until browned, about 2 to 3 minutes. Turn the fish and cook until the fish is firm to the touch, about 1 to 2 minutes more.

6. Place even portions of the shallot and garlic puree in the center of 6 plates. Place the fish over the puree. Sprinkle with the caramelized leeks. Pour some of the vinaigrette on each plate in a circle around the fish. Serve immediately.

makes 6 servings

MO

STRIPED BASS WITH SORREL dairy

6 tablespoons (¾ stick) butter
One 4- to 6-pound striped bass, scaled, cleaned and gills removed
Salt and freshly ground black pepper
3 white mushrooms, sliced
½ cup thinly sliced or chopped shallots
½ cup chopped onion
1 bay leaf
3 sprigs fresh thyme or 1 teaspoon dried
6 sprigs parsley
2 cups dry white wine
2 cups heavy cream
2 cups shredded sorrel
1 large egg yolk

1. Preheat the oven to 425°F. Butter a baking sheet with 2 tablespoons of the butter.

2. Sprinkle the fish inside and out with salt and pepper to taste. Place the fish on the baking sheet and dot it with 3 tablespoons of the butter. Scatter the mushrooms, shallots and onion around the fish. Place the bay leaf, thyme and parsley in the cavity of the fish.

3. Pour the wine over and around the fish and cover closely with heavy-duty aluminum foil. Place in the oven and bake for 20 to 30 minutes. Remove the foil and continue baking for 20 to 30 minutes longer.

4. Pour the cooking liquid and vegetables with herbs into a saucepan. Cover the fish and keep it warm while preparing the sauce.

5. Cook over medium heat until the cooking liquid is reduced to ½ cup. Strain it into a skillet. Add 1½ cups of the heavy cream and cook, stirring, for about 15 minutes. The sauce should be reduced to about 1 cup.

6. Meanwhile, in another saucepan, heat the remaining tablespoon of butter and add the sorrel. Cook until the sorrel is wilted. Add this to the sauce.

7. In a small bowl, blend the remaining ½ cup cream with the egg yolk. Add it to the sauce and cook briefly without boiling.

makes 6 to 8 servings

CC

POACHED ARCTIC CHAR WITH YOGURT-DILL SAUCE dairy

Arctic char is a rich fish, best when slightly undercooked, and does not need a great deal of embellishment. The fish averages around 3 pounds, perfect for 4 servings, and the flesh is the pink color of salmon.

    2 cups dry white wine
    4 cups water
    1 onion
    2 bay leaves
    1 bunch fresh dill
    6 black peppercorns
    Salt
    One 3-pound arctic char, cleaned and left whole
    ½ cup plain yogurt
    3 tablespoons mayonnaise
    Freshly ground black pepper

1. Put the wine in a fish poacher, add the water, onion, bay leaves, a sprig of dill, the peppercorns and salt to taste. Bring to a simmer and cook for 15 minutes.

2. Add the fish to the poacher. The liquid should cover the fish. If not, add more water. Bring to a simmer and cook for 10 minutes. Remove the pan from the heat and allow the fish to remain in the liquid for 40 minutes, or until the liquid is tepid. The fish will be slightly undercooked in the center, which keeps the flesh moist. If you want it well done, simmer it for 15 minutes instead of 10 minutes.

3. Carefully remove the fish from the liquid, put on a platter and either refrigerate until shortly before serving, or, if the fish is to be served within another hour, set it aside at room temperature. If you choose to refrigerate the fish, then remove it from the refrigerator 45 minutes to an hour before serving.

4. Mince enough of the remaining dill to make 3 tablespoons and mix it in a bowl with the yogurt and mayonnaise. Season the sauce with salt and pepper.

5. Peel the skin from the top side of the fish, lift the fillet from the bones and put on a platter. Remove the bones, skin the bottom fillet and place on the platter. Spoon some of the sauce over the fillets, decorate with the remaining dill and serve.

    makes 4 servings

FF

COD WITH MUSHROOMS dairy/pareve

2 tablespoons olive oil
2 tablespoons finely chopped shallots
1 clove garlic, minced
½ pound white mushrooms, sliced
2 pounds cod fillets
Salt and freshly ground black pepper
1 cup dry white wine
2 tablespoons white wine vinegar
4 tablespoons softened unsalted butter or pareve margarine
2 tablespoons finely chopped parsley

1. Preheat the oven to 400°F.
2. Place a large ovenproof skillet over medium heat. Add the olive oil. Sauté the shallots until soft but not brown, then stir in the garlic. Toss the mushrooms with the shallots until they begin to soften, then arrange the cod fillets on the mushrooms in a single layer. Season with salt and pepper, add the wine, place in the oven and bake for about 8 minutes, or until the fish has just turned opaque in the middle. Do not overcook. Transfer the fish and mushrooms to a warm serving platter and cover to keep warm.
3. Add the vinegar to the skillet and cook rapidly until the liquid in the pan just coats the bottom. Swirl in the butter or margarine with a whisk, cooking gently until the sauce begins to thicken. Stir in the parsley, pour over the fish and serve.

makes 4 servings

FF

COD WITH SWEET AND SOUR SAUCE pareve

1 teaspoon olive oil
2 small onions, halved and thinly sliced
Two 1-pound cans plum tomatoes, drained (liquid reserved) and finely chopped
½ teaspoon grated orange zest
3 tablespoons fresh orange juice
2 tablespoons sweet sherry
¼ cup raisins
2 tablespoons balsamic vinegar
1 tablespoon honey
¼ teaspoon ground cinnamon
2 teaspoons salt
Freshly ground black pepper
2 tablespoons toasted slivered almonds
Four 4-ounce cod fillets
2 tablespoons minced scallions

1. Heat the olive oil in a large nonstick skillet over medium heat. Add the onions and turn the heat to medium-low. Cook until the onions are completely wilted and browned, about 10 minutes. Add the tomatoes, ½ cup of the reserved tomato liquid, orange zest and juice, sherry, raisins, vinegar, honey, cinnamon, salt, and pepper to taste. Simmer for 25 minutes.

2. Stir in the almonds. Place the cod fillets in the skillet and cover with the sauce. Simmer over low heat until just cooked through, about 10 minutes. Carefully transfer the fillets to plates using a wide spatula. Spoon some of the sauce over the fish, sprinkle with the scallions, and serve immediately.

makes 4 servings

FF

FLOUNDER SAUTÉ WITH MUSHROOMS AND WILTED SPINACH pareve

2 tablespoons matzoh cake meal
Salt and freshly ground black pepper
Four 3- to 4-ounce flounder fillets or two 8-ounce fillets, split down the center
3 teaspoons olive oil
Juice of ½ lemon
1 scallion, trimmed and minced
2 cups sliced mushrooms
¼ cup dry white wine
4 cups torn spinach leaves, cleaned and dried

1. Place the matzoh cake meal on a plate and season with salt and pepper to taste. Lightly dust the flounder on both sides with the seasoned cake meal. Heat 2 teaspoons of the olive oil in a large, heavy nonstick skillet over medium-high heat. Place the flounder in the pan and sauté on one side for about 90 seconds. Turn the fish over. Squeeze the lemon juice on the fish and sprinkle the scallions evenly over the fillets. Cook for 30 seconds more and divide among 4 warm plates.

2. Place the remaining teaspoon of olive oil in the skillet. Add the mushrooms and season them lightly with salt and pepper. Sauté, shaking the pan constantly, until soft, 3 to 4 minutes. Add the wine, increase the heat to high and continue to cook for about 1 minute until the smell of alcohol disappears. Remove the pan from the heat, add the spinach and toss quickly until it barely wilts. Taste and season again with salt and pepper. Divide the spinach over each flounder fillet and serve immediately.

makes 4 servings

MO

SEPHARDIC FISH WITH EGG AND LEMON SAUCE pareve

Pescado con Huevo y Limón

Fish in a Greek-style egg and lemon sauce is a traditional dish at many Sephardic Seders. It may be served warm or cold.

2 pounds fillet of flounder or fillet of sole
1½ lemons
Few sprigs of parsley
Salt and freshly ground white pepper
5 large eggs
½ teaspoon potato starch
1 tablespoon cold water
1 tablespoon vegetable oil

1. Place the fish in a deep skillet with just enough water to cover. Add the juice of ½ lemon, the parsley and salt and pepper to taste. Bring to a simmer and cook until just done, 10 to 15 minutes.

2. Transfer the fish to a serving platter, draining it well and removing the parsley. The fish may be served hot or cold; if you are planning to serve it hot, cover with foil and keep in a warm oven while preparing the sauce.

3. In a bowl, beat the eggs with the potato starch. Add the juice of 1 lemon, the water and ½ teaspoon salt and beat well.

4. Heat the oil in a small saucepan over very low heat. Remove the pan from the heat and add the egg mixture, stirring vigorously. Return the pan to stove and cook, stirring constantly, until the sauce is thickened and smooth. Be careful not to overcook or the sauce will curdle.

5. Pour sauce over fish and serve. To serve cold, prepare early in the day and refrigerate until ready to serve.

makes 4 to 6 servings

FF

ANGEL FAMILY'S SALMON IN RHUBARB AND TOMATO SAUCE pareve

(FROM *SEPHARDIC HOLIDAY COOKING*)

The Jews of Rhodes eat this fish hot; those in Turkey prefer it cold. It develops a more interesting flavor after 24 hours of refrigeration. A light sprinkling of lemon juice just before serving also enhances the flavor. Although any freshwater fish can be prepared this way, the sweet, fatty flavor of salmon lends itself most readily.

1 pound rhubarb
4 cups water
4 ounces tomato sauce (half an 8-ounce can)
1 teaspoon salt
¼ cup vegetable oil
Pinch of sugar, if needed
2 pounds salmon, cut into 4 to 5 steaks, each about 1¼ inches thick
Lemon wedges for serving

1. Peel the rhubarb and cut into 1-inch chunks. In a pot, combine the rhubarb and 4 cups of water. Simmer until very soft, about 20 minutes. Add the tomato sauce, salt, oil and a tiny pinch of sugar if mixture seems very sour. Simmer for 5 minutes.

2. Add the fish and poach until done, about 15 minutes. Adjust the seasonings in the sauce.

3. Lift the fish from the sauce with a slotted spoon and arrange on a platter or in a pan. Pour the sauce over and chill overnight. Serve with the jellied sauce and lemon wedges on the side.

makes 4 to 5 servings

MS

SALMON FILLETS WITH THYME AND ROASTED TOMATOES pareve

Moira Hodgson's temptingly flavorful recipes appear in *The Times*'s Sunday regional sections distributed in the New York metropolitan area. Since summer's luscious tomatoes are not available at Passover, she suggests a method of roasting that imparts a wonderful, intense flavor to the hothouse or hydroponically-grown tomatoes sold during the holiday season. They become sweet yet sharp, almost caramelized. Roasted tomatoes also enhance fish and chicken and many vegetable dishes where tomatoes are called for, such as Roast Carrots, Tomatoes and Onions with Thyme (page 233).

8 ripe tomatoes (see Note)
2 salmon fillets (about 1 pound each)
Juice of 1 lemon
¼ cup olive oil
Kosher salt and freshly ground pepper to taste
2 teaspoons fresh thyme leaves

1. Preheat the oven to 300°F. Slice the tomatoes very thin and place them on an oiled roasting dish. Roast for 30 minutes to an hour, or until they begin to shrivel and get brown around the edges. Remove from the oven, scrape up with a spatula and set aside. The tomatoes will not hold their shape and will look messy, but this does not matter in the recipe.

2. Preheat the broiler. Sprinkle the salmon fillets with the lemon juice and olive oil and season to taste. Broil for 6 minutes on each side or until the fish is done as you like it. Sprinkle with thyme and tomato pieces and serve.

NOTE: This roasting method works only with ripe tomatoes. Avoid tasteless pale pink ones.

makes 4 servings

MH

JEAN-GEORGES'S BAKED SALMON WITH BASIL OIL pareve
(ADAPTED FROM JEAN-GEORGES VONGERICHTEN)

Chef Vongerichten's elegantly simple method for cooking salmon fillets—baking them at a very low temperature—results in fish with a moist but flaky texture and an intense, rich flavor. The fillets look rather raw when you take them out of the oven, but they are sufficiently cooked.

> Four 6-ounce salmon fillets, skin on
> ⅓ cup light olive oil
> Oil for baking dish
> 1 cup basil leaves
> Kosher salt and freshly ground black pepper
> 4 sprigs of basil for garnish

1. Preheat the oven to 250°F. Season the salmon fillets with a few drops of the olive oil and put them on an oiled baking dish.
2. Wash and drain the basil leaves and dry them thoroughly in a salad spinner. Make a basil oil by pureeing the leaves in a blender with the remaining olive oil until smooth. Season to taste with salt and pepper.
3. Bake the salmon for 10 minutes. If the skin peels away easily and the salmon flesh flakes when tested with a fork, it is done even though it may not look it. (If you prefer it well done, return it to the oven for 3 more minutes.) Sprinkle the salmon with salt and pepper.
4. Put the fillets on heated individual plates and spinkle the basil oil in a circle around it. Put a sprig of basil on top of each fillet and serve.

makes 4 servings

MH

SCROD UNDER HORSERADISH MERINGUE dairy

½ cup plain yogurt
1 tablespoon unsalted butter
½ cup freshly grated horseradish
½ teaspoon salt
6 large egg whites
1 teaspoon sugar
Four 6- to 8-ounce scrod or cod fillets
¼ cup chopped fresh dill

1. Put the yogurt in a strainer lined with cheesecloth and set aside for 4 hours to drain.

2. Preheat the oven to 425°F. Coat a baking dish, large enough to hold the fillets in one layer, with the butter. In a bowl, combine the yogurt, horseradish and salt.

3. In another bowl, beat the egg whites until they form soft peaks. Add the sugar and continue to beat until they form stiff peaks. Carefully fold in the seasoned yogurt.

4. Lay the fillets in the baking dish and cover each with ¼ of the meringue. Bake until cooked through, 8 to 10 minutes, depending on the thickness of the fish. Remove the fillets to individual plates and sprinkle with the dill.

makes 4 servings

MO

SHAD WITH PINEAPPLE-RHUBARB SALSA pareve

2 tablespoons cooking oil
½ cup finely diced onion
1 pound fresh rhubarb stalks, finely minced
½ cup pineapple juice
½ cup sugar
1 cup finely chopped fresh pineapple
1 teaspoon minced, seeded fresh jalapeño pepper
Salt and freshly ground black pepper
1 large shad fillet, about 1½ pounds

1. Preheat the broiler.
2. Heat 1 tablespoon of the oil in a skillet over medium heat. Add the onion and sauté until softened and golden brown. Stir in the rhubarb, pineapple juice and sugar and cook over medium-low heat, stirring often, until the rhubarb is tender, about 10 minutes. Remove from the heat and fold in the fresh pineapple and jalapeño pepper. Season to taste with salt and pepper and set aside.
3. Brush the shad with the remaining oil and season with salt and pepper. Broil the shad until lightly browned and just cooked through, 6 to 8 minutes. Do not turn the fish.
4. Put the shad on a serving platter and spoon the rhubarb salsa in a band running the length of the fillet, then serve.

makes 4 servings

FF

PIERRE TROISGROS'S RED SNAPPER WITH EGGPLANT AND TOMATO pareve

(ADAPTED FROM PIERRE TROISGROS OF THE TROISGROS RESTAURANT IN ROANNE, FRANCE)

Michelin three-star chef Pierre Troisgros created this elegant dish for a feast in Jerusalem in honor of the city's three-thousandth anniversary.

6 tablespoons olive oil, more if needed
1 large onion, diced
2 large tomatoes, peeled, seeded and diced
2 teaspoons fresh thyme leaves
1 bay leaf
1 clove garlic, crushed
2 tablespoons red wine vinegar
2 teaspoons honey
Salt and freshly ground pepper
1 large eggplant (about 1 pound), peeled and cut into ¼-inch rounds
1½ pounds red snapper fillets, deboned, with the skin on one side, cut into 8 rectangular slices

1. In a large saucepan, combine 1 tablespoon of the olive oil and the onion, cover the pan, and sweat the onion for about 10 minutes over medium-low heat. Add the tomatoes, thyme, bay leaf, garlic, 1 tablespoon of the vinegar, the honey and 1 additional tablespoon of the oil. Simmer, uncovered, over medium heat, until much of the liquid has evaporated, about 15 minutes. Discard the bay leaf, and season to taste with salt and pepper.

2. Put the entire mixture into a food processor and puree. Put through a fine sieve.

3. Heat 2 more tablespoons of the oil in a large nonstick pan and fry the eggplant until the rounds are golden brown on both sides. Repeat until all the eggplant has been cooked, adding more oil, if needed, for each new batch. Drain on paper towels; season with salt and pepper.

4. Add the remaining tablespoon of vinegar to the nonstick pan, and stir for 1 minute over high heat to deglaze the pan. Spoon the liquid over the eggplant.

5. Clean the nonstick pan. Working very carefully with the fish fillets, salt and pepper them on both sides. Place the fillets in the pan, and fry them in the remaining 2 tablespoons of oil, over medium heat, for 2 to 3 minutes on each side.

6. For each serving, place the tomato sauce in the middle of the plate, top with several rounds of the eggplant and then, carefully, with 2 fish fillets, skin side up. Serve warm.

makes 4 servings

JN

RED SNAPPER UNDER VEGETABLE PUREE dairy

1 cup low-fat plain yogurt
1 celery root, about ½ pound, peeled and chopped
2 parsnips, about ½ pound, peeled and chopped
2 small boiling potatoes, about ¼ pound, peeled and chopped
1 tablespoon fresh thyme leaves, finely chopped
½ teaspoon salt
1 teaspoon freshly ground pepper
1 cup low-fat milk
2 tablespoons minced fresh chives
1 tablespoon unsalted butter
Four 6- to 8-ounce red snapper fillets
2 tablespoons minced flat-leaf parsley

1. Put the yogurt in a strainer lined with cheesecloth over a large bowl and set aside for 3 hours to drain.

2. Preheat the oven to 425°F. Put the celery root, parsnips, potatoes, thyme, salt, pepper and milk in a saucepan. Bring to a boil over medium-high heat, lower the heat and simmer until the vegetables are tender, about 20 minutes. Pour into a strainer set over a bowl and discard the milk. Push the vegetables through a ricer or food mill and set aside. (The vegetable puree can be prepared ahead of time and refrigerated, covered, for up to 3 days.) When the puree is cool, fold in the strained yogurt and chives.

3. Coat the bottom of a baking dish, large enough to hold the fillets in one layer, with the butter. Lay the fillets in the dish, cover each with ¼ of the puree and bake until cooked through, about 8 to 10 minutes, depending on the thickness of the fish. Sprinkle with the parsley and serve.

makes 4 servings

MO

EDDA SERVI MACHLIN'S
RED SNAPPER JEWISH STYLE pareve

Triglie all'Ebraica
(FROM *THE CLASSIC CUISINE OF THE ITALIAN JEWS*)

Classic Italian-Jewish cuisine is a combination of Italian, Spanish, Middle Eastern and North African cooking, with some recipes said to date back a thousand years. In fact, many vegetables that people now think of as typically Italian were originally used only by Jews; among them are eggplant, beets, artichokes, zucchini and fennel. Garlic, bay leaves, rosemary, vinegar, raisins and pine nuts are also characteristic elements of Italian-Jewish cooking. In Italy, the following recipe is made with *triglie*, a medium-size red fish resembling red snapper in color, but stronger-tasting. Here, red snapper fillets are substituted.

    2½ to 3 pounds red snapper fillets
    Salt
    ½ cup olive oil
    1 teaspoon sugar
    ¼ cup red wine vinegar
    ¾ cup seedless raisins
    ⅓ cup pine nuts

1. Preheat the oven to 400°F.
2. Wash the fillets thoroughly and pat dry with paper towels. Lightly sprinkle them with salt. Lightly oil a large baking dish and arrange the fish in a single layer.
3. In a small bowl, dissolve the sugar in the vinegar and pour over the fish. Pour in the remaining oil and sprinkle with the raisins and pine nuts.
4. Cover with a piece of aluminum foil and bake for approximately 15 minutes. Remove foil and bake another 20 minutes, or until all liquid has evaporated.

makes 6 servings

MH

FILLET OF SOLE WITH RHUBARB pareve/dairy

The honey provides a sweet counterpoint to the rhubarb.

2 stalks rhubarb
4 tablespoons vegetable oil or unsalted butter
2 shallots, minced
Four 4- to 6-ounce fillets of gray sole
2 tablespoons fresh lemon juice
1 tablespoon honey
Freshly ground black pepper
2 tablespoons finely minced parsley

1. Trim the leaves from the rhubarb and cut it into ½-inch dice. Heat 2 tablespoons of the oil or butter in a large skillet over medium heat. Add the rhubarb and shallots and sauté until the vegetables are tender and lightly browned, about 10 minutes. Remove from the pan and set aside.

2. Add another tablespoon of oil or butter to the pan. Pat the fish fillets dry on paper towels and add them to the pan. Sauté just a minute or two on each side until they are barely cooked through. Do not overcook the fish. Remove the fish from the pan and set aside, loosely covered, to keep warm.

3. Add the lemon juice and honey to the pan and cook briefly, then return the rhubarb and the shallots to the pan. Season with pepper. Swirl in the remaining tablespoon of oil or butter.

4. Transfer the fish to each of 4 individual plates, spoon some of the rhubarb mixture over each, sprinkle with parsley and serve.

makes 4 servings

FF

FRESH TUNA WITH
TOMATO COULIS pareve/dairy

4 medium-size ripe tomatoes
2 tablespoons olive oil
2 pounds fresh tuna steaks, 1 to 1½ inches thick, divided into 4 equal portions
½ cup finely chopped onions
3 tablespoons balsamic vinegar
3 tablespoons dry red wine
1 tablespoon minced fresh rosemary
Salt and freshly ground black pepper
¼ cup (½ stick) unsalted butter, in small pieces (optional)

1. Seed and finely chop the tomatoes. Place in a colander over a bowl and allow the excess liquid to drain at least 30 minutes. Set aside.

2. Brush a heavy skillet, preferably cast iron and large enough to hold the fish without crowding, with a little of the olive oil and place over high heat. Heat oil until very hot. Dry the tuna pieces and sear them until they are browned on the outside and still pink in the middle, about 3 minutes on each side. Transfer the fish to a platter, cover loosely with foil and keep warm.

3. Add the remaining olive oil to the skillet. Sauté the onions over low heat until they are tender but not browned. Add the tomatoes and cook until softened, about 5 minutes. Add the vinegar, wine and rosemary and cook over medium-high heat until most of the liquid in the pan has evaporated. Season to taste with salt and pepper.

4. If desired, just before serving, over very low heat with the mixture barely simmering, stir in the butter bit by bit. The sauce should become slightly creamy. When all the butter is incorporated, return the fish to the pan, baste with the sauce, then serve immediately. Once the butter has been added to the pan it is important not to allow the sauce to boil.

makes 4 servings

FF

Asparagus Matzoh Brei (page 103)

Pot Roast Braised in Red Wine (page 179),
Wolfgang Puck's Potato-Onion Latke (page 223),
and Whole Roast Asparagus (page 211)

Gravlax (page 36) with Jean-Georges
Vongerichten's Beet Tartare (page 38)

Southwestern Blackened and Braised
Brisket of Beef (page 176)

Craig Claiborne's Salmon Pâté (page 32)

Joyce Goldstein's Cornish Hens with Apricots, Tomatoes, Onions and Spices
(page 162) with Wolfgang Puck's Moroccan Carrot Salad (page 57)

Striped Bass with Sorrel (page 123)

Carol Wolk's Prize-Winning
Matzoh Balls (page 76)

Craig Claiborne's
Sweet Potato Salad (page 231)

Paul Prudhomme's
Veal Roast with Mango Sauce (page 199)

Salmon Gefilte Fish (page 18)

Charlie Trotter's Lamb Shanks Braised in Red Wine (page 191) with
Union Square Cafe Polenta from Matzoh (page 105)

Barry Wine's Tsimmes Terrine (page 243)

Spa Slaw with Lemon and Orange
Dressing (page 54)

Joyce Goldstein's Pickled Salmon (page 31)

Fresh Tuna with Tomato Coulis (page 138)

Chocolate Macaroons (page 272)

Artichokes in Parsley Sauce (page 210)

Charlie Trotter's Carrot Consommé (page 90)

Pierre Troisgros's Red Snapper with
Eggplant and Tomato (page 134)

Larry Bain's Grandmother's
Haroseth (page 8)

Marion Siner Gordon's Coconut Cake
with Apricot Glaze (page 284)

Andre Balog's Chicken with Fresh Herbs and 40 Cloves of Garlic
(page 150)

Hungarian Hazelnut Torte with
Hazelnut Icing (page 298)

Margareten Family's
Apple Kugel (page 268)

blessings of food and family

a passover memoir

By MIMI SHERATON

Of all the Jewish holidays in the year, none meant more to me as a child than Passover, for it was in every way a joyous and lyrical celebration, bringing with it two brand-new party dresses and wonderfully rich and fragrant foods that I had not tasted for a year.

Best of all, it brought the two Seder dinners, at which I could be among noisy, laughing and warmly affectionate relatives—not only grandparents, aunts and uncles, but first, second and third cousins, some of whom lived near us in Flatbush, and many others who came from places as exotically remote as the Bronx, Yonkers, Forest Hills or the city, by which we meant Manhattan.

Our Passover routine was always the same. We went to my mother's family on the first night and my father's family on the second. If one of my new dresses was a little more elaborate or more expensive than the other, it was saved for the second night, for that to us was a slightly more formal and "special" affair, primarily because we saw my father's family less often than my mother's. In addition, my father's father was a fairly well-known rabbi, and we were all a little in awe of him, loving and kindly though he was.

He was especially impressive on Seder nights and appeared almost kingly, wearing a high white satin hat, somewhat like a crown in shape, and a silken white robe banded in gold metallic ribbon. In keeping with the Passover admonition that one must eat in a leaning position on this holiday, he was ensconced on a sofa piled high with small and large pillows of every shape, each covered in thin white linen with white embroidery tracing leaves, flowers and initials.

The sofa marked the head of the dinner table, which was turned endwise to extend from the living room through the archway and into the adjoining dining room. Every chair, stool and piano bench was mustered to accommodate the twenty or so people gathered around the table. Because of their size, children were always seated within the confines of the archway frame, a position so cramped I can still feel the impulse to crawl under the seat to escape.

My mother had a certain low-key snobbish pride about her Austrian style of cooking, and was slightly condescending toward the Hungarian-Jewish food prepared by Grandfather's third wife. (His first had been my grandmother.) My mother always said that it was better to go to that house on the second night because then one could eat cold beet borscht instead of chicken soup with matzoh balls that would certainly be undercooked and heavy. She also felt that "they" (the Hungarians) were not to be taken seriously as cooks because they put ground almonds and grated carrots in their gefilte fish, additions that rendered the final result heavy and sweet.

But it was a festive event in spite of my mother's discontent, for my grandfather invited all sorts of down-and-out cronies, who loitered around the synagogue, as well as the most distant relatives who had fallen on hard times. One such, named

Trince, was a dry old wisp of a man with flour-white skin and cheeks webbed with a fine network of purple-red burst capillaries, for Trince was a drinker and, on those nights, a fiddler and dancer as well. He sported the most lavish of my grandfather's yarmulkes, a black velvet affair, stitched with gigantic red and blue glass "jewels." By the end of the dinner my father had consumed a great deal of wine, and he sang in the rich and beautiful voice that he retained from the days he spent in my grandfather's choir.

As much as I looked forward to the second Seder night, I was even more eager for the first night to begin, for there I would see the cousins I adored—nine boys in all and I the only girl, the kind of odds I have not often enjoyed since. At my mother's parents', children were seated at a separate table because the main dining table could not accommodate both adults and children, and this meant pranks, laughter, running back and forth to the adult table, teasing, pulling braids, sneaking wine and generally killing time until what seemed like the endless ceremony ended and the eating began.

The Seder at my mother's parents' was not the first glimpse of the food or setting, because my mother, along with an aunt or two, always went over the morning of the Seder dinner to help with preparations, and I went along.

There was fish to be chopped in the huge wooden bowl, since my grandmother believed it had to be chopped, not ground to achieve proper texture. Eggs were mixed with chicken fat, matzoh meal, salt and pepper, and the mix was then chilled several hours so matzoh ball dumplings could be easily formed. There were pots of golden chicken soup simmering almost imperceptibly, sponge cake and almond macaroons baking, bottles of mauve-pink beet borscht being put up for the second night's dinner, and dark red wine was funneled into cut-glass decanters.

The honey-nut confection, noant, was set out to harden, and turkeys or breasts of veal were prepared for roasting. Great, tough horseradish roots were peeled and grated until all eyes were red with tears, and there were thirty or forty hard-boiled eggs to be peeled for the ceremonial dish of eggs in salt water eaten on those two nights. Peeling them was one of my jobs, and I was taught to let them cool in ice water for a few minutes, then to gently tap them on all sides against the sink and roll them between my palms to crack the shells so they would lift off easily without taking off pieces of egg white along with them. Every egg had to be as smooth and perfect as polished alabaster; broken specimens were reserved for the chopped liver that would be served at lunch the next day.

I also opened the walnuts and crushed them with the heavy brass mortar and pestle that now gleams on my own kitchen shelf, and I was appointed official taster of the haroseth, the walnut, apple, wine and ginger salad that represents the mortar that enslaved Jews had used to build the pyramids of Egypt.

There was the table to be set with the best, freshly ironed damask cloths that would soon bear Rorschach blots of red wine and beet-colored horseradish, and the heavy, embossed silver candlesticks and wine goblets had to be polished.

The day of such Seder preparations that stands out above all others took place when I was about eight years old, and my aunt Estelle was at my grandmother's along with her son Wally, aged nine, and by far my favorite cousin.

It was early in the morning and the gefilte fish had not yet been begun. My grandmother added carp to the basic mixture of whitefish and pike, but she liked the carp to be alive until just before it was cooked.

And so a live, golden-scaled carp was swimming in icy water in the bathtub. Wally, feeling sorry for the fish, decided to warm it up a bit and let in steaming hot water. By the time the busy adults in the kitchen were aware of the sound of running water in the bathroom, the fish had rolled over on its side, half cooked. My mother was dispatched to the fish market to replace the carp, but I do not recall any form of punishment meted out to Wally, although I at first feared some terrible fate was in store for us both.

As a surprise for my grandparents, there would always be at this Seder one unexpected guest, one of their sons who lived in some really far-off city such as New Orleans, Tulsa, Omaha or Norfolk. I can still feel the excitement in the room as my aging grandmother and grandfather, trembling with combined laughter and tears, embraced their children whom fate had moved so far away.

ROAST CHICKEN AND MORE

Roasted or poached, chicken is the Friday night favorite of many Jewish families around the world. A wonderful roast chicken needs no adornment, but flavorful variations include a version made with 40 cloves of garlic and another with an herbed mushroom mixture that is cooked inside the bird and later removed from the cavity, combined with wine and served as a garnish.

Alternatives to chicken include Cornish hens prepared with apricots, tomatoes, onions and spices, and succulent roast lemon-pepper duck with honey lemon sauce, a specialty at New York's Union Square Cafe.

CLASSIC ROAST CHICKEN meat

If you would like to stuff the bird, 3 tasty choices are: Potato-Apple-Mushroom Stuffing (recipe follows), Matzoh Ball Stuffing (page 202) and Apple Stuffing (page 203).

One 4-to 5-pound chicken
1 lemon
1 tablespoon olive oil or vegetable oil
Salt and freshly ground black pepper
3 to 4 sprigs parsley
2 medium onions
½ cup dry white wine or chicken stock
1 teaspoon potato starch, for gravy (optional)

1. Remove the package of gizzards, heart, liver and neck from the cavity of the chicken. Except for the liver, these parts can be used to make stock. You may wish to freeze them until you have the innards of several chickens. Sauté the liver and freeze it separately, adding to your supply of frozen livers as you buy whole chickens.

2. Preheat oven to 400°F.

3. Rinse the chicken with cold water and pat it dry on a paper towel. Pull off any excess fat from the back of the cavity near the tail. This fat can be sautéed slowly in a small skillet to use for frying or it can be frozen for future use. Pull out with tweezers or singe over an open flame any large pinfeathers on the wings. Squeeze the juice of half the lemon into the cavity and rub it in.

4. Rub the outside of the chicken with the oil. Season the chicken inside and out with salt and pepper. Tuck the lemon halves and the parsley into the cavity. Quarter one of the onions and tuck the quarters into the cavity.

5. The chicken will hold its shape better if it is trussed. At the very least, tuck the wing tips behind the chicken and, using butcher's cord, tie the legs together. To truss the chicken completely, first loop cord around the tail and crisscross it around the legs, pulling the legs together tightly. Then run the length of cord along the sides of the chicken, just under the drumstick and through the wing joints, pulling the ends together across the back near the neck, securing the extra flap of neck skin under the cord. Tie the cord securely, making for a tight, plump-looking bird.

6. Slice the remaining onion and scatter it in the roasting pan. Position the chicken on a rack and place in the oven. Roast for 13 to 15 minutes a pound, or until the juices run clear when the meaty flesh of the upper thigh is pricked with a sharp fork. If the onions in the pan appear to be browning too rapidly while the chicken is roasting, add a little water to the pan. The onions should become dark brown but should not be allowed to blacken.

7. Remove the chicken to a platter or cutting surface and allow it to rest 10 to 15 minutes before carving.

8. Skim any excess fat from the roasting pan. Add several tablespoons of water to the roasting pan, place it on top of the stove over medium heat and stir, scraping up any browned bits clinging to the pan. Strain the pan juices into a small saucepan. These juices can be seasoned with salt and pepper and used to moisten the portions of chicken or can be used to make a gravy. Add the wine or stock to the juices and bring to a simmer. If gravy is desired, dissolve the potato starch in 1 tablespoon cold water and stir into the juice mixture. Simmer until thickened, then season.

9. Carve the chicken by cutting through the joints to remove the drumsticks and wings, then slicing the breast meat and thigh meat. Arrange the meat on a platter and serve either moistened with pan juices or with the gravy on the side.

makes 4 to 6 servings

FF

POTATO-APPLE-MUSHROOM STUFFING FOR CHICKEN pareve

This may be made a day ahead and refrigerated.

    1 pound tart apples
    1 pound onions
    1 cup orange juice
    ½ cup Port
    ¼ teaspoon allspice
    ½ teaspoon cinnamon
    1½ pounds new potatoes
    ½ pound mushrooms
    Grated rind of 1 orange
    Freshly ground black pepper

1. Wash the apples and quarter. Peel the onions and quarter. Place the apples and onions in a saucepan with the orange juice, Port, allspice and cinnamon. Cover and simmer until tender, 10 to 15 minutes. Drain.

2. Meanwhile, scrub and slice the potatoes about ½ inch thick. Cover and cook in water to cover until tender, about 20 minutes. Drain.

3. Using a food mill, puree the apples. (If you do not have a food mill, peel and core the apples by hand before cooking.) Puree the onions in food processor or food mill. Puree the potatoes in food mill or peel and use potato masher (do not use food processor).

4. Chop the mushrooms medium coarse and mix, in a bowl, with the purees. Season with orange rind and pepper. Use to stuff the chicken or turkey, or reheat in a separate pan on top of stove.

makes 6 servings

MB

DAVID LIEDERMAN'S ROAST CHICKEN AND VEGETABLES meat

Restaurateur and chef David Liederman, owner of New York City's Chez Louis and the David of the David's Cookies retail stores, believes that kosher chicken—which is soaked in water, salted and washed according to Jewish dietary laws—absorbs a trace of salt, which boosts the bird's flavor. In addition, he seeks only 2½- to 2¾-pound chickens and marinates them in a heady herbaceous mélange. "The longer they marinate," he says, "the better they taste."

One 2½- to 3-pound kosher chicken
½ cup olive oil
1 clove garlic, mashed
3 sprigs thyme
4 carrots, peeled, cut in half lengthwise and then across
2 teaspoons salt
1 teaspoon freshly ground black pepper
8 small roasting potatoes, scrubbed
4 small white onions, scrubbed

1. Wash and dry the chicken well. In a shallow dish big enough to hold the chicken, combine the olive oil, garlic and thyme. Add the chicken and baste with the oil, garlic and thyme. Cover and refrigerate for at least 3 hours, and up to 24 hours, basting occasionally and turning to marinate evenly.

2. Ten minutes before cooking, preheat the oven to 450°F and remove the chicken from the refrigerator. Pour the marinade in a large cast-iron pan. Line the bottom of the pan with the carrot slices. Season the chicken inside and out with the salt and pepper and place on top of the carrots. Strew the potatoes and onions around the chicken. Place the pan in the oven and roast for 50 to 55 minutes, or until a meat thermometer reaches between 158° and 160°F when inserted in the thigh. Remove from the oven and allow the chicken to rest for 5 minutes before serving.

makes 4 servings

MO

ANDRE BALOG'S CHICKEN WITH FRESH HERBS AND 40 CLOVES OF GARLIC meat

Andre Balog, who taught kosher cooking in New York City, adds a mixture of fresh green herbs to this traditional French recipe. He considers this a symbolic Passover dish, since the Jews wandered for forty years in the desert before reaching the Promised Land. The garlic flavor is mild because the cloves are cooked whole. Be careful not to slice or otherwise damage the cloves; that releases an enzyme that produces the intense garlic flavor.

4 heads garlic, yielding 40 cloves
2 tablespoons plus ½ cup olive oil
Salt and freshly ground pepper
½ teaspoon sugar
One 4-pound chicken
2 tablespoons chopped parsley
2 tablespoons chopped fresh chives
2 tablespoons chopped fresh basil
1 tablespoon chopped fresh thyme
1 tablespoon chopped cilantro
1 tablespoon chopped fresh chervil
½ bay leaf

1. Separate but do not peel the cloves of garlic.
2. Combine the 2 tablespoons olive oil, salt, pepper and sugar. Roll the garlic cloves in this mixture and set aside.
3. Preheat oven to 425°F.
4. Place the remaining ½ cup olive oil in a Dutch oven, reserving a little to sprinkle over the chicken. Place the chicken in the Dutch oven, then sprinkle olive oil, salt and pepper over the top. Place the garlic around the chicken.
5. Mix the parsley, chives, basil, thyme, cilantro, chervil and bay leaf. Sprinkle over the chicken.
6. Cover and bake for 1 hour. Remove the bay leaf and serve.

makes 6 servings

JN

POLISH ROAST CHICKEN meat

(FROM *JEWISH COOKING IN AMERICA*)
(ADAPTED FROM EDDIE SCHOENFELD)

The intense flavor of this dish belies its simplicity: the secret is the covering of garlic and herbs that permeates the chicken overnight.

4 cloves garlic, or to taste
One 4-pound chicken, cut in 8 pieces
Juice of 1 lemon
Salt and freshly ground black pepper
Sprigs of fresh rosemary, thyme and sage, enough to make a generous handful
¼ cup vegetable oil or olive oil

1. Smash the garlic with a knife and rub into the chicken pieces along with the lemon. Season with salt and pepper to taste and cover with the herbs. Dribble with 2 tablespoons of the oil. Cover and refrigerate overnight, turning the chicken once.

2. Preheat oven to 350°F.

3. Remove the herbs from the chicken. Heat a heavy ovenproof skillet, add the remaining 2 tablespoons oil, and place the chicken skin side down. Brown only on the skin side over medium-high heat, for about 5 minutes.

4. Place the skillet of chicken in the oven and bake about 30 minutes, or until the chicken is crisp and the juices run clear.

makes 6 servings

JN

HELEN NASH'S ROAST CHICKEN WITH DRIED AND FRESH MUSHROOMS meat

(FROM *HELEN NASH'S KOSHER KITCHEN*)

2 ounces dried mushrooms, *cèpes* or porcini
1½ cups boiling water
4 tablespoons olive oil
3 garlic cloves, finely chopped
¾ pounds fresh mushrooms, very coarsely chopped
½ cup flat-leaf parsley, including half the stem, finely chopped
Kosher salt
Freshly ground black pepper (optional)
2 roasting chickens, 2½ to 3 pounds each

1. Preheat the oven to 400°F.

2. Place the dried mushrooms in a small bowl. Pour boiling water over mushrooms. Let soak for about 1 hour. Strain through a sieve lined with a paper towel to absorb sand. Pour the strained liquid into a small saucepan. Set aside. Rinse the mushrooms to remove any remaining sand. Squeeze dry and chop coarsely.

3. In a skillet, heat 3 tablespoons of the olive oil over high heat. Add the garlic and both dried and fresh mushrooms and sauté for 1 minute. Add the parsley. Season with salt and pepper, if desired. Cool.

4. Dry the chickens well. Gently loosen the skin around breasts and thighs. Be careful not to tear skin. Spread the mushroom mixture between the skin and flesh of chickens. Tie the wings together with kitchen twine. Brush with remaining oil. Sprinkle lightly with salt and pepper, if desired. Place chickens on their sides in a roasting pan just large enough to hold them.

5. Roast for 20 minutes. Turn the chickens on their other sides and roast another 20 minutes. Turn the chickens breast side up and roast for 15 to 20 minutes more. The chickens are ready when juices run clear. Remove from the oven. Cut the chickens into eighths. Keep warm.

6. Degrease the roasting pan by pouring off the surface fat and oil. Pour the reserved mushroom liquid and juices from the carving board into the chicken juices that are in the roasting pan. Bring to a boil over high heat, reduce the heat and simmer for 3 to 5 minutes or until liquids thicken into a sauce. Season with salt and pepper to taste, if desired. Pour sauce over chicken or serve separately.

makes 6 to 8 servings

HN

LEMON ROASTED CHICKEN meat

(FROM *A WELL-SEASONED APPETITE*)

4 large lemons
One 4- to 5-pound chicken
1 teaspoon kosher salt
Freshly ground black pepper
2 small onions, peeled and quartered

1. Preheat the oven to 425°F. Using a vegetable peeler, remove the zest from 1 lemon in long, thin strips. Loosen the skin over the chicken breasts and slip the zest in between the skin and the meat. Cut all the lemons in half lengthwise and then across into ¾-inch slices. Squeeze the juice from one of the slices over the skin of the chicken.

2. Season with salt and pepper to taste. Stuff half of the lemon slices and half of the onions into the cavity of the chicken. Place the rest in the center of a roasting pan and place the chicken on top. Roast for 15 minutes, then lower the oven temperature to 375°F. Continue roasting until the juices run clear when the chicken is pricked with a fork in the thickest part of the leg, about 1 hour and 15 minutes longer. Let stand for 10 minutes. Carve, divide among 4 plates and serve.

makes 4 servings

MO

CHICKEN IN POMEGRANATE-WALNUT SAUCE meat

(ADAPTED FROM *THE NEW YORK TIMES LARGE TYPE COOKBOOK*)

Pomegranates are a traditional ingredient in recipes of Jews from the Middle East—from the seeds used since ancient times in haroseth, to the juice that gives this dish its distinctive, sweet flavor. The dish is often served with rice in the Middle East.

5 whole chicken breasts
1 rib celery
½ teaspoon thyme
2 sprigs flat-leaf parsley
1 bay leaf
5 tablespoons pareve unsalted margarine
2 large onions, chopped
3 tablespoons tomato sauce
3 cups finely ground walnuts
2½ cups water
3 tablespoons fresh lemon juice
1 teaspoon salt
1 teaspoon cinnamon
¾ cup pomegranate juice
⅓ cup sugar

1. Place the chicken breasts in a large skillet and barely cover with water. Sprinkle the center of the celery rib with thyme; tie it in cheesecloth with the parsley and bay leaf and add to the skillet. Simmer the chicken over medium heat until tender, about 10 minutes. Cool.

2. Bone the chicken, discarding the skin, and divide each breast into 5 to 8 pieces.

3. Heat the margarine in a large saucepan over medium heat. Sauté the onions until golden. Add the tomato sauce and cook for 5 minutes. Add the walnuts, lower the heat, and cook very slowly, 5 minutes or longer, stirring continuously to avoid sticking. Add the remaining ingredients and stir until well mixed. Cover and simmer for 40 minutes. Add more sugar or salt if needed.

4. Add the chicken to the sauce and cook slowly for 20 minutes. When ready to serve, place the chicken on a serving dish and pour the sauce over it.

makes 10 servings

JH

CLASSIC POACHED CHICKEN meat

One 4-pound chicken, left whole or split
Juice of ½ lemon
Water
2 medium onions
2 whole leeks, well rinsed
2 carrots, peeled
2 stalks celery
2 cloves garlic, peeled
2 sprigs parsley
2 sprigs fresh dill
10 whole black peppercorns
Salt
Matzoh balls (optional)

1. Remove the gizzards, heart, neck and liver from the chicken. Pull off any excess fat from the edges of the cavity. Rinse the chicken in cold water, pat dry on paper towels and rub with the lemon juice. Place in a large, deep pot and cover with cold water to a depth of 2 inches. If necessary to fit the chicken comfortably in the pot, it can be split in half. Rinse the gizzards, heart and neck and add them as well. Reserve the liver for another use. It should not be added to poached chicken because it will make the stock bitter. Bring the water with the chicken to a boil.

2. While the water is coming to a boil, cut the root and top ends off the onions, but do not peel them. The skin will enhance the color of the soup. Trim the roots and most of the green off the leeks and trim the root ends off the carrots. Cut or break the celery if necessary to fit it into the pot. Add the garlic to the pot. Tie the parsley and dill together in a piece of cheesecloth.

3. When the chicken has come to a boil, reduce the heat to a steady simmer and skim the surface of the water, removing the scum as it accumulates. Do this for at least 5 minutes until relatively little scum reappears.

4. Add the vegetables, herbs and peppercorns to the pot. Continue simmering the chicken and vegetables slowly, skimming the surface from time to time, until the juices of the chicken run clear when the thigh is pricked with a sharp fork, about 1 hour. If necessary, additional water can be added to the pot during the cooking.

5. Remove the chicken from the pot, allowing it to drain well. Set it aside, covered, in a shallow bowl.

6. Pour the contents of the pot through a colander set into another large pot or a deep bowl that holds at least 6 quarts. Clean the original cooking pot. Pour the soup through a large, very fine strainer into the cooking pot. If you do not have a large, very fine strainer, use a large strainer with a coarser mesh and line it with a clean linen napkin.

continued

7. Bring the soup to a gentle simmer and cook until it has reduced and concentrated somewhat, 20 to 30 minutes. Do not allow it to come to a boil or it will turn cloudy. When the soup tastes rich enough, season it with salt.

8. While the soup is simmering, retrieve the vegetables you wish to serve with it and cut them into 1-inch pieces. Discard the skin from the chicken. Cut the chicken into serving pieces.

9. Serve the chicken and vegetables in bowls, with matzoh balls, if desired, with the hot soup spooned over them.

makes 4 servings

FF

SAVORY BAKED CHICKEN meat

Whether made with spices or simply garnished with parsley, this dish is a welcome addition to the holiday repertoire: it is effortless, may be served either hot or at room temperature, and the recipe easily can be halved for smaller gatherings.

3 broiling chickens, cut up
Juice of 3 lemons
6 tablespoons extra-virgin olive oil
Salt and freshly ground black pepper
2 teaspoons ground cumin (optional)
1 teaspoon ground oregano
Pinch of allspice (optional)
½ teaspoon cayenne pepper (optional)
1 tablespoon chopped flat-leaf parsley (see Note)

1. Put the chicken pieces in a large mixing bowl. Add the remaining ingredients except the parsley and toss to coat all the pieces.

2. Preheat the oven to 450°F. Line a large baking sheet with a raised edge with heavy-duty foil.

3. Arrange the chicken pieces in a single layer on the baking sheet. Put them in the oven and bake 1 hour, turning the pieces as they brown. Remove the chicken from the oven. Allow it to cool about 10 minutes before moving it to a platter.

4. Serve hot or at room temperature.

NOTE: Sprinkle with parsley if omitting the cumin, allspice and cayenne pepper.

makes 10 to 12 servings

FF

CHICKEN SAUTÉ WITH VINEGAR meat

Two 3½-pound chickens, cut into serving pieces
Salt and freshly ground black pepper
4 tablespoons pareve margarine
⅓ cup finely chopped shallots
3 tablespoons red wine vinegar
2 cups seeded, chopped fresh tomatoes
1 tablespoon chopped fresh tarragon (optional)

1. Sprinkle the chicken pieces with salt and pepper to taste.
2. Heat the margarine in a skillet over medium-high heat and add the chicken pieces. Brown about 12 minutes on one side; turn and brown about 10 minutes on the other.
3. Sprinkle the shallots between the pieces of chicken and add the vinegar. Lower the heat slightly and cook until most of the vinegar evaporates. Add the tomatoes, cover and cook over low heat about 20 minutes.
4. Remove the chicken pieces to a serving platter. Cook the tomato sauce briefly to reduce it slightly. Sprinkle with chopped tarragon, if desired. Pour it over the chicken.

makes 6 or more servings

CC

CHICKEN BREASTS WITH GREEN OLIVES AND TOMATOES meat

This dish is so easy to make, healthy to eat and satisfyingly tasty that you may want to serve it all year round.

4 tablespoons extra-virgin olive oil
2 cloves garlic, minced
Juice of 1 lemon
Salt and freshly ground black pepper to taste
2¼ pounds skinless and boneless chicken breasts
1 medium onion, chopped
1 pound canned plum tomatoes, very well drained and chopped
18 green olives, pitted and coarsely chopped
1 tablespoon parsley, chopped
1 teaspoon fresh thyme leaves or ½ teaspoon dried thyme

1. In a shallow baking dish, combine two tablespoons of the olive oil with half the garlic, the lemon juice and salt and pepper to taste. Add the chicken breasts, turning them in the dish so they are coated with the marinade. Arrange them in a single layer in the dish, cover with plastic wrap and allow them to marinate at room temperature for 30 minutes.

2. Preheat the oven to 375°F.

3. Place the remaining oil in a skillet over medium heat. Add the onion and remaining garlic and sauté until tender but not brown. Add the tomatoes and olives and allow to cook about 15 minutes, until the mixture begins to thicken. Stir in half the parsley and the thyme and season to taste with salt and pepper.

4. Spread the tomato mixture over the marinated chicken breasts. Place in the oven and bake about 20 minutes, until the chicken is done. Remove from the oven and baste to combine the juices in bottom of the pan with the tomato mixture on top. Sprinkle with the remaining parsley and serve.

makes 6 servings

FF

CHICKEN WITH WINE, MUSHROOMS AND OLIVES meat

1½ tablespoons extra-virgin olive oil
1 frying chicken, cut up and patted dry
1 medium onion, finely chopped
2 large cloves garlic, minced
¼ pound fresh shiitake mushrooms, sliced
3 sprigs fresh thyme
12 black European olives, pitted
½ cup dry red wine
Salt and freshly ground black pepper
1 tablespoon minced parsley

1. Heat the oil in a large, heavy ovenproof skillet. Add the chicken pieces and cook over high heat until they are nicely browned. Do not crowd them in the pan. Remove them to a bowl when they are brown. You may have to brown the chicken in several shifts.

2. Preheat oven to 350°F.

3. Lower the heat, add the onion to the fat in the pan and sauté until it is tender. Stir in the garlic, cook another few seconds, then add the mushrooms. Increase the heat to medium high and cook the mushrooms until they begin to brown. Stir in the thyme, olives and wine, scraping the bottom of the pan to loosen any browned particles.

4. Return the chicken to the pan along with any juices that may have been released by the chicken as it cooled. Baste the chicken pieces with the pan juices and season with salt and pepper.

5. Cover and place in the oven. Bake for 40 minutes, basting once or twice during baking. Sprinkle with parsley and serve.

makes 4 servings

FF

CHICKEN BREASTS IN HORSERADISH SAUCE meat

Cooked potatoes pureed in a liquid give the piquant sauce a smooth and creamy texture.

2 whole chicken breasts, split
Freshly ground black pepper to taste
3 tablespoons olive oil
2 tablespoons finely chopped shallots
⅔ cup dry white wine
½ cup thinly sliced onions
2 teaspoons minced garlic
½ cup leeks, white part only, cleaned and finely chopped
1 tablespoon prepared white horseradish
1 bay leaf
1 medium potato (about ¼ pound), sliced as thin as possible
1½ cups chicken stock

1. Sprinkle the breast pieces with pepper.
2. Heat 2 tablespoons of the oil over medium heat in a heavy skillet and add the pieces, skin side down. Cook 5 minutes, or until nicely browned on one side. Turn the pieces and cover closely with a lid. Continue cooking about 10 minutes, turning the pieces occasionally.
3. Pour off the fat from the skillet and scatter the shallots around the chicken pieces. Add two tablespoons of the wine and cook until the liquid has almost evaporated. Remove from the heat.
4. Meanwhile, heat the remaining 1 tablespoon oil in a saucepan and add the onions, garlic and leeks. Cook over medium heat, stirring, until the onions are wilted. Add the horseradish, bay leaf and potato slices and stir. Add the stock and the remaining wine. Bring to a boil and simmer 10 minutes. Remove and discard the bay leaf.
5. Pour the mixture into the container of a food processor and blend until smooth. Pour the sauce over the chicken breasts. Bring to the boil and simmer about 1 minute.

makes 4 servings

FF

JOYCE GOLDSTEIN'S CORNISH HENS WITH APRICOTS, TOMATOES, ONIONS AND SPICES meat

(ADAPTED FROM *BACK TO SQUARE ONE*)

For a variation on roast chicken, chef Goldstein serves this at her Seder table.

¾ cup rendered chicken fat or vegetable oil
6 large Cornish hens or poussins (baby chickens), halved
Salt and freshly ground pepper
4 teaspoons cinnamon
4 cups yellow onions, chopped
1 teaspoon ground cloves
3½ cups dried apricots, soaked in hot water for 1 hour and drained
3 cups canned plum tomatoes, diced, with juice reserved
2 cups chicken stock or water
⅓ cup brown sugar

1. Preheat the oven to 350°F.

2. Melt half of the chicken fat or oil in a large saucepan or skillet. Sprinkle the hens with salt and pepper to taste and 1 teaspoon of the cinnamon, and brown.

3. In another large pan, heat the remaining chicken fat or oil, add the onions, and cook over low heat until the onions are transparent, about 5 minutes. Add the remaining 3 teaspoons cinnamon and the cloves and cook for about 3 more minutes, stirring occasionally. Remove from the heat.

4. Coarsely chop half of the soaked apricots and set aside. Add about ½ cup of the reserved tomato liquid to the remaining half of the soaked apricots and puree in a food processor or blender. Add the pureed apricots, diced tomatoes and 1 cup of the chicken stock to the onion mixture. Bring the mixture to a simmer and cook, uncovered, for 5 minutes.

5. Remove 2 cups of the onion mixture to the food processor or blender and puree. Return the pureed mixture to the pan, add the chopped apricots, brown sugar and remaining 1 cup chicken stock and add enough liquid to make a medium-thick sauce.

6. Place half the sauce in a very large casserole dish. Add the hens or the poussins and cover with the remaining sauce. Bake, covered, for 30 to 40 minutes, or until done.

makes 12 servings

JN

CASSEROLE OF CORNISH HENS AND NEW POTATOES meat

4 Cornish hens or baby chickens (poussins), the smaller the better, but less than
    1 pound each
Salt and freshly ground black pepper
Several sprigs of fresh rosemary and thyme
½ tablespoon unsalted pareve margarine
2 tablespoons minced shallots
2 cloves garlic, minced
½ cup dry white wine
½ cup well-flavored chicken stock
2 pounds small new potatoes, peeled
1 tablespoon chopped fresh parsley

1. Rinse and dry the hens inside and out. Season the cavities with salt and pepper. Tuck some of the herbs into the cavities of the hens. Tuck the wing tips back and tie the legs with butcher's cord.

2. Place the margarine in a large, heavy casserole that will hold the hens. Brown the hens on all sides on top of the stove over medium-high heat. Remove them from the casserole.

3. Preheat the oven to 400°F.

4. Add the shallots to the casserole and sauté over medium heat until tender and barely beginning to brown. Stir in the garlic, cook briefly, then stir in the wine and chicken stock. Remove from the heat.

5. Place the hens in the casserole, cover and put in the oven for 25 minutes.

6. While the hens are roasting, boil the potatoes in salted water until they are just tender, about 20 minutes.

7. When the hens are done, remove them to a warm serving platter. Place the casserole on top of the stove and add the potatoes. Simmer very gently for about 5 minutes, gently turning the potatoes in the sauce. Season to taste with salt and pepper. Add any juices that have drained from the hens onto the serving platter.

8. Wipe the rim of the serving platter with a paper towel. Arrange the hens on the platter and spoon the sauce with the potatoes around them. Sprinkle with parsley and serve.

makes 4 servings

FF

ROAST BREAST OF TURKEY WITH RHUBARB AND DRIED CRANBERRY SAUCE meat

A whole turkey breast, boned and tied and roasted, is an extremely convenient way to cook and serve turkey for small groups, especially if the guests prefer white meat. Because pan drippings are minimal and giblets are nonexistent, the sauce is made by simmering rhubarb, dried cranberries, wine and chicken stock together. Be sure to allow at least 10 minutes for the roast to rest out of the oven before carving.

1 whole turkey breast, boned and tied, about 3½ pounds
3 tablespoons vegetable oil
Salt and freshly ground black pepper
½ cup finely minced onion
½ cup finely minced celery
1 clove garlic, minced
½ cup dry white wine
1 cup chicken stock
¾ cup diced rhubarb
¼ cup dried cranberries
2 tablespoons white wine vinegar
½ cup sugar or honey

1. Preheat the oven to 375°F. Rub the turkey with 2 tablespoons of the oil and season with salt and pepper. Place on a rack in a roasting pan and roast about 1 hour, or until an instant-read thermometer inserted in the center registers 160°F.

2. While the turkey is roasting, heat the remaining oil in a heavy saucepan over medium heat. Add the onion, celery and garlic and sauté until the vegetables are uniformly brown. Stir in the wine, scraping the bottom of the pan.

3. Add the stock, rhubarb, dried cranberries, vinegar and sugar or honey and cook over medium heat and simmer until the sauce thickens, about 20 minutes. Season to taste with salt and pepper, cover and keep at a very low simmer until ready to serve.

4. When the turkey is done, remove it from the oven and allow it to rest at least 10 minutes. Remove the trussing string and slice the meat about ¼ inch thick. Arrange the slices on a warm platter, drizzle with a little of the sauce and pass the rest alongside.

makes 6 servings

FF

SLOW-ROASTED DUCK WITH PEPPERED PINEAPPLE CHUTNEY meat

Although the duck must cook for more than 8 hours, the slow process at very low heat results in a moist, practically spoon-tender meat. The fat is completely rendered as the bird roasts, through many openings pricked in the skin, so that a quick browning is all that is needed to crisp the skin before serving. And the accompanying spicy-sweet chutney is a luscious counterpoint to the richness of the meat.

1 duckling, about 5 pounds
3 lemons
6 cloves garlic, peeled and crushed
Salt and freshly ground black pepper
½ fresh pineapple, peeled, cored and diced
½ cup finely chopped onion
3 tablespoons cider vinegar
6 tablespoons brown sugar, or to taste
½ teaspoon whole black peppercorns, crushed

1. Preheat oven to 200°F.

2. Rinse the duck, pat it dry and pull any excess fat away from cavity. Using a skewer or sharp fork, prick the skin all over, piercing it horizontally to penetrate into the layer of fat, not the flesh. Halve two lemons and place them in the cavity along with the garlic and salt and pepper to taste. Put the duck on a V-shaped roasting rack placed in a roasting pan. Place it in the oven and pour about an inch of water into the pan. Roast for 8 hours.

3. Raise the oven temperature to 425°F and roast about 20 minutes longer, just until the skin is crisp and brown.

4. While the duck is roasting, place the pineapple in a heavy saucepan. Add the juice and grated rind of the remaining lemon, along with the onion, vinegar, sugar and crushed peppercorns. Bring to a boil and cook over medium-high heat for 20 to 25 minutes, until most of the liquid has evaporated and the mixture is thick. Adjust the amount of sugar to taste. The chutney should be somewhat tart. It can be made either shortly before the duck has finished roasting or earlier in the day and refrigerated, then rewarmed for serving.

5. Remove the duck from the oven. Cut it in sections and arrange on a platter. Serve with warm chutney.

makes 4 servings

FF

UNION SQUARE CAFE'S ROAST LEMON-PEPPER DUCK WITH HONEY LEMON SAUCE meat
(ADAPTED FROM MICHAEL ROMANO)

Chef Romano complements the richness of the duck with a mouthwatering sauce that is simultaneously sweet, spicy and citric. And it is an excellent choice for a busy cook: as a *Times* food reporter, Amanda Hesser, pointed out in an article about chefs' techniques, this elegant dish can be prepared a day in advance, refrigerated, and finished off an hour or so before serving.

for the duck:
>   2 tablespoons minced lemon zest
>   1 teaspoon minced fresh thyme
>   1 teaspoon coarsely ground black pepper
>   1 teaspoon kosher salt
>   Two 5-pound ducks with neck, giblets and liver removed

for the sauce:
>   2 tablespoons unsalted pareve margarine
>   2 shallots, sliced
>   1 clove garlic, sliced
>   ½ jalapeño pepper, with seeds, finely chopped
>   2 tablespoons chopped fresh thyme
>   2 tablespoons chopped fresh sage
>   2 tablespoons chopped fresh rosemary
>   ¼ cup honey
>   ⅓ cup lemon juice
>   3 tablespoons potato starch
>   2 cups veal stock or chicken broth

1. In a small bowl, combine the lemon zest, thyme, black pepper and salt. Using your fingers, loosen the skins of the ducks over the breastbones, legs and thighs. Tuck the lemon-pepper mixture evenly beneath the skin, covering each breast, leg and thigh. Tie the legs together with kitchen twine.

2. Preheat oven to 425°F. Heat a roasting pan in the oven for 10 minutes. Place the prepared ducks on a rack in the roasting pan and cook 1 hour 10 minutes. Remove the ducks from the pan, and bring to room temperature. Quarter the ducks, trimming off any excess fat. Cover, and refrigerate for up to 24 hours.

3. To prepare the sauce, place the roasting pan over medium-high heat and add the margarine, shallots, garlic and jalapeño. Sauté until softened, about 2 minutes. Add the thyme, sage and rosemary and sauté 1 minute more. Add the honey and lemon juice.

4. Make a paste of the potato starch and 1 tablespoon water, stirring constantly until the water is completely absorbed. If the paste is brittle or lumpy, blend in an additional 1½ teaspoons of water. Add the paste to the pan. Add the veal stock or chicken broth and reduce the liquid until the sauce lightly coats the back of a spoon, about 5 minutes. The sauce may be cooled and refrigerated for up to 24 hours.

5. To serve, preheat the oven to 450°F. In a small pan over medium heat, reheat the sauce. Heat an ovenproof skillet over high heat and add the duck pieces, skin side down. Cook over high heat until the skin begins to sizzle, about 1 minute. Reduce the heat to low and crisp the duck skin, 5 to 7 minutes. Cover with a lid or foil and reheat in the oven for 10 minutes. Transfer to a warm platter and serve with sauce.

makes 4 to 6 servings

AH

BRISKET
AND
BEYOND

Pot roast and brisket are great Passover favorites, especially for families of Eastern European origin, with recipes cherished from one generation to the next. The preparation of brisket can be very basic—using only onions and broth—or it can be flavored with more than a dozen different spices. It is delectable sliced and served cold with horseradish, gherkin pickles, Rhubarb Chutney (page 172) or other spicy condiments. And leftover haroseth complements it wonderfully. Pot roasts, too, offer a range of culinary possibilities—classic, or sweet and sour, or with wine. Many cooks prepare them a day ahead, refrigerating them overnight so they can absorb the flavors of the sauce. Sliced, covered with sauce and reheated, they are mouthwatering. Leftovers of either brisket or pot roast are a fine addition to a beef broth or other meat-based soup. Beef is also the basis of two tasty and traditional stews often served at Persian Seders, one made with eggplant and tomatoes, the other with dill, cilantro and other green herbs. And a matzoh "crust" filled with ground beef, raisins, nuts and spices makes a delectable pie.

Although the ancient practice of sacrificing lambs on the eve of Passover has led to different interpretations of how the meat is prepared for the holiday (see page 187), there are any number of versatile lamb preparations. They include Wolfgang Puck's Braised Moroccan-Style Lamb with Almonds, Prunes and Dried Apricots; lamb shanks braised in either red wine, as chef Charlie Trotter prepares them, or braised in white wine with orange and rosemary; or a Persian stew with okra in a sweet-and-sour sauce.

Veal, too, makes a wonderful Passover meal. Breast of veal, a traditional favorite, becomes even more a Passover specialty when served with a matzoh-ball stuffing. And for a very special meal, nothing beats Paul Prudhomme's Veal Roast with Mango Sauce—a magnificent dish created to honor the three thousandth anniversary of Jerusalem.

CLASSIC BRISKET meat
(ADAPTED FROM FLORENCE AARON)

A basic brisket that is a great holiday favorite. For maximum tenderness, be sure to slice the meat against the grain.

> 1 whole brisket, 6 to 7 pounds
> 2 tablespoons beef fat rendered from the brisket, or vegetable oil
> 2 large onions, sliced very thin
> 1 cup well-seasoned beef stock
> Salt and freshly ground black pepper to taste

1. Preheat the broiler.
2. Place the brisket on a rack in a broiling pan and broil, turning, until the outside is browned on both sides.
3. Preheat oven to 350°F.
4. Heat the beef fat in a large roasting pan or in a 7- to 8-quart heatproof casserole and sauté the onions. When the onions are brown, stir in the stock. Place the meat in the pan or casserole, cutting it in half if necessary. Cover the pan and place it in the oven.
5. Bake the brisket for 3 to 4 hours, or until very tender. Allow to cool, then refrigerate overnight.
6. Remove the congealed fat from the sauce and reheat the meat in the sauce. Or, for speedier preparation, slice the meat and reheat slices in the sauce. Season the sauce with salt and pepper. If the brisket is whole, slice the meat and serve it in the sauce or with sauce on the side.

makes 12 to 15 servings

FF

RHUBARB CHUTNEY pareve

This relish studded with spices and raisins can dress up a simple roast duck or chicken, a pot roast, brisket, or even grilled fish. It will keep for several months in the refrigerator. Select rhubarb stalks that are fresh-looking and slender. Do not be tempted to use the leaves. They contain oxalic acid, which can be toxic.

    4 cups coarsely diced rhubarb
    2 cups brown sugar
    ½ cup lemon juice
    ½ cup cider vinegar
    2 tart apples, peeled and coarsely diced
    1 cup raisins
    3 tablespoons minced fresh ginger
    10 black peppercorns
    4 whole cloves

1. Place the rhubarb, sugar and lemon juice in a heavy saucepan. Bring to a simmer and add the remaining ingredients.

2. Continue to simmer 20 minutes or so, until the rhubarb is tender but still holds its shape.

makes 4 half-pints

NOTE: The chutney will keep for many months in the refrigerator. For pantry storage, transfer the mixture to sterilized jars, seal with sterilized lids and process for 5 minutes in a boiling water bath, or alternatively, place the hot mixture in freshly sterilized jars, seal the jars with sterilized lids and invert the jars on the countertop for 5 minutes. (This is a new method that has proved safe.)

FF

BRISKET WITH SUN-DRIED TOMATOES meat
(ADAPTED FROM MELANIE NUSSDORF)

This brisket in an intense tomato sauce is a specialty of Melanie Nussdorf, a lawyer in Washington, D.C.

One 5-pound brisket of beef
Salt and freshly ground black pepper
2 red bell peppers, seeded and coarsely chopped
2 white onions, peeled and coarsely chopped
3 tablespoons olive oil
3 medium carrots, peeled and sliced ½ inch thick
½ cup parsley, chopped
1 cup sun-dried tomatoes (not packed in oil)
¼ cup ketchup
1 cup beef broth
3 tablespoons brown sugar

1. Preheat the oven to 350°F. Sprinkle the brisket with salt and pepper to taste and place it, fat side up, in a heavy roasting pan.

2. Sauté the red peppers and onions in the olive oil until lightly browned. Remove from the heat and scatter the mixture over the top of the brisket. Add the carrots, parsley and sun-dried tomatoes.

3. In a small bowl, mix the ketchup, beef broth and brown sugar together. Add enough water to make 2 cups of liquid, and pour around the brisket. Make sure the sun-dried tomatoes are covered by liquid. Cover the pan tightly with a lid or heavy-duty aluminum foil. Bake for 2½ hours. Take the brisket out of the pan and cool.

4. Trim off all the visable fat from the cooled brisket and slice diagonally, against the grain. Return the meat to the heavy pan with the vegetables and gravy. When ready to serve, reheat for half an hour in a 350°F oven.

makes 12 servings

JN

BARRY WINE'S STRINGED-BEEF BRISKET meat

Once cooked, the brisket is shredded and returned to its wine-based sauce to absorb even more flavor. It may be made a day ahead and reheated. Chef Wine likes to serve this with his Spicy Tomato Sauce (recipe follows) and his Vegetable-Matzoh "Salad" (page 65).

6 pounds beef brisket, cut in 1½-inch squares
Kosher salt and freshly ground black pepper
¾ cup peanut oil
1 carrot, peeled and chopped
1 whole leek, trimmed, washed and diced
1 celery stalk, diced
2 tablespoons pureed garlic
1 onion, chopped
2 cups Cabernet Sauvignon wine
12 cups good veal stock or beef stock
1 bay leaf
2 tablespoons dried thyme
½ cup Cognac

1. Season the meat with salt and pepper. Heat half of the peanut oil in a skillet. Add the meat and cook over medium-high heat until browned on all sides. Remove the meat and set aside.

2. Add the remaining oil to the same skillet, lower heat to medium and lightly brown the carrot, leek, celery, garlic and onion. Remove the vegetables and add ⅓ cup of the red wine to deglaze the pan.

3. Place the meat, vegetables and deglazed juices in a stockpot. Add the remaining ingredients with the exception of 2 tablespoons of Cognac. Add salt and pepper to taste. Bring to a simmer, cover and cook until the meat is tender, about 2 hours.

4. Remove the meat and, using a fork, split apart to shreds. While doing this, allow the sauce to reduce over low heat, uncovered, until thick enough to coat a spoon. Adjust the seasoning and return the shredded meat to the sauce. You can do this much a day or so ahead. When ready to serve, reheat if necessary.

5. Add the remaining Cognac and serve mounded up on a platter. If desired, surround by matzoh "salad" and pass the spicy tomato sauce.

makes 10 to 12 servings

JN

BARRY WINE'S SPICY TOMATO SAUCE FOR BRISKET pareve

Chef Wine serves this with his stringed brisket (page 174).

⅔ cup olive oil
4 pounds plum tomatoes, sliced ⅓ inch thick
Kosher salt and freshly ground black pepper to taste
3 sprigs fresh thyme or 1 teaspoon dried
3 fresh jalapeño or other hot peppers, thinly sliced

1. Preheat oven to 300°F.
2. Drizzle a little oil on a cookie sheet and place the sliced tomatoes on top. Sprinkle with salt and pepper and lay the thyme and half the sliced peppers evenly over the tomatoes.
3. Bake for 40 minutes until the tomatoes are concentrated, dryish and wrinkled.
4. Puree the tomatoes with the thyme and the cooked peppers in a food processor, adding the remaining olive oil slowly. Strain this mixture through a fine strainer.
5. Add as much of the remaining peppers as needed to suit your taste. Puree and serve at room temperature as a sauce.

makes 2 cups

JN

SOUTHWESTERN BLACKENED AND BRAISED BRISKET OF BEEF meat

(ADAPTED FROM LENARD RUBIN)

As a child in Bethel, Connecticut, Lenard Rubin grew up eating Passover Seder dishes typical of Eastern Europe. Now, as a chef in Scottsdale, Arizona, Mr. Rubin is rethinking traditional foods. His brisket is blackened with over a dozen different spices.

¼ cup vegetable oil
One 6-pound beef brisket, boneless and trimmed of most fat
¼ cup Southwestern seasoning blend (combine to taste ginger, cayenne pepper, cinna-
    mon, thyme, garlic powder, onion powder, paprika, coarsely ground black pepper,
    kosher salt, dried basil, dried oregano, white pepper, chili powder, cumin)
3 medium onions, chopped
2 large carrots, chopped
2 ribs celery, chopped
3 cloves garlic, chopped
2 bay leaves
6 cups chicken stock (or enough to cover)
1 tablespoon pareve margarine
Salt and freshly ground pepper

1. Heat the vegetable oil over medium-high heat in a 6-quart pan or Dutch oven.

2. Coat one side of beef with half the seasoning blend, patting well. Place beef in the hot oil and cook until brown and crisp on first side. Turn beef over and coat the other half with the remaining spice blend, and cook that side. Remove the meat from the pan.

3. Add the onions, carrots and celery to the pan and cook, stirring, until the onions are golden brown. Add garlic and cook for 1 minute. Add bay leaves, brisket and enough chicken stock to cover the brisket.

4. When the stock is boiling, cover the pan with a tight-fitting lid and reduce the heat to low to simmer. Cook until very tender, 2½ to 3 hours.

5. Remove the beef from the pan and set aside. Skim the excess fat from the stock and strain the liquid. (Or make the brisket a day in advance, refrigerate it and remove the fat after it congeals.) Cook the sauce until it reduces to half its volume. Slowly whisk in margarine. Season with salt and pepper to taste. Add the brisket and reheat.

makes 10 to 12 servings

JN

BASIC POT ROAST meat

This recipe is best if the beef is cooked the day before and then reheated, which greatly improves the flavor. Though first-cut brisket is more expensive and leaner than the thicker cut, it tends to be less succulent. Use first cut only if a low-fat recipe is necessary.

1 tablespoon olive oil
4 pounds boneless brisket in one piece, preferably second-cut
2 cups finely chopped onions
1 cup finely chopped carrots
1 cup finely chopped celery
3 cloves garlic, minced
3½ cups beef or veal stock
Salt and freshly ground black pepper
1½ teaspoons dried thyme
1 bay leaf
2 tablespoons tomato paste

1. Preheat the oven to 350°F.
2. Heat the oil in a heavy 3-quart casserole. Add the beef and cook over medium-high heat until browned on all sides. Remove the meat from the casserole and add the onions, carrots and celery. Cook over medium-low heat until tender and lightly browned. Stir in the garlic, then add the stock.
3. Bring to a simmer, scraping the bottom of the pan. Stir in the salt and pepper to taste, thyme and bay leaf. Return the meat to the casserole.
4. Cover the casserole and place in the oven. Bake for about 2 hours until the meat is tender.
5. To serve at once, remove the meat from the casserole and set aside. Strain the cooking liquid and puree the vegetables in a food processor or a blender. Return the cooking liquid to the casserole and stir in the pureed vegetables and the tomato paste. Bring to a boil and cook for about 5 minutes until the sauce has thickened slightly. Season to taste with salt and pepper.
6. Slice the meat against the grain and arrange on a platter. Spoon some of the hot sauce over the slices and pass the rest alongside.
7. Alternatively, the meat can be refrigerated overnight in the cooking liquid and the next day Steps 5 and 6 of this recipe can be followed.

makes 6 to 8 servings

FF

SWEET-AND-SOUR POT ROAST meat

3 pounds brisket of beef in one piece
1 cup dry white wine
⅓ cup cider vinegar
1 tablespoon vegetable oil
2 cups chopped onions
1 cup chopped carrots
3 cloves minced garlic
½ cup raisins
½ teaspoon ground ginger
3 tablespoons brown sugar
1 cup beef or veal stock
½ cup canned crushed tomatoes
2 bay leaves, crushed
Salt and freshly ground black pepper
1 to 2 tablespoons fresh lemon juice

1. Place the meat in a deep bowl, add the white wine and vinegar and allow to marinate in the refrigerator for 6 to 8 hours.

2. Preheat the oven to 350°F.

3. Remove the meat from the marinade, reserving the marinade, and pat the beef dry. Heat the oil in a heavy 3-quart casserole. Add the beef and cook over medium-high heat until browned on all sides. Remove the meat from the casserole and add the onions and carrots. Cook over medium-low heat until tender and lightly browned. Stir in the garlic, then add the raisins, ginger and brown sugar. Add the stock, the reserved marinade and the tomatoes. Bring to a simmer, scraping the bottom of the pan. Stir in the bay leaves and salt and pepper to taste. Return the meat to the casserole.

4. Cover the casserole and place in the oven. Bake for about 2 hours, or until the meat is tender.

5. To serve, remove the meat from the casserole and slice it against the grain. Arrange on a platter. Reheat the sauce and check seasonings. Add some or all of the lemon juice if the sauce does not seem tart enough. Spoon some of the hot sauce over the meat and pass the rest.

6. Alternatively, the meat can be refrigerated overnight in the cooking liquid and the next day the meat can be sliced and the sauce reheated before serving.

makes 6 to 8 servings

FF

POT ROAST BRAISED IN RED WINE meat

You'll need plenty of advance time for this pot roast because the meat must marinate in the refrigerator overnight, but not more than 16 hours, to absorb the flavor of the wine before it is cooked.

3 pounds boneless beef brisket in one piece
2 cups dry red wine
2 cups sliced onions
1 tablespoon olive oil
3 cloves garlic, minced
1 cup well-flavored beef or veal stock
Salt and freshly ground black pepper
1 bay leaf
Several sprigs of fresh rosemary

1. Place the meat in a bowl, add the wine and ½ cup of the onions. Cover and refrigerate overnight, but no more than 16 hours.

2. The next day, remove the meat from the wine marinade, reserving the marinade. Pat the meat dry on paper towels. Preheat the oven to 350°F.

3. Heat the oil in a heavy 3-quart casserole. Add the beef and cook over medium-high heat until browned on all sides. Remove the meat from the casserole. Add the remaining 1½ cups onions and cook over medium-low heat until tender and lightly browned. Stir in the garlic.

4. Add the stock and the reserved marinade. Bring to a simmer, scraping the bottom of the pan. Stir in the salt and pepper to taste, bay leaf and rosemary. Return the meat to the casserole.

5. Cover the casserole and place in the oven. Bake for about 2 hours, or until the meat is tender.

6. To serve at once, remove the meat from the casserole and slice it against the grain. Arrange on a platter. Reheat the sauce and check the seasonings. Spoon some of the hot sauce over the meat and pass the rest alongside.

7. Alternatively, the meat can be refrigerated overnight in the cooking liquid, and the next day the meat can be sliced and the sauce reheated before serving.

makes 6 to 8 servings

FF

WEYL FAMILY'S BOILED BEEF WITH HORSERADISH meat

Pot-au-feu

(FROM *THE JEWISH HOLIDAY KITCHEN*)

Pot-au-feu was served at Seders that Guy Weyl attended as a child in Alsace, and he and his wife, Eveline, continue the tradition at their home in Massachusetts. They serve it accompanied by horseradish, cranberries and gherkin pickles.

> 8 pounds flanken (short ribs) or beef shanks, with bones
> 4 leeks, white part only
> 1 medium onion
> 2 cloves
> 2 medium purple turnips, peeled
> 6 medium carrots, scraped
> 3 ribs celery
> 2 bay leaves
> 1 teaspoon dried thyme
> ½ cup parsley sprigs
> Kosher salt and freshly ground pepper

1. Place the meat in a large pot. Cover with cold water and bring to a boil. Remove the meat, rinse the pot and fill again with cold water. Add the meat again, bring to a boil and skim.

2. Wash the leeks thoroughly. Slice lengthwise in two. Remove the grit and add leeks to the pot.

3. Peel the onion, halve, stud with the cloves and add to the pot. Cut the turnips in quarters and the carrots in chunks. Add the turnips, carrots and remaining ingredients to the pot. Bring to a boil, then reduce the heat to low and simmer, covered, for 2½ hours. Remove from heat and return to room temperature. Pour off the broth. Overnight, refrigerate the broth in one container and the meat and vegetables in another.

4. Once the fat has congealed on the soup, remove it and continue to refrigerate the broth until ready to serve. You can use the broth to cook *Matzeknepfle* (page 78) and as a soup for the Seder.

5. Slice the meat and reheat with the vegetables and some of the broth. Serve as a main course. Horseradish, cranberries, gherkin pickles, *Matzeknepfle*, and Onions and Prunes (page 221) are good accompaniments.

makes 8 servings

JN

ILANA AMINI'S MEAT AND EGGPLANT GOULASH meat

Choresh Bademjon

Two cloves of garlic can be added to this hearty Persian stew as the beef begins to cook.

1 large ripe eggplant
Coarse kosher salt
½ cup vegetable oil
2 large onions, sliced thin
2½ to 3 pounds lean beef chuck, cut in 1- to 1½-inch cubes
2 teaspoons salt
½ teaspoon freshly ground white pepper
3 ripe, peeled plum tomatoes (optional)
One 8-ounce can tomato sauce

1. Peel the eggplant and cut lengthwise into slices about ¾ inch thick. Sprinkle with coarse salt and let stand at room temperature for about 1 hour, or until brown juices drain off. Set aside.

2. Heat ¼ cup oil in a 2½- to 3-quart Dutch oven or stewpot over moderate heat. Add the onions and gently sauté until soft and golden brown. Stir in the meat and add half of the salt and pepper. Cover and simmer gently over moderate heat until the meat is completely tender, about 2 hours. Stir frequently to prevent scorching and add water only if the cooking liquid evaporates.

3. While the meat cooks and when the eggplant slices have drained, pat them dry. Add the remaining ¼ cup oil to a skillet. Gently cook the eggplant slices over medium heat in a single layer. Turn the eggplant slices so that each side is light golden brown and tender. The eggplant should be done in about 7 minutes. Set aside.

4. If fresh tomatoes are used, add them half an hour before the beef is finished cooking. Add the tomato sauce 15 minutes before end of cooking time.

5. Five or 10 minutes before serving, lay the eggplant slices over the top of the beef and reheat together. Adjust the seasonings.

NOTE: This can also be prepared with lamb or veal, using stewing cuts such as shoulder.

makes 4 to 6 servings

MS

ILANA AMINI'S GREEN HERB STEW meat

Choresh Cormeh Sabzi

For Persian Jews, the green herbs signify the spring season.

2½ to 3 pounds lean beef chuck
¾ cup vegetable oil, approximately
2 large onions, sliced thin
2 teaspoons salt, or to taste
½ teaspoon freshly ground white pepper
1 medium leek
3 cups chopped spinach leaves
2 cups chopped parsley
½ cup cilantro, chopped (optional)
¾ cup fresh dill, chopped
Lemon juice (optional)

1. Trim the beef of fat and cut in 1- to 1½-inch cubes.
2. Heat half of the oil in a 2½- to 3-quart Dutch oven or other stewpot over very low heat. Add the onions and sauté until just slightly brown. Add the beef and stir. Add half the salt and pepper. Cover and let simmer gently but steadily over low heat for about 2 hours. Stir at intervals to prevent scorching, and check to be sure there is enough liquid, adding water only if necessary.
3. While beef is cooking, prepare the greens. Wash the leek thoroughly and chop the white and green portions separately.
4. Heat the remaining oil in a deep skillet or wide saucepan over medium heat. Add the white portions of leek and sauté until they begin to soften, about 5 minutes. Add the green portions of leek and sauté until they begin to soften, about 5 minutes. The leeks should not take on color. Add the chopped spinach and sauté for 5 minutes. Add the parsley and sauté for 5 minutes. Add the cilantro, if desired, and sauté for 5 minutes. Add the dill and sauté for 5 minutes. By this time the mixture should be reduced to a near sauce, but should still be bright green. Remove from the heat.
5. When the meat is thoroughly cooked, stir in the green sauce and reheat together for about 5 minutes before serving. Adjust seasonings, adding lemon juice to taste.

NOTE: This stew can also be made with lamb or veal, using stewing cuts such as shoulder. At other times of the year, Mrs. Amini adds ½ cup large dried lima beans to beef as it starts to cook.

makes 4 to 6 servings

MS

CLAUDIA RODEN'S MATZOH-MEAT PIE meat
(ADAPTED FROM *THE BOOK OF JEWISH FOOD*)

This particular blend of raisins, nuts, spices and meat is characteristic of the Arab world.

1 large onion, chopped
3 tablespoons vegetable oil
1½ pounds ground lamb or beef
Salt and freshly ground black pepper
1 teaspoon cinnamon
½ teaspoon allspice
2 tablespoons raisins
2 tablespoons pine nuts or walnuts
1 cup warm beef stock
5 to 6 matzohs
1 small egg, lightly beaten

1. In a skillet, fry the onion in 2 tablespoons oil over medium-high heat for about 10 minutes until golden. Add the ground meat and spices. Cook, stirring, until meat has browned but is still moist, about 10 minutes. Add raisins.

2. In another small pan, fry the nuts in the remaining 1 tablespoon oil for about 1 minute, stirring the nuts or shaking the pan until the nuts are lightly colored. Add to the meat mixture and stir.

3. Place the stock in a large, shallow, rectangular pan. Soak matzohs, one at a time, pressing them gently to absorb the liquid.

4. Press 2 or 3 softened matzohs into a 9-inch pie plate. (You may have to tear or cut matzohs with a scissors to accomplish this.) Place the meat mixture on top of matzohs, and use the remaining softened matzohs to cover pie.

5. Preheat the oven to 375°F. Brush the top with the beaten egg and bake for about 30 minutes, or until the top is golden.

makes 4 to 6 servings

LS

MARGARETEN FAMILY'S PASSOVER MEAT LOAF meat

2½ pounds ground chuck
2 large eggs, lightly beaten
1 cup tomato sauce (see Note)
1 large onion, grated
1 large clove garlic, minced
¼ cup matzoh meal
Salt and freshly ground black pepper
½ cup chicken or beef stock

1. Preheat the oven to 350°F.
2. In a bowl, combine the ground chuck, eggs, tomato sauce, onion, garlic, matzoh meal and salt and pepper to taste.
3. Pack the mixture into a 9-inch loaf pan, pour the stock over the top and bake for 1½ hours. (It can also be formed into 2 smaller loaves, placed side by side in a baking pan and baked for 1 hour.)

NOTE: The Margareten family uses canned Horowitz-Margareten tomato sauce with mushrooms. Crushed drained canned tomatoes or tomato puree may be substituted and, if you wish, some chopped mushrooms sautéed in a little oil may be added to the mixture.

makes 6 to 8 servings

FF

NICHOLAS STAVROULAKIS'S ALBONDIGAS meat

(ADAPTED FROM *THE COOKBOOK OF THE JEWS OF GREECE*)

Albondigas, Spanish meatballs, are a staple of Sephardic cuisine, and so are the honey and cinnamon used to flavor the sauce.

- 1 pound ground beef
- 1 large egg
- 3 tablespoons matzoh meal
- Salt and freshly ground pepper
- 2 cloves garlic, minced
- 1 tablespoon pine nuts
- 2 tablespoons chopped parsley
- 1 teaspoon ground cumin
- 2 tablespoons olive oil

for the sauce
- 1 small onion, finely chopped
- 2 cloves garlic, finely chopped
- Salt and freshly ground pepper
- 4 large tomatoes, peeled, seeded and chopped
- ¼ teaspoon cinnamon
- 1 tablespoon honey
- ½ cup water
- 2 tablespoons chopped parsley

1. In a bowl, combine the beef, egg, matzoh meal, salt and pepper to taste, garlic, pine nuts, parsley and cumin. Form into meatballs the size of walnuts.

2. Heat the oil in a heavy skillet over medium-high heat and brown the meatballs, about 10 minutes. Remove the meatballs and set aside.

3. To make the sauce, in the same skillet, add the onion, garlic, and salt and pepper to taste and sauté over medium heat until the mixture is soft, about 5 minutes. Add the tomatoes and stir well. Add the cinnamon and honey; simmer, uncovered, over medium heat until the tomatoes are reduced to a sauce, about 15 minutes.

4. Add the water and the meatballs and simmer over low heat, covered, for 30 minutes. Sprinkle with the parsley before serving.

makes about 2 dozen meatballs

JN

lamb

The ancient custom of sacrificing lambs on the eve of Passover and eating the meat at the Seder ended with the destruction of the Second Temple in 70 C.E. (Common Era). The practice was forbidden by the code of Jewish law called the Shulkhan Arukh. Those Jews who favor a strict interpretation of that ruling will not eat roasted meat or poultry of any kind at the Seder. Jews who accept a looser interpretation of the law will eat lamb if it is not roasted, but that has been further complicated by the changing definition of roasting.

Roasting once meant cooking over an open fire. Today, however, it generally means cooking in an oven without liquid. And according to the Union of Orthodox Jewish Congregations of America, lamb "must be cooked in a pan with liquid."

WOLFGANG PUCK'S BRAISED MOROCCAN-STYLE LAMB WITH ALMONDS, PRUNES AND DRIED APRICOTS meat

(ADAPTED FROM ADVENTURES IN THE KITCHEN)

In this recipe, chef Puck combines almonds, dried prunes and apricots with lamb to create an extremely festive and tasty dish.

1 boned and trimmed lamb shoulder, about 2 pounds
2 teaspoons ground cumin
1½ teaspoons freshly ground black pepper
½ teaspoon chopped fresh thyme
1 teaspoon kosher salt, plus more to taste
3 tablespoons olive oil
1 large onion, coarsely chopped
1 large carrot, peeled and coarsely chopped
1 rib celery, coarsely chopped
2 cloves garlic, thinly sliced
1 teaspoon chopped fresh rosemary
1 cup dry red wine
2 cups lamb or low-sodium chicken broth, plus up to ½ cup, if needed
1 medium tomato, trimmed and coarsely chopped
1 cup blanched whole almonds, lightly toasted (see Note, page 6)
½ cup pitted prunes
½ cup dried apricots

1. Preheat the oven to 450°F.

2. Lay the lamb out, skin side down, and sprinkle with 1 teaspoon of the cumin, ½ teaspoon of the pepper, and the thyme. Roll and tie well with butcher's string. Sprinkle the outside with ½ teaspoon of the pepper and ½ teaspoon of the salt.

3. Heat 2 tablespoons of the olive oil in a large ovenproof casserole. Add the lamb and cook over medium-high heat until browned on all sides. Remove the lamb from the casserole.

4. Add the remaining 1 tablespoon oil to the casserole. Add the onion, carrot, celery and garlic. Cook, stirring, over medium-high heat until vegetables soften, about 5 minutes. Stir in the remaining teaspoon cumin, the rosemary and the red wine. Bring to a boil and cook about

3 minutes, stirring with a wooden spoon and scraping browned bits off the bottom of the casserole. Stir in the broth, tomato, ½ teaspoon salt and ½ teaspoon pepper. Return the lamb to the casserole, cover, place in the oven and bake until meat is almost tender, about 1 hour.

5. Remove the casserole from the oven and take out the meat. Remove the vegetables from the pot with a slotted spoon and place them in a blender. Blend until smooth. Scrape the mixture back into the pot and stir well. Place over medium heat and cook about 5 minutes to thicken slightly. Return the meat to the sauce and surround with the almonds, prunes and apricots. Cover and bake until the meat is very tender and the fruit is soft, about 15 minutes.

6. Remove the lamb from the casserole, cut and remove the string and cut the lamb into thin slices. If the sauce is too thick, thin with a little additional broth. Divide the lamb among 8 plates and spoon some sauce over the top. Serve immediately, passing any remaining sauce separately.

makes 8 servings

MB

SLOWLY BRAISED LAMB meat

This recipe is based on a French technique of extremely slow cooking, which results in very tender meat.

1 boned shoulder of spring lamb, about 3½ pounds, rolled and tied
Salt and freshly ground black pepper
3 tablespoons vegetable oil
1 cup finely chopped onions
½ cup washed and finely chopped whole leeks
3 cloves garlic, minced
½ cup chicken or veal stock
½ cup dry white wine
2 tablespoons fresh lemon juice
3 sprigs fresh tarragon or 1 teaspoon dried
2 whole scallions, finely chopped
2 tablespoons finely minced parsley
Sprigs of parsley for garnish

1. Season the lamb with salt and pepper to taste. Preheat the oven to 250°F.

2. Heat the oil in a casserole large enough to hold the lamb over medium heat. Brown the lamb on all sides; it should take at least 15 minutes. Remove the lamb from the pan and set aside.

3. Add the onions and leeks to the casserole and sauté over medium-low heat until tender and just turning golden. Stir in the garlic.

4. Return the lamb to the casserole and add the stock, wine, lemon juice, tarragon and scallions. Bring to a simmer, cover and place in the oven.

5. Bake the lamb for 5 hours; by then it should be extremely tender. Remove the lamb from the casserole.

6. Strain the sauce into a heavy saucepan. Skim off as much fat as possible. Place the solids in a blender or food processor along with 1 tablespoon of the minced parsley. Puree, adding a little of the sauce if necessary. Add this puree to the sauce, reheat and check seasonings.

7. Remove the strings from the lamb. Slice the roast down the middle the long way, then cut it into chunks. Layer the meat into a bowl or loaf pan that holds 5 to 6 cups, then unmold onto a warm serving platter. Sprinkle the remaining minced parsley over the top, garnish the platter with parsley sprigs and serve, with the sauce on the side.

makes 6 to 8 servings

FF

CHARLIE TROTTER'S LAMB SHANKS BRAISED IN RED WINE meat

The lamb shank is the meat of the foreleg, usually on the bone. It is sturdy, sinewy meat that can be rendered succulent and meltingly tender with long, slow braising. Chef Trotter's version calls for 6 or more hours of virtually unattended braising. Although the cooking will tie up the oven at a low temperature for many hours, the meat can be prepared early in the day or the day before and reheated if that is more convenient.

8 lamb shanks, the smaller the better
Salt and freshly ground black pepper
2 tablespoons olive oil
2 medium onions, chopped
2 carrots, peeled and diced
12 cloves garlic, chopped
1½ cups dry red wine
6 to 8 cups lamb, beef or chicken stock
Water as necessary
1 tablespoon fresh lemon juice
3 tablespoons finely chopped flat-leaf parsley

1. Preheat the oven to 250°F.
2. Season the lamb shanks with salt and pepper. Heat the oil over medium-high heat in a heavy roasting pan large enough to hold all the lamb shanks. Brown the lamb shanks, 2 or 3 at a time, removing them from the casserole as they are done.
3. Reduce the heat to low and add the onions, carrots and garlic to the roasting pan. Cook the vegetables slowly until they are tender and just beginning to brown. To deglaze the pan, add the red wine and bring it to a simmer, gently scraping the bottom of the pan to loosen any particles that may adhere to it.
4. Return the lamb to the pan, add 6 cups of the stock, bring to a simmer and cover with aluminum foil. Put the pan in the oven and slowly braise for about 6 hours, checking from time to time that there is enough liquid in the pan. Add stock or water as necessary. Though the meat does not have to be submerged, there should be a couple of inches of liquid. Turn the lamb in the pan and baste it at least once during the cooking.
5. Remove the lamb from the pan. It should be very tender. Skim as much fat as possible from the cooking liquid and strain the liquid into a saucepan, pressing as much of the solids as

continued

possible through the strainer. If necessary, bring to a simmer over medium-high heat and reduce liquid to 2 cups. Add the lemon juice. Season the sauce to taste with salt and pepper.

6. To serve, reheat the lamb in the oven if necessary. Spoon a little of the sauce over the lamb on a platter. Sprinkle with parsley. Reheat the remaining sauce and serve it alongside.

makes 8 servings

FF

LAMB SHANKS BRAISED WITH GREEN OLIVES meat

¼ cup extra-virgin olive oil
2 sprigs rosemary, needles stripped from the branches and minced
2 cloves garlic, minced
⅛ teaspoon red pepper flakes
3 pounds lamb shank, trimmed of fat and cut into 2-inch cubes
1 cup dry white wine
½ cube chicken bouillon
1 large ripe tomato (about 1 pound), peeled, seeded and chopped
¾ cup green olives in brine, drained, rinsed and pitted
Salt and freshly ground black pepper to taste

1. Warm the oil in a large heavy skillet or Dutch oven and sauté the rosemary, garlic and red-pepper flakes over low-medium heat for 4 or 5 minutes, until the garlic begins to turn golden. Add enough lamb to fit comfortably in the pan; increase the heat to medium and sauté the shanks, turning them several times, until they are evenly browned. Transfer them to a platter. Repeat until all the lamb is cooked, adding oil as needed.

2. Add the wine and the bouillon cube to the skillet and cook over medium-high heat until the liquid has reduced by about half. Return the lamb to the pan, add the tomato, cover and cook over very low heat for about 1 hour, until the lamb is easily pierced with the tip of a knife.

3. Let the lamb sit for a few hours or overnight and reheat it. Skim off any fat, cover and simmer for half an hour, stirring in the olives during the last 5 to 10 minutes. Adjust the seasoning with salt and pepper and serve.

makes 4 to 6 servings

FF

SPRING LAMB SHANKS BRAISED IN WHITE WINE meat

This recipe borrows some of its details from the Italian veal-shank dish *osso buco*.

¼ cup olive oil or vegetable oil
8 medium to small lamb shanks, about 6 pounds total
½ cup finely chopped onion
½ cup washed and finely chopped whole leeks
½ cup finely chopped celery
3 cloves garlic, minced
1½ cups dry white wine
4 sprigs fresh rosemary
4 large sprigs Italian parsley
2 bay leaves
Salt and freshly ground black pepper
2 tablespoons finely minced parsley
1 tablespoon finely grated lemon peel
2 teaspoons potato starch
1 tablespoon cold water
Juice of 1 lemon

1. In a large, heavy, covered casserole or roasting pan, large enough to hold the lamb shanks, heat half the oil. Add the lamb shanks, a few at a time, and brown them well on all sides over medium-high heat. Remove from the pan.

2. Preheat the oven to 350°F.

3. Add the remaining oil to the pan, lower the heat and sauté the onion, leeks and celery until they are soft and lightly browned. Stir in all but ½ teaspoon of the garlic, then add the wine. Simmer for a few minutes, scraping the browned particles from the bottom of the pan.

4. Stir in the rosemary, parsley sprigs and bay leaves. Season the mixture with salt and pepper, then return the lamb to the pan. Cover and place in the oven to bake until the lamb is very tender, about 3 hours.

5. While the lamb is baking, mix the remaining ½ teaspoon garlic with the minced parsley and lemon peel and set aside.

6. When the lamb is tender, remove it from the pan. Bring the liquid to a simmer on top of the stove and taste it for seasoning, adding more salt and pepper if necessary. Dissolve the potato starch in the cold water and stir it in to thicken the sauce, then stir in the lemon juice.

Return the lamb to the pan and baste it with the sauce. Keep warm until ready to serve or, if desired, prepare it in advance and reheat it just before serving.

7. Transfer the lamb to a platter and spoon the sauce over it. Sprinkle with the minced parsley, garlic and lemon peel mixture and serve.

makes 8 servings

FF

BRAISED LAMB SHANKS WITH ORANGE AND ROSEMARY meat

Matzoh polenta (page 105) makes a wonderful accompaniment for these savory lamb shanks.

2 tablespoons vegetable oil
4 lamb shanks
Kosher salt and freshly ground pepper
Matzoh meal for dredging meat
1 onion, chopped
2 cloves garlic, minced
1½ cups chopped Italian plum tomatoes
2 cups dry white wine
¼ cup orange liqueur
1½ cups chicken stock, preferably homemade
3 strips orange peel
1 teaspoon fresh rosemary or ½ teaspoon dried

1. Heat 1 tablespoon of the oil over medium-high heat in a heavy skillet or casserole big enough to hold the lamb shanks in one layer. Season the shanks with salt and pepper and dredge them lightly in matzoh meal, then brown them on all sides. Remove to a plate and pour off the fat from the casserole.

2. Heat the remaining oil in a casserole. Add the onion and garlic and cook them over moderate heat until they are soft, but not brown. Add the tomatoes, wine, orange liqueur, stock, orange peel and rosemary and bring to a boil over medium-high heat. Return the shanks to the casserole. Reduce the heat and simmer for 1 to 1½ hours or until they are tender.

3. Remove the shanks from the sauce. Degrease the sauce and return the shanks to the casserole. Heat them through and serve.

makes 4 servings

MH

LAMB STEW WITH ARTICHOKES meat

3 jumbo artichokes, stalks intact
2 lemons
3 tablespoons olive oil
2 pounds lamb shoulder in 1-inch pieces, fat trimmed
Kosher salt and freshly ground black pepper
3 large spring onions, sliced, or 1 medium onion, chopped
1 clove garlic, minced
1 cup dry white wine
1 cup water
1 teaspoon fresh thyme leaves
1 egg
⅓ cup chopped mint leaves

1. Cut off the end of the artichoke stalks; slice the tops off the artichokes horizontally about ⅓ of the way down. Discard the tough lower outer leaves. With a paring knife, trim away any dark green bits and trim the outside of the stalks. Cut the artichokes in half vertically. With a spoon, scrape out the chokes. Cut each half with its stalk into thirds vertically and put into a bowl of water into which you have squeezed the juice of half a lemon. This will stop them from turning brown.

2. Heat the oil in a large casserole over moderate heat. Drain the artichokes and pat them dry with a towel. Brown them lightly in the oil and set them aside. Season the lamb with salt and pepper and brown the meat a few pieces at a time in the oil over medium-high heat. Remove to a bowl.

3. Add the onions and garlic and cook over moderate heat until soft. Add the wine, water and thyme, scraping up the cooking juices. Return the lamb pieces to the pan. Cover and simmer gently for 1 hour. Add the artichokes and cook for another 30 minutes or until they are tender. Correct the seasoning.

4. Beat the egg in a small bowl with the juice of the remaining 1½ lemons. Whisk in ¾ cup of lamb cooking juices. Off heat, add the egg mixture to the lamb and stir well. Sprinkle with mint and serve.

makes 4 servings

MH

DAISY INY'S IRAQI SWEET AND SOUR LAMB WITH OKRA meat

Bamia

(FROM *THE BEST OF BAGHDAD COOKING*)

2 pounds boneless shank or shoulder lamb, cut into 1- to 1½-inch cubes
Freshly ground black pepper
1 small onion, chopped
Dash turmeric
3½ cups water
3 large stalks celery, sliced
1 pound fresh okra, washed and trimmed
2 heaping tablespoons tomato paste
6 tablespoons fresh lemon juice
Salt
2 tablespoons finely chopped parsley
1 tablespoon finely chopped celery leaves
½ cup coarsely chopped fresh mint or 1 heaping teaspoon of dried mint
3 tablespoons sugar, or to taste

1. Sprinkle the lamb cubes with pepper. Cover with cold water and bring to boil. Boil 15 to 20 minutes. Drain and rinse lamb in cold water.

2. Return the lamb to the pot with the onion. Sprinkle the turmeric over the lamb and add a few dashes of pepper. Pour in 3 cups cold water. Cover partially and cook over medium heat for about 1 hour until lamb is cooked about halfway.

3. Add the celery stalks and cook another 45 minutes to 1 hour, adding additional water, if necessary, to cover three-quarters of the meat.

4. Add the okra and tomato paste. When mixture begins to boil, add the lemon juice and season with salt. Add additional water, if necessary. Cook 15 minutes longer.

5. Stir in the parsley, celery leaves and mint. Simmer, partially covered, for 15 minutes longer.

6. Add the sugar and cook a few minutes longer.

NOTE: This dish may be prepared ahead, refrigerated until serving time and reheated.

makes 8 servings

MB

PAUL PRUDHOMME'S VEAL ROAST WITH MANGO SAUCE meat

Chef Prudhomme, of K-Paul's Louisiana Kitchen in New Orleans, created this roast veal for a dinner in Jerusalem celebrating the city's three thousandth anniversary. Although the rib-eye roast is expensive, the results are spectacular.

1 teaspoon salt
1 teaspoon onion powder
1 teaspoon garlic powder
1 teaspoon cayenne pepper
1 teaspoon freshly ground white pepper
1 teaspoon freshly ground black pepper
1 teaspoon dried basil
1 large mango, peeled and diced
2½ cups veal or beef stock
1 rib-eye veal roast, boned to yield 3 to 3½ pounds
2 tablespoons olive oil

1. Preheat the oven to 325°F.

2. In a small bowl, combine the salt, onion and garlic powders, cayenne, white and black peppers, and basil. Set aside.

3. Place the mango and 2 cups of the stock in a saucepan, and bring to a boil over high heat. Lower the heat, allowing the mixture to thicken, and cook until the stock is reduced to about 1½ cups, for about 20 minutes. Add 1 teaspoon of the seasoning mix, and remove from the heat. Puree in a blender or food processor, and set aside for a few hours until ready to use.

4. To prepare the roast, cut a series of pockets ¾ inch apart, each pocket about 1 inch wide and 1 inch deep. With your hands, work 5 teaspoons of the seasoning mix into the pockets and along the outside of the roast.

5. In a large nonstick skillet, heat the olive oil over high heat. Sear the meat on all sides.

6. Transfer the meat to a roasting pan. Add the remaining ½ cup of stock to the skillet to deglaze, scraping up any bits from the bottom. Pour the contents of the skillet over the meat. Cover the pan, and roast the veal until it is medium rare, with an internal temperature of 125°F, about 45 minutes to 1 hour.

7. Serve ½-inch slices of the roast topped with the mango sauce.

NOTE: It is delicious accompanied by sautéed peppers, eggplant and squash seasoned with the remaining teaspoon of seasoning mixture.

makes 6 servings

JN

MIMI SHERATON'S BREAST OF VEAL WITH MATZOH BALL STUFFING meat

(FROM *FROM MY MOTHER'S KITCHEN*)

Breast of veal is a succulent but underutilized cut that requires a long roasting time. In this dish, the roast isn't stuffed with actual matzoh balls. Instead, the matzoh ball ingredients are mixed together lightly so that they do not become too dense or hard, transforming them into a perfect Passover stuffing. The stuffing should be made just before you roast the meat, so it's easiest if you prepare it after rinsing the meat.

1 breast of veal, 8 to 9 pounds
4 cloves garlic
Salt, freshly ground black pepper and sweet paprika
Stuffing (page 202)
1 teaspoon powdered ginger
2 to 3 tablespoons chicken fat or pareve margarine
2 medium onions, coarsely chopped
2 carrots, scraped and coarsely diced
2 cups tomato juice
1 to 2 cups water, or as needed
2 to 3 sprigs of parsley

1. Have the butcher cut a pocket as large as possible in the veal breast, but be sure he does not cut through to the edges of the top. The fat should not be trimmed from the top of the veal, as it will keep the meat moist during cooking. Have the butcher saw notches between the ribs on the underside of the breast so it will be easy to carve between them, but be sure he does not cut into the pocket area, either on top or bottom, or the stuffing will ooze out. Rinse the veal and pat dry.

2. Preheat the oven to 375°F.

3. Crush 2 cloves of garlic and rub around the inside of the pocket. Rub also with a little salt, pepper and paprika. Stuff the pocket with the stuffing. Do not cram it too full, as stuffing will expand. Leave 1- to 1½-inch margin at the opening of the pocket, or it will be messy to sew. When the breast is stuffed, sew the opening with small stitches, using a large needle and unwaxed cotton kitchen thread.

4. Rub the outside of the breast, top and bottom, with salt, pepper, paprika and ginger. Place the fat, onions, carrots and the 2 remaining cloves of garlic in the bottom of a covered

roasting pan. Place the veal breast on top of the vegetables and slide the pan, uncovered, into preheated oven.

5. Check after a few minutes, and when the fat has melted, baste the top of roast. Let the roast remain uncovered for 20 to 30 minutes, or until top of breast and vegetables begin to turn golden brown. When brown, pour 1 cup of the tomato juice over the roast and add water to the bottom of the pan. Add the parsley, cover the roasting pan, slide back into oven and, after roasting for 10 minutes, reduce heat to 350°F.

6. Roast, covered, for about 3½ hours, including the time taken for the roast to brown. Check every half hour to see if more tomato juice and water are needed to keep vegetables from burning, and to baste the roast. It will probably take all the tomato juice and 1 to 2 cups of water.

7. When the meat near the back of the ribs can be pierced easily with a long-pronged fork, the roast is done. Remove it to a heated platter and keep warm. Skim as much fat as possible from the pan juices. Pour the juices through a strainer into a large saucepan, discarding the parsley but forcing through the cooked carrots, onion and garlic. Skim again. Adjust the seasoning and if gravy is too thick (which it should be), thin with a little water. Simmer on top of the stove to reheat. Remove the thread from breast of veal and carve meat, cutting slices between ribs to include stuffing.

8. Arrange on a heated platter. Serve gravy on the side in a heated sauceboat. Green salad or asparagus would usually be the only accompaniment.

makes 8 to 10 servings

MS

MIMI SHERATON'S MATZOH BALL STUFFING meat
(FROM *FROM MY MOTHER'S KITCHEN*)

The ingredients for matzoh balls become a stuffing if the recipe is made just before the meat is roasted. Do not let the mixture set, as when making matzoh balls. The recipe may be halved to stuff half a breast of veal or a chicken of not more than 6 pounds.

6 large eggs
2 large egg yolks
½ cup cold water
6 heaping tablespoons rendered and solidified chicken fat
1 teaspoon salt
⅛ teaspoon freshly ground white pepper
1½ cups matzoh meal
1 large onion, finely chopped
2 tablespoons finely minced parsley

1. In a bowl, lightly beat the eggs plus yolks with water. Add 5 tablespoons of chicken fat and stir with a fork until the fat dissolves. Add salt and pepper. Stir in the matzoh meal.

2. In a skillet, sauté the chopped onion in the remaining 1 tablespoon of fat until it is very soft and bright yellow over low heat for about 5 minutes. Do not let it brown. Add a little more fat if needed. Stir the onion into the matzoh mixture along with the parsley. Adjust the seasoning with salt and pepper. Stuff into poultry or veal breast at once. Roast the veal as soon as it is stuffed.

makes stuffing for a 9-pound breast of veal

MS

BREAST OF VEAL
WITH APPLE STUFFING meat

The stuffing recipe may be halved to stuff a chicken of not more than 6 pounds.

One 8-to 10-pound breast of veal
1½ cups chicken fat or vegetable oil
3 cups chopped onions
1 cup matzoh meal
2 tart apples, cored and diced
¼ cup chopped parsley
Salt and freshly ground black pepper
¼ to ½ cup water
2 cups sliced onions
6 unpeeled cloves garlic, or more, to taste
6 carrots, coarsely chopped

1. Have the butcher trim the breast of excess fat, cut a pocket into it and crack the large, flat bone to which the ribs are attached to make carving easier.

2. Heat the fat in a large skillet. Add the chopped onions and sauté slowly until softened but not brown. Stir in the matzoh meal, apples, parsley, and salt and pepper to taste. Mix well. Add enough water to make the mixture moist so it holds together without being gummy. You should have about 4 cups of stuffing. Remove from the heat and allow to cool.

3. Just before cooking, stuff the pocket of the veal with the stuffing and skewer the opening closed.

4. Preheat oven to 350°F.

5. Scatter the sliced onions, garlic and carrots in the bottom of a large roasting pan. Place the stuffed breast of veal on top and rub it with salt and pepper. Add enough water to the pan to cover the vegetables but not the roast. Cover the pan with aluminum foil, place in the oven and roast for 2 hours. Uncover the roast and roast for another hour or so until the top is crisp and brown. Transfer the roast to a large carving board.

6. With a slotted spoon, remove the vegetables from the roasting pan and place them in a sieve suspended over a bowl. Skim as much fat as possible from the juices remaining in the pan. Press the vegetables through the sieve and stir them back into the juices in the pan. Place over medium-high heat and cook, stirring and scraping the pan to loosen any particles clinging to it. Taste the sauce for seasoning.

continued

7. Slice the roast into portions, cutting down between the ribs. Arrange the slices, each with a rib and stuffing, on a serving platter. Pass the sauce on the side. To serve a half-portion, cut the slice of meat and stuffing away from the bone and divide it in half.

makes 8 servings

FF

TAGLIO BIANCO VEAL ROAST meat
(ADAPTED FROM ANDREE ABRAMOFF)

This is a simple roast that is easy to prepare and traditionally served at Sephardic tables. The name *taglio bianco* refers to the "white cut" of the expensive veal tenderloin. The less costly shoulder cut will be somewhat darker in color.

3 pounds veal tenderloin or shoulder, tied at 1-inch intervals with string
2 to 3 cloves garlic, slivered
3 tablespoons matzoh-meal cake flour
Salt and freshly ground black pepper
¼ cup light (not extra-virgin) olive oil
3 tablespoons fresh lemon juice

1. Cut small deep slashes in the meat and insert the slivers of garlic. Roll the meat in the matzoh-meal flour and dust off any excess. Sprinkle with salt and pepper.

2. Heat the oil over medium heat in a large, heavy pot with a nonreactive enamel, stainless-steel, or dark gray anodized aluminum finish. Sear the roast until nicely browned. Add the lemon juice, lower the heat, and simmer, covered, for 50 minutes to 1 hour. Check from time to time, adding a tablespoon of water if the liquid in the pan seems to be evaporating. At just under an hour, the roast should be medium, registering 140°F on an instant-read meat thermometer inserted in the thickest part. If you prefer veal well done, cook longer, but not beyond a reading of 180°F.

3. Remove the roast from the pan and set aside for 30 minutes. Just before serving, reheat the pan juices and check for seasoning. Slice the meat and serve with hot pan juices. Some Sephardim traditionally serve this with rice, but matzoh-meal polenta (page 105) is also an excellent accompaniment.

makes 8 servings

FF

MAKING A TSIMMES— AND OTHER VEGETABLE DISHES

Not surprisingly, root vegetables are popular among Ashkenazi. Carrots, one of the few sweet-tasting vegetables that were available to Jews of Eastern Europe, are a great favorite, whether served plain or in soufflés, puddings, purees or salads. Combined with potatoes, they are mainstays of tsimmes, a stew of vegetables and fruits that may also contain meat. Contemporary variations of this traditional dish are a Southwestern version and a layered tsimmes terrine with asparagus. Artichokes, eggplants and other Mediterranean vegetables are especially favored by Sephardim and Jews of the Middle East. Spinach is particularly popular during Passover because its color evokes the spring season.

Regular potato pancakes are always a favorite, but for variety also try low-fat potato "muffins" or Wolfgang Puck's plate-size version. Butternut Squash Ratatouille from Anne Rosenzweig, Beet Crisps, Leek Croquettes, and Onions and Prunes are mouthwatering.

And for a special treat, there is even "Lasagna"—layers of eggplant, tomatoes and mushrooms, minus the pasta.

ARTICHOKES, SEPHARDIC STYLE pareve
(ADAPTED FROM ANDREE ABRAMOFF)

These artichokes, spicy and topped with a splash of vinegar to create a warm vinaigrette, are similar to those served in Mrs. Abramoff's home when she was growing up in Cairo.

8 medium artichokes
1 lemon, cut in half
4 cloves garlic, very finely minced
1 teaspoon hot red pepper flakes
½ cup chopped flat-leaf parsley (packed)
2 tablespoons kosher salt
Oil for deep frying
½ cup red wine vinegar

1. Cut off the stems flush with each artichoke and trim off the coarse outer leaves. With a sharp knife, slice off about 1 inch of top of each artichoke and, using scissors, snip the prickly points off the leaves. Rub the cut areas with half the lemon. Then juice the lemon.

2. Fill a large, deep pan with salted water and bring to a boil. Add the lemon juice and artichokes. When the water returns to a boil, cover and cook over medium heat for 20 to 25 minutes, until the artichokes are tender and a leaf can be removed easily. Drain the artichokes upside down until cool.

3. In a small bowl, combine the garlic, hot pepper flakes, parsley, and salt.

4. When the artichokes have cooled, remove the fuzzy choke and center leaves from each artichoke by gently spreading the center of the artichoke open and pulling out the choke or scooping it out with a spoon.

5. Fill each artichoke with the parsley mixture, tucking it between the leaves and in the center. Set aside or refrigerate until ½ hour before serving.

6. Heat the oil for deep-frying to a depth of 2 to 3 inches in a deep saucepan, deep fryer, or wok. When the oil has reached 375°F, fry the artichokes for 30 seconds each, until the leaves begin to curl. Drain briefly on paper towels.

7. Sprinkle each with a tablespoon of red wine vinegar and serve.

makes 8 servings

FF

ARTICHOKES IN PARSLEY SAUCE pareve/meat

48 baby artichokes
Juice of 1 lemon
3 tablespoons olive oil
2 cloves garlic, sliced
1 cup water, vegetable stock or chicken stock
1½ cups flat-leaf parsley, stems removed
Salt and freshly ground black pepper

1. Preheat oven to 400°F.
2. Trim the artichokes by slicing off ½ inch of the top, slicing off any stems and pulling off the tougher outer leaves.
3. Toss the artichokes with the lemon juice and olive oil in an ovenproof dish. Scatter the garlic on top and drizzle with ¾ cup of the water or stock. Cover and bake about 30 minutes until the artichokes are tender.
4. Transfer the cooking liquid and garlic to a blender and add the parsley. Add the remaining ¼ cup of water or stock. Puree. Season to taste with salt and pepper.
5. Toss the artichokes with the parsley mixture and serve warm or at room temperature.

makes 6 servings

FF

WHOLE ROAST ASPARAGUS pareve
(ADAPTED FROM *RED, WHITE & GREENS* BY FAITH WILLINGER)

The lemon and orange enhance the delicate flavor of the asparagus.

  1 pound fresh asparagus of medium thickness and uniform size, trimmed and peeled,
      if necessary
  2 to 3 tablespoons olive oil
  Salt and freshly ground pepper
  2 tablespoons fresh lemon juice
  1 tablespoon orange juice

1. Place the asparagus in a single layer in a large nonstick skillet and drizzle with 1 tablespoon of olive oil. Shake the pan to coat the asparagus with the oil and place over medium heat. Cook the asparagus, shaking the pan every few minutes to brown evenly.

2. Lower the heat and continue cooking until asparagus is tender, about 10 to 15 minutes (time may vary, depending on size of asparagus). Test by poking asparagus stems with a toothpick or knife. Transfer to a serving dish. Season with salt and pepper to taste. Drizzle with 1 to 2 tablespoons of olive oil. Combine the lemon juice and orange juice and sprinkle over the asparagus. Serve immediately.

makes 3 to 4 servings

MO

ASPARAGUS WITH
HORSERADISH SAUCE pareve/dairy

This may be made with sweet butter for dairy meals.

1 tablespoon fresh horseradish
2 tablespoons water
8 tablespoons (1 stick) unsalted pareve margarine or unsalted butter, cut into 8 pieces
16 to 18 hot, freshly cooked asparagus spears

1. Combine the horseradish and water in a saucepan and stir. Do not boil, but heat almost to the boiling point.

2. Add the margarine or butter, piece by piece, and swirl it around until the sauce is well blended and smooth. Serve the hot sauce over the asparagus.

makes 4 to 6 servings

CC

ASPARAGUS WITH RED AND YELLOW PEPPER COULIS pareve

For a beautiful presentation, try steamed asparagus served on a colorful two-tone sauce made with red and yellow peppers.

    2 yellow bell peppers
    4 red bell peppers
    1 cup extra-virgin olive oil, plus oil for drizzling
    Balsamic vinegar to taste
    Kosher salt and freshly ground black pepper to taste
    40 fresh asparagus spears of uniform size
    Fresh tarragon leaves for garnish

1. Cut the peppers in quarters and remove the stems and seeds. In boiling water, simmer the red peppers in one pan, the yellow peppers in another for 10 minutes. Drain.

2. Combine the red peppers in a blender or food processor with half the olive oil and puree. Add vinegar, salt and pepper to taste. Set aside. Wash out the container. Repeat the process with the yellow peppers.

3. Cut the tough stems from the asparagus. With a vegetable peeler, pare away the tough skin from the lower half of the stalk. Rinse the asparagus in cold water.

4. Place the asparagus in a steamer basket over boiling water. Steam until tender but firm. Drain and sprinkle with olive oil. Cool to room temperature before serving.

5. On eight individual plates, pour two tablespoons red pepper sauce on one side, two tablespoons yellow pepper sauce on the other. Arrange asparagus on top. Garnish with tarragon.

    makes 8 servings

MH

BEET CRISPS pareve

(FROM *THE PLEASURE OF YOUR COMPANY*)

4 large beets, peeled
Vegetable oil for deep-frying
Kosher salt to taste

1. Using a vegetable peeler, cut the beets into long, flat, thin strips. Pour enough oil into a large pot to reach a depth of about 3 inches. Heat the oil to 375°F.

2. Fry the beets in small batches until they are browned and crisp. Remove with a slotted spatula and place on paper towels to drain well. Just before serving, place in a bowl and toss with salt.

makes 6 to 8 servings

MO

ROASTED CARROTS WITH GARLIC pareve

1½ pounds large carrots (3 to 4 carrots), peeled
4 cloves garlic, sliced
2 tablespoons olive oil
Salt and freshly ground black pepper
1 tablespoon chopped fresh cilantro leaves
1 tablespoon chopped Italian parsley leaves

1. Preheat the oven to 425°F.

2. Slice the carrots on an angle about ¾ inch thick. Put the carrots in a baking dish that will hold them snugly in a single layer. Add the garlic, oil, salt, pepper, cilantro and parsley, and toss all the ingredients together to mix well.

3. Rearrange the carrots in a single layer, then put the dish in the oven and roast until the carrots are tender and beginning to brown, which takes about 40 minutes. Turn the carrots once during roasting so they cook evenly. Serve hot or at room temperature.

makes 4 servings

FF

BAKED EGGPLANT AND TOMATO, WITH OR WITHOUT FENNEL dairy

1½ pounds eggplant
Salt
½ cup olive oil
½ cup chopped onions (or ¼ cup onion and ¼ cup chopped fresh fennel bulb)
1 large clove garlic, minced
2 pounds ripe tomatoes, peeled, seeded and chopped
1 teaspoon minced fresh thyme
Freshly ground black pepper
½ cup crumbled feta cheese
1 tablespoon minced parsley

1. Quarter the eggplant lengthwise, then cut into slices ½ inch thick. Place in a bowl, toss with about 1 teaspoon salt and allow to sit for 30 minutes.

2. Meanwhile, heat 2 tablespoons of the oil in a large skillet over medium heat. Add the onions, or onion and fennel, and sauté until tender but not brown. Add the garlic and cook another minute or so.

3. Stir in the tomatoes. Cook the tomato mixture over high heat, stirring occasionally, until the excess liquid evaporates, about 20 minutes. Stir in the thyme and salt and pepper to taste. Set aside.

4. Preheat the oven to 400°F. Rinse and dry the eggplant pieces.

5. Heat half the remaining oil in a large heavy skillet over medium-high heat and sauté about half the eggplant pieces until lightly browned. Remove and repeat with the remaining oil and eggplant pieces. Arrange the eggplant pieces, slightly overlapping, in a fairly shallow 6- to 8-cup baking dish. Season the eggplant lightly with salt and pepper. Spoon the tomato mixture over the eggplant and top with crumbled feta cheese.

6. Bake 10 minutes, lower the heat to 350°F and bake about 15 minutes longer. Sprinkle with the parsley and serve.

makes 6 servings

FF

ANGEL FAMILY'S
LEEK CROQUETTES pareve/dairy

Keftes di Prasa
(FROM *SEPHARDIC HOLIDAY COOKING*)

For best flavor, the croquettes should be made the day before you plan to serve them.

> 12 very large leeks
> 3 matzohs
> 3 large eggs
> 1 teaspoon salt
> ¼ teaspoon freshly ground black pepper
> Matzoh meal, for dredging
> Vegetable oil, for frying
> 2 lemons, cut in quarters

1. Buy the largest, thickest leeks you can find for this: if you buy them in bunches and find that one or two in a bunch are thin, buy extras. Trim off the roots and all of the tough outer green leaves. You will use the white and only the tenderest yellow green center stalk leaves—about 6 to 7 inches in all. Split each leek down the middle, then cut in small pieces. Soak in several changes of cold water until leeks are completely free of sand. About four changes should do.

2. Place the leeks in a saucepan with unsalted water to cover. Cook for about 45 minutes, or until leeks are completely soft and mashable. Drain well. When cool enough to handle, pick up small bunches of the cooked leeks and squeeze out as much water as possible. This will reduce the leeks to a near pulp. Chop briefly or cut coarsely with a knife.

3. Soak the matzohs in warm water for about 10 minutes, or until completely soft. Squeeze out as much water as possible. The matzohs will also be close to a pulp.

4. In a bowl, beat eggs, salt and pepper into matzohs, then beat in leek pulp. You should have a mixture that will be sticky and soft, but that can be molded into small patties about 2 inches in diameter and close to a ½ inch thick. If mixture is too liquid to mold, add matzoh meal by teaspoonfuls until mixture can be shaped.

5. Shape into patties and dredge very lightly on all sides in matzoh meal.

6. Fry slowly in hot oil until the first side is golden brown. Turn and fry second side. Total frying time should be about 10 minutes per batch. Drain on paper towels, then place in a baking dish. Cover loosely and store in the refrigerator overnight.

continued

7. Before serving, preheat the oven to 250°F. Sprinkle the croquettes liberally with lemon juice and bake for about 20 to 30 minutes, or until thoroughly warm. Serve at once.

NOTE: If you plan to serve the croquettes with a dairy meal, fry them in unsalted butter, with or without a little vegetable oil added to retard burning. The butter improves the flavor.

makes about 30 croquettes

MS

UNION SQUARE CAFE SAUTÉED MUSHROOMS pareve

Chef Michael Romano tops his Matzoh Meal Polenta (page 105) with these mouthwatering mushrooms, which also make a tasty side dish for roast meats or poultry and a superb appetizer. If you want to serve them separately, simpy double the recipe for 4 to 6 portions.

2 tablespoons olive oil
½ pound assorted mushrooms, cleaned and very thinly sliced (use any combination of
    white, shiitake, cremini or wild mushrooms)
½ teaspoon garlic
¼ cup white wine
1 tablespoon lemon juice
¼ teaspoon salt
⅛ teaspoon freshly ground black pepper
1 tablespoon chopped parsley

1. Heat the oil in a 2-quart sauté pan over high heat until it just begins to smoke. Add the mushrooms and sauté to brown and soften them, about 3 to 5 minutes.

2. Add the garlic, white wine and lemon juice and toss together to blend the flavors. Season with salt and pepper and cook 1 to 2 minutes.

3. Serve the mushrooms and their juice spooned over the matzoh polenta and sprinkled with parsley. Or serve them as an appetizer or side dish, sprinkled with parsley.

makes 4 to 6 servings as a topping or 2 to 3 servings as a side dish or appetizer

FF

MUSHROOM AND CABBAGE CASSEROLE dairy

Without the sour cream or yogurt topping, this hearty casserole becomes a good side dish for roast chicken or pot roast.

3 tablespoons vegetable oil
12 ounces fresh white mushrooms
1 large onion, sliced
2 cloves garlic, minced
1 tablespoon minced fresh ginger
2 pounds green cabbage, cored and coarsely shredded
2 cups vegetable stock
1 cup dry white wine
Salt and freshly ground black pepper
1 bay leaf
2/3 cup sour cream or plain yogurt

1. Preheat the oven to 375°F.

2. On top of the stove, heat the oil in a heavy 3-quart casserole over medium-high heat. Add the mushrooms and sauté until they begin to brown. Lower the heat to medium, stir in the onion and sauté until tender. Stir in the garlic and ginger.

3. Add the cabbage, stock and wine. Bring to a simmer, mix to distribute the ingredients and season to taste with salt and pepper. Add the bay leaf, cover and place in the oven.

4. Bake 2 to 2½ hours until most of the liquid is absorbed. Remove bay leaf. Check seasonings. Serve topped with sour cream or yogurt.

makes 6 servings

FF

ONIONS AND PRUNES pareve/meat

A wonderful complement to roasted poultry and meats. Schmaltz gives the dish a richer flavor.

¼ cup goose fat or cooking oil
1½ pounds onions, peeled and diced
Salt to taste
¾ pound pitted prunes

1. Place the goose fat or oil in a medium-large skillet over low heat. Add the onions and a little salt and cook for 1½ hours, adding a little water if necessary.
2. Meanwhile, soak the prunes in water to cover for half an hour; drain and then simmer very slowly with the onions for half an hour more.

makes 6 to 8 servings

JN

POTATO PANCAKES pareve

Latkes

(ADAPTED FROM SUSAN KOPALD)

Latkes—you can serve them with brisket and applesauce, top them at dairy meals with sour cream, and even eat them plain. They are so tasty, satisfying and versatile that you may want to freeze a batch or two to have on hand for instant access: simply put the pancakes on a baking sheet in the freezer after they have been fried and drained on absorbent paper. After they are frozen, store them in a plastic bag. When you have an urge for them, remove the latkes from the freezer and heat them at 450°F for several minutes before serving.

    6 Idaho or russet potatoes (medium to large)
    2 large yellow onions
    2 large eggs, slightly beaten
    4 to 6 tablespoons matzoh meal
    Salt and freshly ground white pepper
    ¼ cup minced parsley (optional)
    Vegetable oil

1. Peel the potatoes and put them in cold water until ready to grate.
2. Grate the potatoes and onions, either by hand or in a food processor, but do not puree them. They must be rough. Squeeze out as much liquid as possible into a bowl and return the starchy sediment to the mixture.
3. Add the eggs and matzoh meal. Add the seasonings and the parsley, if desired.
4. Heat 1 inch of oil in a skillet over medium heat. Place 1 tablespoon of batter for each pancake in the skillet, flattening and spreading them out. The pancakes should be thin. Fry, turning once, so that pancakes are golden brown and crisp on both sides. Drain on paper towels. To keep pancakes warm while frying other batches, place them on a baking sheet lined with absorbent paper in a 250°F oven. Serve with applesauce or, at dairy meals, with sour cream.

NOTE: After frying the first batch, it may be necessary to add more matzoh meal to the remaining potato mixture to absorb any accumulated liquid. If you prefer to make them early in the day, keep the pancakes at room temperature on a baking sheet and reheat before serving. Do not refrigerate because that will make them soggy.

    makes 4 to 6 servings

CC

WOLFGANG PUCK'S POTATO-ONION LATKE pareve

Chef Puck's variation on potato latkes: one large pancake that is sliced into servings.

2½ tablespoons olive oil
1 medium onion, peeled and thinly sliced
3 large baking potatoes, peeled
1½ teaspoons salt
1 teaspoon freshly ground black pepper

1. Preheat the oven to 400°F.
2. Heat 1 tablespoon of the olive oil in a medium skillet. Add the onion and sauté over medium-high heat until golden brown.
3. Cut the potatoes across into ⅛-inch slices, place in a bowl and toss with the remaining olive oil.
4. Lightly grease a 10-inch nonstick or cast-iron baking pan or ovenproof skillet. Arrange half of the potatoes in the pan in a single layer, and season with salt and pepper. Cover with the onions, top with the remaining potatoes, and season with salt and pepper.
5. Bake until the potatoes are golden brown and crisp, about 30 minutes. If the underside of the potatoes is not browned when the potatoes are tender, finish over high heat on top of the stove. Loosen from the pan with a spatula.
6. Cut into 6 equal slices and serve.

makes 6 servings

MB

POTATO PANCAKES WITH FIRE-ROASTED PEPPERS pareve

(ADAPTED FROM CHEF ALLEN'S)

The strips of red pepper impart a distinctive color and flavor to these latkes, a specialty of Chef Allen's restaurant in North Miami.

1 red bell pepper
1 tablespoon olive oil
4 large Idaho baking potatoes
1 medium onion
1 tablespoon minced garlic
½ cup matzoh meal
2 large eggs, beaten
Salt and freshly ground white pepper to taste
Vegetable oil for frying

1. Coat the red pepper with the olive oil. Roast over an open flame, or put on a baking sheet in a 450°F oven for 10 minutes, charring well. When the outside is charred thoroughly, remove the pepper from the heat and put in a brown bag (this will make it easier to peel). When cool, remove the skin and seeds, and cut in julienned strips.

2. Grate the potatoes coarsely by hand, and then grate the onion. Combine the garlic, matzoh meal, eggs, salt and pepper. Add the pepper strips.

3. In a heavy-bottomed sauté pan, heat ¼ inch of vegetable oil over medium heat. Using 3 tablespoons of batter, make patties about ½ inch thick. Brown one side until golden, about 2 to 3 minutes; turn and brown the other side. Do not crowd the pancakes; make sure there is at least an inch between them. Serve immediately.

makes about 8 pancakes

JN

FAYE LEVY'S LOW-FAT POTATO LATKE "MUFFINS" pareve
(ADAPTED FROM *THE LOW-FAT JEWISH COOKBOOK*)

These are more like mini-kugels (puddings) than latkes (pancakes).

2 tablespoons vegetable oil
2 medium onions, chopped
1¼ teaspoons paprika
1¾ pounds baking potatoes, peeled
2 large eggs, lightly beaten
1 teaspoon salt, or to taste
½ teaspoon freshly ground black pepper

1. Preheat the oven to 400°F. Use a little of the oil to grease a nonstick 12-muffin tin.
2. Heat 1 tablespoon vegetable oil in a heavy nonstick skillet over medium heat. Add the onions and sauté until softened, about 10 minutes. Stir in 1 teaspoon paprika; remove from the heat.
3. Coarsely grate the potatoes by hand or in a food processor. Put them in a large strainer, and press out the excess liquid. Transfer to a bowl, and stir in the onions, eggs, salt and pepper.
4. Put a scant ⅓ cup of the potato mixture in each muffin tin. Smooth the tops lightly, brush with the remaining oil and sprinkle with a little paprika. Bake about 40 minutes until brown at the edges and firm.
5. Remove the "muffins" and serve at once, or leave in the pans to keep warm for 15 minutes or so.

makes 12 "muffins" for 6 servings

FF

POTATO KUGEL pareve

For Ashkenazi Jews, potato pudding is a favorite at all times of the year.

Vegetable oil for greasing casserole
6 medium potatoes, peeled
3 large eggs
½ cup matzoh meal
½ teaspoon potato starch
1½ teaspoons salt
Freshly ground black pepper to taste
1 onion, grated (optional)

1. Preheat the oven to 350°F. Grease a 1½-quart casserole.
2. Grate the potatoes into cold water, then drain. There should be 3 cups.
3. In a bowl, beat the eggs until they are thick. Stir in the potatoes and remaining ingredients, including the onion, if using.
4. Turn the mixture into the casserole and bake, uncovered, about 1 hour.

makes 6 to 8 servings

JH

LEMONY POTATOES
AND SCALLIONS meat

2 pounds small red new potatoes
2 tablespoons olive oil
2 cloves garlic, minced
2 cups chicken broth
2 tablespoons fresh lemon juice
Salt and freshly ground black pepper
½ cup finely chopped scallions

1. Peel the potatoes and place in a bowl of water so they do not discolor.

2. Heat the oil in a large skillet or casserole that has a cover over medium-high heat, dry the potatoes and add them. Cook for several minutes to coat the potatoes with oil. Lower the heat and add the garlic, chicken broth, lemon juice and salt and pepper to taste. Cover the pan tightly and slowly simmer until the potatoes are tender when pierced with the point of a knife, about 25 minutes. Check the potatoes from time to time to make sure they are not sticking.

3. Remove the potatoes to a warm serving dish and cover to keep warm.

4. Increase the heat in the pan and boil the cooking liquid, uncovered, until it is reduced and somewhat thickened. Add the scallions and cook a minute or so longer, then pour the sauce over the potatoes in a serving dish and serve.

makes 6 servings

FF

ROASTED-PEAR-POTATO-AND-WATERCRESS PUREE WITH TOASTED WALNUTS pareve

2 large baking potatoes, pricked with a fork in several places
3 firm but ripe Bosc pears
1½ cups stemmed watercress
1 teaspoon salt
Freshly ground black pepper
¼ cup toasted walnuts, coarsely chopped (see Note, page 6)

1. Preheat the oven to 450°F. Place the potatoes on a baking sheet and roast for 20 minutes. Peel, halve and core the pears. Place the pears on the baking sheet with the potatoes, and roast until the potatoes and pears are soft, about 40 minutes.

2. Meanwhile, bring a pot of water to a boil. Add the watercress and blanch for 1 minute. Drain well. Place the watercress and the pears in a food processor and process until smooth, stopping to scrape down the sides of the bowl.

3. Cut the potatoes in half lengthwise and scoop out the flesh. Pass the potato through a ricer into a medium-size bowl. Stir the pear mixture into the potato until smooth. Season with the salt and pepper to taste. Divide among 4 plates and sprinkle with the toasted walnuts. Serve immediately.

makes 4 servings

MO

SPINACH WITH GARLIC AND LEMON *pareve*

(FROM *A WELL-SEASONED APPETITE*)

    1 tablespoon olive oil
    4 cloves garlic, minced
    16 cups spinach leaves, stemmed, washed and torn, about 3 pounds
    4 teaspoons fresh lemon juice
    1 teaspoon salt
    Freshly ground black pepper

1. Heat 1 teaspoon of oil in a large skillet. Add the garlic and cook over medium heat, stirring constantly, for 20 seconds.

2. Add the spinach by handfuls, tossing it in the skillet, until all of it fits. Cook, stirring, for about 2 minutes.

3. Remove from the heat and toss in the remaining oil and lemon juice, and the salt and pepper to taste. Divide among 4 plates and serve.

makes 4 servings

MO

ANNE ROSENZWEIG'S BUTTERNUT SQUASH RATATOUILLE

pareve/meat

Apples add a sweetness to this vegetable mélange. Chef Rosenzweig suggests serving the ratatouille with roasted meat. It can be made ahead and carried in a covered dish to a Seder.

2 medium butternut squash, peeled, halved, fibers scooped out and cut into ¾-inch cubes
3 teaspoons vegetable oil
1 cup carrots, peeled and cut into ¼-inch dice
1 cup leeks, cleaned and cut into ¼-inch dice
1 cup zucchini, cut into ¼-inch dice
1 cup Golden Delicious apples, peeled, cored and cut into ¼-inch dice
½ cup minced shallots
1 cup vegetable or chicken broth
2 teaspoons salt
Freshly ground pepper

1. Preheat the oven to 375°F. Place the squash in a roasting pan and toss with 2 teaspoons of the oil. Roast until just tender, tossing from time to time, about 25 minutes.

2. Heat the remaining teaspoon of oil in a large, nonstick skillet over moderately high heat. Add the roasted squash and the carrots and cook for 3 minutes, stirring occasionally. Add the leeks and cook for 2 minutes, stirring occasionally. Add the zucchini, apples and shallots and cook for 3 minutes longer, stirring occasionally. Stir in the vegetable or chicken broth and salt and pepper to taste, and simmer until the vegetables are tender but not too soft, about 15 minutes. Serve warm.

makes 10 to 12 servings

MO

CRAIG CLAIBORNE'S
SWEET POTATO SALAD pareve

A delicious side dish for cold roast chicken.

1½ pounds sweet potatoes (about 3 large)
Juice of 4 limes
2 large apples
1 cup thinly sliced and then chopped celery
6 ounces coarsely chopped cashews or pecans
1 cup, approximately, mayonnaise, freshly made if possible

1. Quarter the potatoes, place in a pot with enough water to cover the potatoes, bring to a simmer and cook until tender, about 20 minutes. Drain potatoes and allow them to cool enough to peel. Quarter lengthwise, then cut into cubes. Place in a mixing bowl and sprinkle with lime juice. Chill.

2. Peel, core and dice the apples. Add to the potatoes together with the celery and nuts. Add enough mayonnaise to coat well. Chill before serving.

makes 4 to 6 servings

CC

BAKED SWEET POTATOES WITH RED ONIONS pareve/dairy

3 medium red onions, peeled, cut into paper-thin round slices
3 medium sweet potatoes, about 1 pound, peeled and cut into thin round slices
2 cups apple cider or apple juice
2 teaspoons brown sugar
½ teaspoon salt
¼ teaspoon freshly ground black pepper
1 tablespoon fresh thyme leaves
1 tablespoon unsalted butter or pareve margarine, cut into small pieces

1. Preheat the oven to 350°F. In a 9-inch round or oval gratin dish, place the red onions and sweet potatoes in alternate layers.

2. Put the apple cider or apple juice, brown sugar, salt and pepper in a small saucepan and stir over medium heat until the sugar dissolves. Pour the hot liquid over the onions and sweet potatoes and sprinkle with the fresh thyme.

3. Distribute the pieces of butter or margarine over the top and cover the gratin dish with foil. Bake for 1 hour. Remove the foil and continue baking, basting often, until the onions and sweet potatoes are tender, about 30 minutes.

makes 4 to 6 servings

MO

ROAST CARROTS, TOMATOES AND ONIONS WITH THYME pareve

The vegetables become almost caramelized, their flavors emphasized by the roasting process.

1 ½ pounds carrots
12 plum tomatoes
2 large onions
2 tablespoons olive oil
2 teaspoons fresh thyme leaves or 1 teaspoon dried
Kosher salt and freshly ground black pepper to taste

1. Preheat oven to 350°F. Slice the carrots into 1-inch pieces. Peel the tomatoes by dropping them into boiling water, leaving them for 1 minute and then draining them and slipping off their skins. Cut them in half and scrape out the seeds. Cut the onions into thick slices.

2. Pour the oil over the bottom of a baking dish about 9 by 13 inches and spread out the onions, tomatoes and thyme. Season with salt and pepper and stir the vegetables lightly to make sure they are coated with the oil. Bake for 30 minutes, stirring from time to time.

3. Add the carrots, stir to coat with oil and continue roasting for 1 hour.

makes 6 servings

MH

VEGETARIAN "LASAGNA" dairy

This lasagna-style casserole is made with layers of eggplant, tomatoes, mushrooms and cheese, but without pasta. It is perfect for a crowd and, for smaller gatherings, the recipe can easily be halved.

4 medium-large eggplants, about 5 pounds total
6 tablespoons extra-virgin olive oil
1½ pounds fresh mushrooms, sliced
1 cup chopped onions
1½ cups chopped sweet red pepper
6 cloves garlic, minced
8 cups well-drained canned Italian plum tomatoes, about four 28-ounce cans
2 teaspoons chopped fresh oregano
1 teaspoon chopped Italian parsley
Salt and freshly ground black pepper
4 tablespoons unsalted butter
4 tablespoons potato starch
5 cups whole milk
4 cups shredded mozzarella cheese
⅔ cup matzoh meal
1 cup, about 4 ounces, freshly grated Parmesan cheese

1. Preheat the broiler. Line a large broiler pan with foil.
2. Slice the eggplants ½ inch thick, discarding the stems and the very bottom slices. Place as many of the slices as fit in a single layer on the broiler pan and broil until lightly browned, turning the slices once to brown both sides. Repeat until all the slices have been browned, then set them aside.
3. Heat 3 tablespoons of the oil in a very large, heavy nonstick skillet over high heat. If you do not have a very large skillet, one that holds 4 quarts, use 2 skillets. Add the mushrooms and stir-fry until they have wilted. Remove them from the pan and place in a bowl.
4. Add 1 tablespoon oil to the pan or pans along with the onions, sweet pepper and garlic. Reduce the heat to medium-low and cook the vegetables, stirring until soft, about 10 minutes.
5. Add the tomatoes to the pan, bring to a simmer and cook until fairly smooth, about 20 minutes. Add the oregano and parsley and season with salt and pepper to taste. Mix half the tomato sauce with the mushrooms and set the rest aside.
6. Melt the butter in a medium-size saucepan over medium-low heat. Whisk in the potato starch, then slowly whisk in the milk. Cook over medium heat, whisking constantly,

until the sauce comes to a simmer and is thickened and smooth. It will not be a very thick sauce. Season to taste with salt and pepper and remove from the heat. Mix in the shredded mozzarella.

7. Use ½ tablespoon of oil to grease two baking dishes, each about 9 by 13 inches and 2 inches deep (see Note). Spread a little of the plain tomato sauce in the bottom of each dish.

8. Place a layer of eggplant in each dish, using a total of ⅓ of the eggplant. Spread with ½ the tomato and mushroom mixture, then sprinkle with ⅓ of the matzoh meal. Spoon on half the mozzarella and white sauce mixture. Then repeat the layers of eggplant, mushrooms and tomato mixture, matzoh meal and mozzarella and white sauce mixture.

9. Finally, top each baking dish with a layer of eggplant and spread with a thin layer of the plain tomato sauce. Sprinkle with the remaining matzoh meal, then sprinkle on the Parmesan cheese. Drizzle with the remaining oil. Cover the baking dishes with foil. If the dishes are prepared more than two hours before serving, they should be refrigerated.

10. When ready to bake, have the baking dishes at room temperature. Preheat the oven to 350°F. Place the baking dishes in the oven and bake for 15 minutes. Uncover the dishes and bake 25 to 30 minutes longer, until the ingredients bubble and the top lightly browns.

11. Meanwhile, reheat the remaining tomato sauce.

12. When the baking dishes are removed from the oven, allow them to stand for 5 minutes before serving. Serve a dish of the tomato sauce alongside.

NOTE: If you cannot fit both baking dishes in your oven at one time, bake the second one after the first has come out of the oven. In that case, cover the first one with aluminum foil after you take it out of the oven. If both "lasagnas" are prepared in advance, they can be refrigerated, then brought to room temperature and reheated at 425°F for about 15 minutes before serving.

makes 12 to 16 servings

FF

VEGETABLE GRATIN pareve

1 small eggplant, halved lengthwise, then thinly sliced crosswise

2 small yellow squash, thinly sliced crosswise

1 tablespoon kosher coarse salt

4 carrots, peeled and thinly sliced

1 medium onion, finely chopped

2 cloves garlic, finely chopped

1 teaspoon tomato paste

¼ cup white wine

1 medium tomato, thinly sliced

1 yellow bell pepper, seeded, deveined and sliced lengthwise into ½-inch strips

1 red bell pepper, seeded, deveined and sliced lengthwise into ½-inch strips

1 tablespoon chopped fresh thyme

1 teaspoon freshly ground black pepper

2 tablespoons olive oil

6 sprigs flat-leaf parsley, stems removed, finely chopped

1. Preheat the oven to 375°F. Lightly cover the eggplant and squash slices with the salt and set aside for 30 minutes. Rinse the slices under cold running water and pat them dry.

2. Put the carrots, onion and garlic in a large skillet with a heavy bottom. In a small bowl, dissolve the tomato paste in the white wine and pour it over the carrots. Stir to combine.

3. Arrange the eggplant, tomato, yellow pepper, squash and red pepper, in that order, in alternating rows on top of the carrot mixture. The sliced vegetables should be loosely packed. Sprinkle the thyme over the gratin and season with the black pepper. Drizzle with the olive oil, cover the pan with foil and bake for 45 minutes. Remove the foil and continue to bake for an additional 30 minutes.

4. Garnish with the parsley.

makes 4 to 6 servings

MO

ROASTED ROOT VEGETABLES pareve/dairy

1 ½ tablespoons olive oil
1 bunch beets
1 small rutabaga, about ½ pound
¾ pound Yukon gold potatoes (about 6)
3 carrots, peeled
2 large parsnips, peeled
5 cloves garlic, peeled and halved
3 tablespoons unsalted butter or pareve margarine
Salt and freshly ground black pepper

1. Coat your hands with a little of the oil to prevent the beets from staining. Remove the stems from the beets, then peel and quarter them. Set aside in a small bowl.

2. Peel the rutabaga and cut in 1½-inch chunks. Put in a large bowl. Scrub the potatoes, quarter them and put them in the bowl. Cut the carrots and parsnips in 1½-inch chunks and add them to the bowl. Pour the remaining olive oil over the vegetables and toss.

3. Preheat the oven to 400°F. Arrange all the vegetables except the beets in a shallow baking dish large enough to hold them in a single layer, but with little room to spare. Scatter the garlic cloves into the dish. Then tuck in the beet quarters. Dot with butter or margarine and season to taste with salt and pepper.

4. Put in the oven and bake 45 minutes. Gently toss the vegetables in the dish and bake another 45 minutes until they have browned along the edges and are very tender. Serve from the baking dish.

makes 6 servings

FF

tsimmes

Although the expression "making a *tsimmes*" means making a fuss, the preparation of most *tsimmes* is a relatively simple process. Vegetables and fruits—and meat, if desired—are combined and cooked in liquid for a long time, so that the flavors of the ingredients blend. The traditional *tsimmes* usually contains root vegetables—carrots, white potatoes, sweet potatoes—and dried fruit; with the addition of beef browned with onions, it becomes the classic meat version. Fresh fruits, canned fruits, fruit juices, and other vegetables are other favorite ingredients for the *tsimmes* pot. Some people serve *tsimmes* in place of potatoes; others like to serve it in addition to potatoes. And the meat version especially makes a hearty main course. In recent years, some chefs have created innovative variations of *tsimmes:* Lenard Rubin's Southwestern Tsimmes Stuffed in Anaheim Chiles, for example, or Barry Wine's Tsimmes Terrine—a colorful layered loaf embedded with whole asparagus—which is a feast for the eye as well as the palate.

CARROT TSIMMES meat/pareve

1 tablespoon chicken fat or pareve shortening
10 to 12 medium carrots, diced, about 2 pounds
¼ teaspoon salt
1 teaspoon sugar
½ cup raisins
⅛ teaspoon ground ginger
3 tablespoons water

1. Melt the fat in a skillet over medium heat. Add the carrots and cook for 1 minute, stirring constantly.

2. Add the remaining ingredients, bring to a boil and simmer. Cook, covered, until tender, about 15 minutes. Drain, if necessary, and serve.

makes 6 servings

JH

CARROT AND APPLE TSIMMES pareve

1 pound carrots, peeled and quartered
1 McIntosh apple, cored, peeled and quartered
¼ cup sugar
Grease for casserole
2 tablespoons pareve unsalted margarine
Dash of salt
½ teaspoon cinnamon

1. Preheat oven to 350°F.

2. In a food processor, coarsely grate the carrots and apple. Sprinkle the mixture with the sugar and set aside.

3. Grease a heavy 1-quart casserole with a lid with pareve unsalted margarine. Bring 1 cup water to a boil and transfer it to the casserole. Add salt, the carrot mixture and the margarine, and sprinkle with the cinnamon. Cover and bake 1 hour, until carrots are soft.

makes 4 to 6 servings

JN

CYREL DEITSCH'S SWEET POTATO AND CARROT TSIMMES pareve/dairy

(ADAPTED FROM *SPICE AND SPIRIT: THE COMPLETE KOSHER JEWISH COOKBOOK*)

This classic tsimmes can be prepared with or without the canned fruits.

12 cups salted water
6 medium sweet potatoes, peeled and diced (about 3 pounds)
1 pound carrots, peeled and diced
Salt
Vegetable oil for pan
½ cup pitted prunes, halved
1 cup orange juice
¼ cup brown sugar
½ teaspoon cinnamon
2 tablespoons butter or pareve margarine
One 20-ounce can pineapple chunks, drained (optional)
1 can Mandarin orange pieces, drained (optional)

1. In a large pot, bring the water to a boil. Add the sweet potatoes and carrots and simmer, uncovered, about 15 minutes or until tender. Drain and mash. Add salt to taste. Place in a greased 6-quart casserole with the prunes.

2. Preheat the oven to 350°F. In a bowl, combine the orange juice, brown sugar and cinnamon, and pour over the sweet potatoes. Bake, covered, for 30 minutes. Uncover and taste. If the tsimmes tastes sweet enough, dot with butter or margarine, bake, uncovered, 15 minutes more. Otherwise, add pineapple chunks and mandarin oranges, then dot with butter or margarine, and bake an additional 15 minutes.

makes 4 to 6 servings

JN

VILNA TSIMMES meat

A Lithuanian version of the classic meat tsimmes.

3 pounds flanken or chuck, cut into 2-inch stewing cubes
2 teaspoons salt, or to taste
3 medium onions, sliced
3 tablespoons chicken fat or pareve margarine
Water or beef broth
3 large white potatoes, peeled and quartered
2 large sweet potatoes, peeled and quartered
5 large carrots, scraped and sliced into 2-inch chunks
12 ounces pitted prunes
¼ cup brown sugar
Dash of nutmeg
½ teaspoon cinnamon
Grated zest and juice of 1 orange
Freshly ground black pepper to taste

1. Sprinkle meat with salt. Brown the meat with the onions in 2 tablespoons of the chicken fat or margarine over medium heat.

2. Add water or beef broth to cover, lower the heat and simmer, uncovered, for 1 hour.

3. Preheat the oven to 350°F. Place the meat, onions and liquid in a 4-quart casserole, surrounded by the white potatoes, sweet potatoes, carrots, prunes, brown sugar, nutmeg, cinnamon and grated orange zest and juice. If needed, add more water or beef broth to cover. Cover the casserole and bake 1 hour.

4. Uncover, season with salt and pepper, and cook an additional 2 hours or until the liquid is absorbed and the top turns crusty.

makes 6 to 8 servings

JN

BARRY WINE'S TSIMMES TERRINE meat

This beautiful terrine alternates layers of a classic tsimmes: carrots and sweet potatoes, prunes and white potatoes. Onions and asparagus spears are other original variations on the traditional recipe.

4 whole leeks, with green part
3 carrots, peeled and coarsely chopped
2 medium-size sweet potatoes, peeled and cut in large chunks
¼ pound chicken fat
¼ cup brown sugar
¼ cup cider or apple juice
Kosher salt and freshly ground pepper
Juice of ½ lemon
½ teaspoon cinnamon
3 large onions
3 tablespoons vegetable oil
1½ cups water
6 large eggs
3 large Maine potatoes, peeled
12 ounces pitted prunes
16 to 20 pencil-size asparagus spears (see Note)

1. Up to two days before serving, cut the leeks open down the center and clean the grit from them. Then blanch in a pot of simmering water and remove to iced water. Dry.

2. In a 375°F oven, in a casserole dish, bake the carrots and sweet potatoes with the chicken fat, brown sugar, cider or apple juice, salt and pepper to taste, lemon juice and cinnamon until the vegetables are soft, about 1 hour. Puree the mixture.

3. Dice the onions and sweat them slowly in a covered heavy pan with the oil, cooking slowly over low heat until the onions are translucent, about 20 minutes, stirring occasionally. In a food processor or blender, puree the onions and adjust the consistency by adding about a cup of water until the mixture has reached the texture of whipped cream.

4. When the carrot–sweet potato mixture is cool, fold in 3 of the eggs and 1 cup of the onion puree. Set aside.

5. Cook the Maine potatoes in a pot of boiling water until tender and mash until smooth, mixing in the remaining onion puree. Add salt and pepper to taste. When cool, add the remaining 3 eggs and fold in well.

6. Heat the prunes with about 1 inch of water until soft, drain and puree.

continued

7. In boiling water, cook the asparagus for about 2 minutes and then plunge into iced water. Dry.

8. For each terrine—this recipe makes two—grease a loaf pan. Lay the dry leeks across the pan to line it, alternating tops and bottoms from one side to the other so that the ends overlap the top by about 2 inches.

9. Put one quarter of the sweet potato–carrot mixture in the pan. Bury 4 to 5 asparagus spears in the sweet potato–carrot mixture. Atop the layer of sweet-potato mixture, spread a thin layer of prunes. Atop that, put half the white-potato mixture. Cover with the second quarter of the sweet potato–carrot mixture, again pushing in 4 to 5 asparagus spears. Repeat for the second terrine.

10. Seal the terrine by folding the leeks over the top. Put the pan in a larger pan containing about an inch of very hot water. Cover the terrine with foil and bake for 1 hour at 375°F.

11. Cool completely outside the oven in the pan with the water. When completely cool, weigh down with heavy cans or a wrapped brick and place in the refrigerator for 1 day. Slice while chilled with a very sharp slicing knife, making sure to wipe the knife after each slice. Warm slightly in the oven and serve.

NOTE: For a more traditional tsimmes, or if asparagus is not available, substitute 20 additional pitted prunes, whole and cooked until soft, for the asparagus.

makes 2 terrines

JN

SOUTHWESTERN TSIMMES STUFFED IN ANAHEIM CHILES pareve
(ADAPTED FROM LENARD RUBIN)

Using cilantro and Anaheim chiles, chef Rubin created a Southwestern variation of the traditional tsimmes.

12 ounces pitted prunes
6 medium carrots, peeled and diced
3 medium sweet potatoes (about 2 pounds), peeled and diced
6 tablespoons honey
½ teaspoon nutmeg
½ teaspoon cinnamon
½ teaspoon salt
1 tablespoon fresh lemon juice
¼ cup orange juice
1½ teaspoons chopped cilantro
12 green or red Anaheim chiles
Pareve margarine for greasing pan

1. Preheat the oven to 250°F.
2. Combine all the ingredients except the chiles in greased 3-quart baking dish. Cover and bake, stirring occasionally, until vegetables are soft but not mushy, 3 to 4 hours. Let cool.
3. Dice the mixture to facilitate stuffing into chiles. This can be prepared a day ahead.
4. Roast the chiles over flame or under broiler until skin turns black and bubbly, turning frequently so skin burns evenly (do not overcook; when peeled, the chiles should remain green and crunchy). Under cold running water, peel the burnt skin off by rubbing with your fingers. Or place the chiles on a cookie sheet in a 450°F oven. Roast about 20 minutes, turning occasionally, until skin turns black. Remove to a plastic or paper bag and leave until cool. Peel off the skin.
5. With a sharp knife, make a slit from the bottom of the stem to the point of each chile.
6. Gently peel out the seeds and rinse the inside of the chile.
7. Pat each chile dry and stuff with chopped tsimmes so the chile is slightly overstuffed, causing the slit to open, exposing the filling.
8. Bake in a preheated 350°F oven for 10 to 15 minutes.

makes 10 to 12 servings

JN

lessons of a passover pupil

By MOLLY O'NEILL

Six years ago, when my husband began to drop hints about establishing a Jewish home for the sake of his daughter, I was delighted. Despite my midwestern, Episcopalian roots, I knew enough about his traditions to welcome the opportunity to buy a special set of dishes for the Sabbath, a new white tablecloth and to plan candle-lit Friday evenings—an annual calendar of ritual, much of which is centered around the table.

Although I look forward to any pretext for ceremonial celebration, after five Jewish years I'm convinced that my anticipation speaks to a deeper yearning for community, tradition and ritual. It is, after all, not the white "grappa" plates from Vietri or the Florentine damask cloth that have sanctified Shabbat in our home. Rather, it is the weekly repetition, the gradual development of over three hundred Fridays, of a ritual that begins with boisterous singing and mellows into a quiet contentment to which we look forward.

We've had only five chances to practice Pesach and we've been, so far, voyeurs at others' Seders. Perhaps this history, along with the prominence of Passover itself, has left us tentative about making a Seder of our own. My husband thinks we are gathering ideas when, like wandering Jews, we travel from Seder to Seder. I'm starting to realize that the wandering itself has become our tradition; how poetic that seems. But for the first few years I thought we were pursuing the Pesach of others in order to learn. As matters turned out, I learned mostly by my mistakes.

Invited to a close friend's house during the first year my husband and I were together, we offered to bring the matzoh balls and to provide as well an appetizer for the Seder. Incapable of declining good intentions, my friend agreed. In a pathetic attempt to banish my lack of lifelong Seder experience with an exercise in inventive cooking, I spent days perfecting matzoh balls with ground chick-peas and Middle Eastern seasoning that I'd learned from a Yemenite in Israel. My husband roasted eggplant for baba ganoush on our terrace for two consecutive evenings.

The final preparations made us nearly an hour late for the Seder. Our tardiness, I thought, probably explained why the baba ganoush was never served, and why the Yemenite matzoh balls met with a tepid reaction. But the brisket and chicken, potatoes, pickled beets, glazed carrots and dense hazelnut torte were consumed with a passionate voracity I'd previously witnessed only among epicureans in citadels of haute cuisine.

When she invited us the next year, however, my friend mentioned that, well, she just had this thing for the matzoh balls made from the recipe on the box. And having considered the issue carefully, I concluded that she wanted to make her own matzoh balls. Cheerfully, I learned from my first mistakes.

Lesson 1: When invited to a Seder, know the dietary restrictions of your host. At other times of the year, my friend would have welcomed the foods we brought. But not at Passover, when chick-peas and Middle Eastern seasonings are foods forbidden to observant Ashkenazim and some Sephardim.

Lesson 2: Be prompt, even—or particularly—if this means rushing the food preparations. There is, after all, the legacy of unleavened bread to heed.

For the second night of Passover we went to the home of other friends, who happened to be superb cooks. We offered to bring the kosher wine, which we did, and in a surge of good will or grandiosity we also brought six bottles of a delicious wine substitute, for anyone who didn't consume alcohol. It was never served. One guest, who I knew didn't keep a kosher home, reckoned that since the bottles lacked a label certifying rabbinical approval, it might connote the possibility of fermentation, which could suggest the presence of yeast. And that would certainly violate the Seder observance.

Lesson 3: Tradition is an important ingredient in any Seder dish.

Lesson 4: Even people who eat pork-fried rice with shrimp at Chinese restaurants can be kosher at Passover.

We traveled to Washington, D.C., the next year for a gourmet Seder punctuated by a pageant the hostess's children have performed for years. The pageant was delightful and the meal was delicious: a four-hour progression of appetizers, golden matzoh ball soup, fork-tender brisket with a heady horseradish sauce and heaping platters of grilled vegetables, each in a different herb marinade. And more than enough time between courses to clean our plates. It all seemed like a great combination, but near the end we were too tired and too full to really appreciate orange-scented almond cake or the battery of East European–style cookies and pastries that accompanied the coffee. We also missed the last plane back to New York.

Lesson 5: A Seder is more than dinner. Each course has significance, and collecting them into a single menu is a ritual that takes time to observe.

We booked a hotel room the following year when we accepted the Seder invitation of friends in Philadelphia. Our hosts, a former student radical who is now an Orthodox rabbi and his wife, an artist, had somehow passed the experience of their lives through the fine mesh sieve of Hasidic tradition.

Their Seder was designed to engage each person around the table on a number of levels.

We all were asked, for instance, to bring for the Seder plate a taste that represented something we wished to be freed of. We were asked to talk about the taste and what it represented. I remember a preponderance of bitter ingredients—fresh horseradish, of course, but also ginger root, chile peppers and raw dandelion greens. There was a lot of talk about forgiveness as an antidote to bitterness. The evening became a junction of ancient mysticism and trendy notions of self-help that miraculously resonated in harmony around the table. The conversation was more intense than the flavors of the food.

Lesson 6: Ritual comes alive when it becomes up-close and personal.

We've attended an Italian Seder, a Yemenite Seder, a Russian Seder and a French Seder. At the Yemenite Seder, the food was distinctive. The balls floating in our clear chicken broth were made from ground chick-peas and chick-pea flour, and the brisket had been braised, à la cholent, with apricots and figs. At the other Seders, the differences were more cultural and aesthetic. A museum-quality Kiddush cup from Murano, for instance, dappled light on the guests through a rosy prism as it was lifted above the candelabra for the blessing. Romanoff cutlery was a nice touch. A three-hundred-year-old matzoh cradle, a family treasure from the south of France, deepened the sense of history around the table.

Just as our family Shabbat emerged from trial and error, our sense of Pesach has emerged in a somewhat surprising way. The Seder-to-Seder wandering we thought of as a prelude is, in fact, our tradition. We can never replicate the whole as well as its parts: the variety of soft lights, the disparate textures of the gefilte fish, the different flavors and buoyancy of the matzoh balls we've been served. All this, including our own mistakes—a few

Seders that ended late and some that ended too early—is weaving the texture of our Pesach.

Most important, were we to make our own Seder, my husband, stepdaughter and I would lose the rare experience of being guests. We'd miss the satisfaction of being simultaneously powerless over an evening's proceedings and completely at ease in a familiar structure.

Last year, I quizzed my young stepdaughter. "How is this night different from all other nights, Miss Samuelson?" I asked. "We go to other people's houses!" came the quick reply. "We don't have to stay home!"

That's true, and we all have a lot more to learn.

BEFORE THE AFIKOMEN
desserts
and sweets

From fruit compotes for those who are calorie conscious to chocolate cakes for those who are not, Seder desserts can be an enormously satisfying conclusion to the Passover meal.

For traditionalists, fruit is a favorite: in salads or compotes, puddings or soufflés. For a real show-stopper, try the pyramid-shaped apple meringue from artist Claude Monet's repertoire.

The macaroon, which dates back to monks in eighth-century Europe, has become a typical part of Passover at Seders around the world. Other popular holiday sweets are meringues, orange squares, nut cookies, chocolate crisps—and even Passover brownies. Fritters, which can be topped with a lemon-flavored sauce or syrup, or with jam, fruit or cinnamon sugar, are also served frequently.

Then there are the cakes and tortes, in which matzoh cake flour or ground nuts is substituted for regular flour and stiffly beaten egg whites provide the leavening. The most basic and beloved Passover cake is sponge cake—an airy, citrus-tinged conclusion to any meal. Nut tortes range from plain to those that are filled and frosted—some made even more fancy with accompaniments like chocolate sauce and coconut jam. There is also a Passover cheesecake and, for chocoholics, a variety of chocolate cakes—including a holiday version of seven-layer cake—so good, you might want to serve them year-round.

Finally, to conclude a meal, or for a sweet treat at any time during the holiday, try a traditional homemade brittle with walnuts and honey.

compote

A compote, flavored with spirits or not, is a favorite Seder dessert and a perfect accompaniment to cakes and macaroons. At meatless meals, a scoop of ice cream or a dollop of yogurt provides a creamy contrast to the tangy flavors. Making a compote is simply a matter of simmering fruits, dried or fresh or a combination, with a little liquid and sweetening plus spices. Wine or juice or even tea can be used as the liquid, each imparting its distinctive flavor to the dessert. Compotes can be served immediately or can be made in advance and kept refrigerated for a long time. Individual dried fruits can be poached in liquids that enhance their intense flavors—prunes in red wine, for example, or figs in ginger syrup.

DRIED FRUIT COMPOTE pareve

This compote, flavored with citrus and honey, is excellent for children and for others who do not want the flavor of wine or Cognac.

½ pound mixed dried fruit (apples, apricots, pears, peaches, prunes, figs)
1 teaspoon freshly grated orange peel
½ teaspoon freshly grated lemon peel
1 tablespoon honey, or to taste
1 orange, juiced
2 tablespoons chopped toasted almonds (see Note, page 6), or crumbled dry macaroons (optional)

1. In a saucepan, simmer the fruit in water to cover until soft, 15 to 20 minutes. Remove the fruit to a bowl and cook the liquid in the saucepan until it's reduced to ½ cup.

2. Add the orange and lemon peels, honey and orange juice to the saucepan. Cook, stirring, until the honey has melted. Pour the mixture over the fruit. Leave at room temperature.

3. Just before serving, sprinkle the fruit with the almonds or macaroon crumbs, if desired.

makes 3 to 4 servings

MH

FRUIT COMPOTE IN RED WINE pareve

½ cup slivered orange peel
½ cup honey
2 pounds mixed dried fruit (apples, apricots, pears, peaches, prunes, figs)
1 bottle dry red wine
½ cup orange juice (approximately)
2 cinnamon sticks

1. Place the orange peel and honey in a heavy saucepan and simmer slowly until the peel begins to look translucent, about 10 minutes.

2. Add the remaining ingredients and simmer until the fruit is tender, about 40 minutes. If too much of the liquid evaporates during cooking, add a little additional orange juice or some water.

3. Remove from the heat and cool to room temperature. Remove the cinnamon sticks, then chill before serving. Spoon into individual goblets or bowls.

makes 6 servings

FF

MACEDOINE OF FRUIT IN VERMOUTH pareve

½ cup sweet or dry vermouth
¼ cup sugar
¼ teaspoon cinnamon
1 small to medium pineapple, cut into wedges
3 navel oranges, peeled and cut into sections
18 large grapes, halved and seeded

1. In a bowl, combine the vermouth, sugar and cinnamon and let stand in the refrigerator 1 hour.

2. Pour off the liquid into another bowl and discard the sugar sediment. Pour the liquid over the prepared fresh fruit and marinate in the refrigerator for at least 1 hour before serving.

makes 6 servings

CC

SHERRIED PEARS pareve

2 large ripe pears
1 tablespoon fresh lemon juice
1½ cups water
3 tablespoons sugar
½ cup sweet sherry

1. Peel, core and halve the pears. In a bowl, toss them with the lemon juice.
2. In a saucepan, bring the water and sugar to a boil. When the sugar has dissolved, add the pears, lower the heat and simmer until the pears are just tender, about 10 minutes.
3. Drain the pears, transfer to a shallow serving dish and pour the sherry over them. Turn them in the sherry once or twice. Serve the pears while still warm.

makes 2 servings

FF

PRUNES POACHED IN RED WINE pareve

(FROM *A WELL-SEASONED APPETITE*)

Zest of 2 oranges, removed in long strips
3 tablespoons black peppercorns
½ cup fresh orange juice
One 750-milliliter bottle Merlot or other dry red wine
1 cup sugar
2 pounds pitted prunes

1. Tie the orange zest and peppercorns in a piece of cheesecloth and place in a large saucepan. Add the orange juice, wine and sugar and stir to combine.

2. Place over medium heat and simmer for 10 minutes. Remove from heat and add the prunes. Refrigerate overnight.

3. Serve at room temperature. At dairy meals, spoon over vanilla ice cream.

makes 8 servings

MO

GINGERED FIGS pareve/dairy

Try serving this with cream or vanilla ice cream at dairy meals.

1 pound dried figs
3 tablespoons fresh lemon juice
1 tablespoon freshly grated lemon zest
1 large piece fresh ginger
Sugar
4 thin slices lemon
Heavy cream, whipped (optional)

1. Wash the figs and clip off the stems. Put in a saucepan and add cold water to cover, 2 tablespoons lemon juice and 1 tablespoon lemon zest.

2. Add the ginger and bring the mixture to a boil. Boil until the figs are puffed and soft, 20 to 30 minutes. Drain, reserving the liquid. Place the figs in a serving dish.

3. Measure the liquid and return to the saucepan. Add half as much sugar as liquid and simmer over low heat until syrupy. Add 1 tablespoon lemon juice and 4 slices of lemon.

4. Pour the syrup with the lemon slices over the figs. Serve chilled, with whipped cream at dairy meals.

makes 6 servings

CC

STRAWBERRIES SABRA dairy

For an elegant dessert, spoon this fruit-liqueur mixture into a Nut Meringue (page 275). It may be served without whipped cream at meat meals.

1 pint strawberries
2 large navel oranges, preferably Jaffa oranges from Israel
2 tablespoons Sabra liqueur or orange-flavored liqueur
1 cup heavy cream
2 tablespoons sugar
1 tablespoon freshly grated orange zest
Pinch of cinnamon

1. Rinse and hull the strawberries and place them in a large bowl.

2. Peel the oranges, removing all the pits. Hull the oranges over the bowl of berries to catch any juice. Use a small, sharp knife to cut each section free of its surrounding membrane, allowing the sections to fall into the bowl of berries as they are released.

3. Add the liqueur to the fruit and gently toss. Divide the fruit among 4 long-stemmed goblets. Refrigerate until ready to serve, but do not prepare more than 1 hour in advance.

4. Just before serving, in a chilled bowl, whip the cream until softly peaked. Add the sugar and orange zest and whip until cream holds its shape. Spoon the cream over the fruit in the goblets, dust with cinnamon and serve.

makes 4 servings

FF

STRAWBERRY FLOATING ISLANDS pareve

A combination of meringue "islands" in a sea of strawberry puree.

8 large egg whites, at room temperature
Pinch of salt
1 ⅓ cups sugar
3 pints ripe strawberries, hulled
Juice of ½ lemon
Pinch of cinnamon

1. In a mixing bowl, beat the egg whites with the salt until softly peaked. Add ¼ cup of the sugar and beat until stiff. Gradually add all but ⅓ cup of the sugar, beating constantly, until the egg whites are stiff and glossy.

2. Heat a large pot of water until the steam rises from the top, but before it has come to a simmer. Using 2 large tablespoons or an ice cream scoop, form large ovals or rounds of the egg-white mixture and drop them into the water. Poach for 2 minutes, turn once and poach another 2 minutes. You may have to do this in batches. Remove the meringues as they are done and drain them on absorbent paper. Refrigerate for at least 1 hour.

3. In a food processor or blender, puree 2 pints of the strawberries. Transfer to a bowl and season the puree with the remaining sugar and the lemon juice. Mix in the cinnamon. Refrigerate the puree. Slice the remaining strawberries in half lengthwise and refrigerate. To serve, spoon the strawberry puree into a shallow serving bowl and float the meringues on top. Scatter the sliced strawberries around and over the meringues and serve.

makes 8 servings

FF

FRESH BERRY GRATIN pareve

The egg-yolk mixture is basically a zabaglione. Adding a pinch of starch is a chef's trick to help keep it from separating.

1 pint raspberries
1 pint strawberries
¾ cup amaretto or other sweet liqueur
6 large egg yolks
1 teaspoon potato starch
⅓ cup sugar

1. Pick over the raspberries. Hull the strawberries and slice them in half. In a bowl, mix the berries with 2 tablespoons of the liqueur. Refrigerate.

2. Place the egg yolks in a bowl that will fit over a pan of simmering water to create a double boiler. Beat the egg yolks with the potato starch to dissolve the starch, then continue beating until the egg yolks have thickened slightly. Beat in ¼ cup of the sugar. Set the bowl over a pan of simmering water over low heat and beat the mixture vigorously.

3. Add half the remaining amaretto or other liqueur and continue beating. As the egg-yolk mixture thickens and lightens, gradually add the remaining amaretto or liqueur. Continue beating the mixture until it is very thick and light, taking care to regulate the heat so the yolks do not coagulate.

4. Remove the pan from the heat, stir the mixture again and refrigerate until just before serving time.

5. Preheat the broiler. Spread the berries in a shallow gratin dish at least 9 inches in diameter. Spread the egg-yolk mixture over the berries, covering them completely. Sprinkle with the remaining sugar.

6. Place the gratin dish under the broiler and cook for a minute or two, just until the top becomes brown and glazed. Place the gratin dish on a serving dish and serve at once, gently scooping portions of berries and gratin onto each plate.

makes 6 to 8 servings

FF

DRIED APRICOT MOUSSE pareve

This is a particularly subtle and refreshing mousse.

½ pound dried apricots
1 cup dry white wine
2 apples, peeled, cored and sliced
Juice of ½ lemon
½ to ¾ cup sugar, or to taste
3 large egg whites
2 tablespoons toasted almonds (see Note, page 6)

1. In a saucepan, simmer the apricots in the wine with the apples, lemon juice and sugar, covered, until soft, 15 to 20 minutes. Remove from the heat, cool and puree in a food processor.

2. Meanwhile, in a bowl, beat the egg whites until they form stiff peaks. Using a whisk, fold them into the apricot puree.

3. Spoon the mousse into wineglasses or individual bowls. Chill for 1 to 2 hours. Just before serving, sprinkle with the almonds.

makes 4 to 6 servings

MH

MALVINA KINARD'S
COFFEE MACAROON CRÈME dairy
(FROM *THE NEW YORK COOKBOOK*)

This recipe has been in the Kinard family for over eighty years. It is a welcome addition to the more traditional Passover macaroon fare.

1½ tablespoons unflavored gelatin
¼ cup cold water
2 cups strong, hot coffee
⅓ cup sugar
½ teaspoon almond extract
1½ cups heavy cream
1 cup macaroon crumbs

1. In a mixing bowl, dissolve the gelatin in the cold water. Add the hot coffee, sugar and almond extract and stir to dissolve the sugar and gelatin. Cover and refrigerate until the mixture begins to set, 1 to 1½ hours.

2. Meanwhile, in another bowl, whip the cream until it forms soft peaks. Cover and refrigerate.

3. When the coffee mixture has begun to set, remove it from the refrigerator. Fold in the whipped cream and macaroon crumbs. Spoon into 6 dessert cups or wineglasses and refrigerate for about 6 hours.

makes 6 servings

MO

ALMOND PUDDING pareve

(FROM *JEWISH COOKING IN AMERICA*)

This light and delicate dessert is a satisfying conclusion to a heavy meal.

> 4 large eggs, separated
> ½ cup plus 2 tablespoons sugar
> ¾ cup ground blanched almonds
> ½ teaspoon almond extract
> Oil for the pan
> Matzoh meal for the pan
> 1 pint strawberries or 1 cup strawberry puree

1. Preheat the oven to 350°F.

2. In an electric mixer, beat the egg yolks until foamy. Add the sugar and mix until the egg yolks are very pale and fluffy. Add the almonds and the extract and mix until well blended.

3. In another bowl, beat the egg whites until stiff peaks form.

4. Fold the egg whites into the yolk mixture and turn into an 8-inch soufflé dish or springform pan that has been greased and then floured with matzoh meal. Bake for 30 to 35 minutes, or until golden. The pudding will rise slightly during cooking; it will settle as it cools. Let cool slightly.

5. Top with fresh strawberries or strawberry puree and serve.

makes 6 to 8 servings

JN

APPLE MERINGUE pareve

(ADAPTED FROM MONET'S TABLE: THE COOKING JOURNALS OF CLAUDE MONET)

The meringue topping turns this simple apple dish into an elegant dessert, and its pyramid shape evokes the Exodus from Egypt.

> 10 tart apples, peeled, cored and sliced
> 1 cup plus 2 tablespoons sugar
> 2 large egg whites
> 1 tablespoon grated lemon zest

1. Place the apples in a saucepan with enough water to cover, add 1 cup of the sugar and bring to a simmer. Cook until the apples are tender, about 25 minutes. This step may be done in advance, but the apples should be reheated before continuing with the recipe.

2. Preheat oven to 300°F.

3. Drain the apples and place them in a round baking dish, mounding them into a pyramid.

4. In a bowl, beat the egg whites until they begin to peak, then gradually beat in the 2 tablespoons of sugar and the lemon zest. Continue beating until the egg whites hold firm peaks but are not dry.

5. Cover the apples with the meringue, place in the oven and bake 15 minutes until the meringue begins to brown. Serve immediately.

makes 6 servings

FF

MATZOH-APPLE SCHALET pareve

Charlotte aux Pommes
(FROM *THE JEWISH HOLIDAY KITCHEN*)

An elegant soufflé-like pudding.

4 matzohs
Vegetable oil to grease pan
2 large eggs, separated
¼ cup sugar
½ teaspoon cinnamon
Grated zest and juice of 1 lemon
½ cup raisins
3 McIntosh apples, peeled, cored and diced
½ cup hazelnuts or almonds, coarsely ground

1. Soak the matzohs in cold water until soft. Squeeze dry.

2. Preheat oven to 350°F. Grease an 8- or 9-inch springform pan with vegetable oil.

3. In a large bowl, mix the egg yolks, sugar, cinnamon, lemon zest and juice. Add the raisins, apples and nuts. Mix well. Add the matzohs and mix.

4. In another bowl, beat the egg whites until stiff peaks form. Fold into the mixture.

5. Add the mixture to the springform pan. Bake for 1 hour, or until golden. Cool and serve at room temperature.

makes 6 to 8 servings

JN

MARGARETEN FAMILY'S
APPLE KUGEL pareve

Whole wheat matzohs give this a wholesome flavor.

4 sheets whole wheat matzoh, crushed
6 large eggs
1½ cups sugar
½ cup ground walnuts
1 cup raisins
¼ cup fresh orange juice
Grated rind of 1 orange
6 tart apples, peeled, cored and sliced
1½ tablespoons cinnamon, mixed with ¼ cup sugar
¼ cup melted pareve margarine

1. Preheat the oven to 350°F. Grease a 9- by 12-inch baking pan.
2. Place the crushed matzoh in a bowl, cover with warm water and allow to soak briefly. Squeeze out as much water as possible; you can transfer the matzoh to a strainer and press out the water.
3. In a mixing bowl, beat the eggs until frothy. Add the sugar, beating well. Stir in the drained matzoh and add the walnuts, raisins, orange juice and rind. Spread half this mixture into the baking pan.
4. In another bowl, toss the apple slices with the cinnamon and sugar mixture and spread half of the apples into the pan. Spread remaining matzoh mixture over the apples, then top with remaining apples. Pout the melted margarine evenly over the top.
5. Bake 45 minutes. Serve warm or at room temperature.

makes 8 servings

FF

SEPHARDIC PASSOVER RAISIN PUDDING pareve

Babanatza

Vegetable oil to grease pan
5 matzohs
Water to cover matzohs
1¼ cups raisins
Boiling water to cover the raisins
6 large eggs, well beaten
1½ cups coarsely chopped walnuts
¼ cup vegetable oil
¼ cup honey
½ cup sugar
1 tart apple, peeled, cored and diced

1. Preheat the oven to 350°F. Grease a 9-inch square baking pan or a 10-inch pie pan with vegetable oil.

2. Soak the matzohs in the water until soft and drain well. Soak raisins in boiling water to soften, and drain. In a mixing bowl, combine matzohs and raisins. Add the eggs and mix well.

3. In another bowl, combine the walnuts, oil, honey, sugar and apple and add to the matzoh mixture. Mix well. Pour into the prepared pan and bake 1 hour.

4. Remove from the oven and immediately cover tightly with foil. Allow to come to room temperature before serving. Kept tightly covered, *babanatza* improves after 24 hours.

makes 8 to 12 servings

FF

macaroons

Macaroons date back to monks in eighth-century Europe. The earliest record has been traced to Cormery, France, in the year 791, where the confections were made at the local monastery, supposedly in the shape of monks' navels. Their name comes from the Venetian word *macarone*, which means fine paste.

Exactly where and how the cookies became part of the Jewish observance of Passover is unclear. But today macaroons in their many variations are eaten during the holiday around the world.

The macaroon most familiar to American Jews at Passover is a sweet, chewy almond-paste variety, often with coconut, that comes out of a can. Those made by hand offer a greater variety of tastes and textures. Macaroons are delicious plain, but they can also be dipped in chocolate, filled with raspberry jam, flecked with walnuts, spiked with chocolate chips, flavored with coffee, sprinkled with coconut, drizzled with honey or pressed together like a sandwich. Try making the classic almond macaroon, the rich chocolaty macaroon and even a "pralinized" version made with pecans and brown sugar.

SEPHARDIC-STYLE MACAROONS pareve
(ADAPTED FROM EVA CAPSOUTO)

Eva Capsouto serves this airy almond confection at the Seder she holds at Capsouto Frères, her family's Manhattan restaurant.

> 3 cups (15 ounces) blanched almonds
> 1 cup sugar
> 3 large egg whites
> Confectioners' sugar, for dusting

1. If necessary, blanch the almonds by putting them in boiling water for 2 minutes. Remove, drain and peel. When cool, grind the almonds in a food processor.

2. Preheat oven to 325°F. Line 2 cookie sheets with parchment paper and set aside. In a medium bowl, mix the ground almonds, sugar and egg whites. Drop from a teaspoon onto the cookie sheets, leaving ½ inch between macaroons. Bake 12 to 15 minutes, or until lightly brown. Dust with confectioners' sugar when cool.

makes 2 dozen macaroons

DK

CHOCOLATE MACAROONS pareve

(ADAPTED FROM DORIS SCHECHTER)

These intensely rich morsels are one of the most popular varieties of macaroons sold at Doris Schechter's restaurant and bakery, My Most Favorite Dessert Company, in Manhattan.

1⅔ cups blanched almonds (8 ounces)
3 large egg whites
1 cup sugar
3 ounces semisweet chocolate, melted and cooled to room temperature
7 ounces sweetened shredded coconut

1. Preheat the oven to 350°F. Line 2 cookie sheets with parchment paper.
2. Grind the almonds in a food processor, and set aside. In a large bowl, beat the egg whites until stiff. Alternately fold in the sugar and ground almonds; then gently fold in the melted chocolate and the coconut. Drop from a teaspoon onto the lined cookie sheets, leaving ½ inch between macaroons. Bake 20 minutes.

makes 2 dozen macaroons

DK

MISSISSIPPI PRALINE MACAROONS pareve

(FROM *JEWISH COOKING IN AMERICA*)

The late Felicia Schlenker, one of the first Jews to live in Natchez, Mississippi, "pralinized" a recipe for Viennese Passover nut meringue kisses by substituting brown sugar and pecans for sugar and almonds.

> 3 large egg whites
> 1 cup brown sugar
> 1 cup roughly chopped pecans
> Pareve margarine for greasing cookie sheet
> 24 pecan halves for topping

1. Preheat the oven to 275°F.
2. Beat the egg whites to form peaks. Gradually add the sugar and beat until the whites are stiff. Stir in the chopped nuts.
3. Spoon a heaping teaspoon of macaroon mixture on a greased cookie sheet. Press down to shape into a macaroon. Place a pecan half on top. Bake for 30 minutes, checking occasionally, until cookies are hard but still shiny.

makes about 2 dozen cookies

JN

PERI WOLFMAN-GOLD'S CHOCOLATE COCONUT MERINGUES

pareve

Peri Wolfman-Gold, an owner of a housewares shop in SoHo, prizes this family recipe, which she first tasted at her mother-in-law's table more than twenty-five years ago. The meringues are light and deeply chocolaty, but not too sweet.

2 large egg whites
⅔ cup sugar
4 ounces unsweetened chocolate
1½ cups finely grated unsweetened coconut

1. Preheat oven to 350°F. Line 2 baking sheets with parchment paper.
2. In a mixing bowl, using an electric mixer, whip the egg whites until soft peaks form. Gradually beat in the sugar, continuing until stiff peaks form.
3. Melt the chocolate in a microwave oven or a double boiler. With a rubber spatula, gently fold the melted chocolate and half the coconut into the bowl of egg whites. Fold in the remaining coconut.
4. Drop heaping tablespoons of the batter onto the lined baking sheets. Bake about 12 minutes, or until the meringues are firm. Turn the oven off, but leave the cookies in the oven with door ajar 15 minutes longer.

makes 3 dozen cookies

EL

NUT MERINGUES pareve

These meringues are delicious vessels for Strawberries Sabra (page 260) or a scoop of sorbet or, at dairy meals, ice cream.

4 large egg whites
1 teaspoon vanilla extract
1 cup minus 1 tablespoon sifted sugar
1 cup pine nuts

1. In a mixing bowl, beat the egg whites until foamy. Continue beating and add the vanilla.

2. Add the sugar, about 1 tablespoon at a time, beating constantly. Fold in the nuts.

3. Preheat the oven to 225°F. Cover a baking sheet with parchment paper. Drop meringue off a large tablespoon onto the paper, in the shape of circles or eggs.

4. Bake for 1 hour for soft, crunchy meringues. Watch carefully; if the meringues begin to take on color, turn off the oven and let the meringues remain in the oven until dry.

5. Remove the meringues from the paper with a spatula. If the meringues stick, cover them for a few minutes with a damp towel. Make indentation in centers to hold sorbet, if desired.

6. Store in airtight container until ready to use.

makes 12 meringues

MB

ILANA AMINI'S WALNUT COOKIES

pareve

This is a good way to use egg yolks left over from macaroons and meringues.

    4 extra-large egg yolks
    ½ cup sugar
    3½ cups coarsely chopped walnuts
    Grated rind of 1 lemon (optional)

1. Preheat the oven to 325°F.
2. In a mixing bowl, beat the egg yolks with the sugar until very thick and almost white.
3. Mix the chopped walnuts and lemon rind, if desired, into the yolk mixture.
4. Drop teaspoonfuls of batter onto ungreased cookie sheet, leaving 2 inches between them.
5. Bake for about 10 minutes, or until cookies are dry and firm. Remove from the cookie sheet when cool.

makes about 40 cookies

MS

ROSALYN TAUBER'S ORANGE MARMALADE BARS pareve

¼ cup unsalted pareve margarine
1 cup sugar
1 cup matzoh cake meal
½ cup plus 1 tablespoon potato starch
2 large eggs
1 cup orange juice
⅓ cup orange marmalade or strawberry preserves
1 teaspoon cinnamon
¼ cup chopped nuts
1 tablespoon unsalted pareve margarine, melted

1. Preheat the oven to 350°F.
2. In a mixing bowl, cream the margarine and ¾ cup of the sugar together until light and fluffy.
3. In another bowl, sift together the matzoh cake meal and potato starch and add to the margarine mixture. Stir gently until smooth.
4. In another bowl, beat together the eggs and orange juice. Add to the cake meal mixture, stirring gently. Grease a 9-inch square pan with margarine and lightly sprinkle potato starch on the bottom. Pour half of the batter into the prepared pan.
5. Spoon the marmalade or preserves over the batter and top with remaining batter. In a small bowl, combine the remaining sugar, cinnamon, nuts and melted margarine and sprinkle over the top of the batter. Bake 30 to 35 minutes. Cool in the pan. Cut into squares.

makes 16 squares

JH

MARGARETEN FAMILY'S PASSOVER BROWNIES pareve

½ cup (1 stick) unsalted pareve margarine
¾ cup unsweetened cocoa powder
1 cup sugar
2 large eggs, well beaten
⅓ cup matzoh cake meal
½ tablespoon instant coffee
⅓ cup ground walnuts
16 walnut halves

1. Preheat the oven to 350°F. Grease an 8-inch square baking pan with margarine.
2. Melt the margarine and set aside to cool.
3. In a mixing bowl, mix the cocoa and sugar. Stir in the margarine, eggs, matzoh cake meal, coffee and ground nuts, beating until smooth. Add 2 tablespoons cold water and beat again.
4. Spread the batter into the prepared pan and place the nut halves evenly on top, in 4 rows of 4.
5. Bake 25 minutes. Allow to cool completely in the pan, then cut into 16 squares with a walnut half centered in each square.

makes 16 brownies

FF

ROSALYN TAUBER'S FROSTED CHOCOLATE NUT SQUARES pareve

for the squares

½ cup (1 stick) unsalted pareve margarine
2 ounces bittersweet chocolate, preferably Elite or Lieber brand
3 large eggs
1 cup sugar
¼ cup matzoh cake meal
2 tablespoons potato starch
1 teaspoon liqueur
½ cup chopped nuts

for the frosting

3 ounces bittersweet chocolate, preferably Elite or Lieber brand
3 tablespoons strong coffee or the liqueur used in the squares
½ cup (1 stick) unsalted pareve margarine

1. Preheat the oven to 350°F. Grease a 9-inch square baking pan with margarine.

2. In a saucepan over low heat, melt the chocolate and margarine.

3. Put eggs and sugar in a bowl and beat until very light and fluffy.

4. In another bowl, sift together the cake meal and potato starch. Add the dry ingredients, alternately with the chocolate mixture, to the egg mixture, mixing well with each addition, beginning and ending with dry ingredients.

5. Stir in the liqueur and nuts. Pour mixture into the greased pan. Bake 25 minutes. Cool in the pan.

6. Meanwhile, make the frosting. Place the chocolate and coffee or liqueur in the top of a double boiler over hot water. Stir until melted and smooth.

7. Remove the top of the double boiler from the heat and beat in the margarine 1 tablespoon at a time, making sure that it is blended in well before adding the next tablespoon. Cool slightly before using to frost the squares.

8. Frost the baked and cooled mixture with the frosting. Refrigerate. Cut in squares and serve at room temperature.

makes 25 squares (with about 1 cup frosting)

JH

PHYLLIS WERTHEIMER'S CHREMSLACH WITH FOAMY LEMON SAUCE pareve

(FROM *THE KOSHER GOURMET*)

Chremslach, crisp balls of deep-fried matzoh dough, can be served hot or cold with jam, cinnamon sugar, fresh or canned fruit or the accompanying Foamy Lemon Sauce. If you're making the lemon sauce, you'll need to prepare it in advance so it will have time to chill. However you serve them, these fritters make a lovely dish for dessert or brunch. If you can't find tea matzohs, substitute 13 regular matzohs.

     14 tea matzohs
     7 large eggs, separated
     1¼ cups sugar
     1 teaspoon grated lemon rind
     ½ teaspoon salt
     ⅛ teaspoon nutmeg
     1 cup matzoh meal
     ¾ cup chopped nuts
     Vegetable oil for frying
     1 recipe Foamy Lemon Sauce (optional) (recipe follows)
     Confectioners' sugar (optional)

1. Soak the matzohs in water until soft. Squeeze out the excess water and place the matzohs in a bowl. Add the egg yolks, sugar, lemon rind, salt, nutmeg, matzoh meal and nuts. Mix well.

2. In another bowl, beat the egg whites until stiff but not dry, and fold into the matzoh mixture.

3. In a large, heavy pot, add the vegetable oil to a depth of 1½ to 2 inches. Heat the oil to 365°F. Drop the mixture by tablespoonfuls into the oil. Fry until golden, turning once. Drain on paper towels and serve with the Foamy Lemon Sauce or dust with confectioners' sugar, if desired.

makes about 6 dozen

FOAMY LEMON SAUCE pareve

1 tablespoon potato starch
1 cup sugar, or to taste
1½ cups water
Juice of 1 lemon
2 large eggs, separated

1. In a saucepan, mix the starch and sugar together. Gradually stir in the water. Add the lemon juice and the yolks, slightly beaten, and mix.
2. Bring the mixture to a boil, stirring, and cook 1 minute. Remove from the heat.
3. In a bowl, beat the egg whites until stiff but not dry, and fold into the hot mixture. Chill and serve cold.

makes about 1 quart

SEPHARDIC PASSOVER BUENUELOS WITH LEMON-HONEY SUGAR SYRUP

pareve

6 matzohs
6 large eggs, beaten
⅓ cup sugar
3 tablespoons matzoh meal
¼ teaspoon cinnamon
Vegetable oil for deep-frying
Sugar Syrup (below)
2 cups finely chopped walnuts

1. Break the matzohs into small pieces and soak in cold water. Drain very well. In a bowl, combine the matzohs, eggs, sugar, matzoh meal and cinnamon, and mix well.

2. In a large pot, add vegetable oil to a depth of 1½ to 2 inches and heat oil to 375°F. Drop the batter by teaspoonfuls into the hot oil and fry until golden brown, turning once. Drain on paper towels.

3. Using tongs, dip the *buenuelos* into sugar syrup and then roll in chopped nuts.

makes about 4 dozen

sugar syrup

1 cup sugar
1 cup water
¼ cup honey
2 teaspoons fresh lemon juice

1. In a small, deep saucepan, combine the sugar and water. Bring to a boil and cook until thickened (the temperature should reach about 250°F on a candy thermometer).

2. Stir in the honey, then bring to a simmer. Add the lemon juice, mix well and remove from the heat.

makes about 1 cup

FF

TED'S SPONGE CAKE pareve

The "Ted" of this recipe, which appeared in a 1950 article without a byline, is not identified, but his sponge cake is a classic.

8 large eggs, separated and at room temperature or a little warmer
1 lemon, juice and finely grated rind
1½ cups sugar
1 cup, less 1 tablespoon, matzoh cake meal, sifted three times

1. Preheat the oven to 350°F.
2. Lightly grease the bottom of a 9-inch tube pan. Line with wax paper. Dampen the paper with a little cold water, if desired.
3. In a bowl, beat the yolks well. Add the lemon juice and rind and mix with a spoon. In another bowl, beat the egg whites until very stiff. Gradually add the sugar to the egg whites, beating after each addition. Gently fold in the yolk mixture.
4. Gently fold in the cake meal, a tablespoonful at a time. Turn into the prepared pan and bake 40 to 50 minutes.

NOTE: Matzoh cake meal should not be confused with matzoh meal. Both are made of crushed matzoh, but their textures differ. Cake meal is fine and floury; matzoh meal is coarser and more like fine cookie crumbs. They are not interchangeable.

makes 8 servings

MARION SINER GORDON'S COCONUT CAKE WITH APRICOT GLAZE *pareve*

¼ cup matzoh meal
½ cup potato starch
⅛ teaspoon salt
7 large eggs, separated
1 cup sugar
Juice of ½ lemon
Apricot Glaze (below)
Coconut Frosting (below)

1. Preheat the oven to 300°F.
2. Sift together the matzoh meal, potato starch and salt.
3. In a bowl, beat the egg yolks with the sugar and lemon juice until thick and lemon colored. In another bowl, beat the egg whites until stiff and fold into the yolk mixture. Fold in the sifted dry ingredients and pour the batter into a 9-inch, ungreased springform pan. Bake 30 minutes.
4. Increase the oven heat to 325°F. Bake 15 minutes longer, or until a cake tester comes out clean. Invert to cool.
5. Cut crosswise into layers and spread with the Apricot Glaze, then frost with the Coconut Frosting.

makes 8 to 10 servings

apricot glaze

Heat the contents of one 12-ounce jar of apricot preserves over low heat. When dissolved, force the mixture through a fine sieve. Use as a glaze while hot.

makes about 1¼ cups

coconut frosting

1 tablespoon unflavored gelatin
½ cup cold water
½ cup boiling water
½ cup sugar
3 large egg whites, stiffly beaten

Juice of ½ lemon
1 fresh coconut, grated or approximately 4 cups dried grated unsweetened coconut

1. In a bowl, soften the gelatin in the cold water. Then dissolve by adding the boiling water. Add the sugar and stir until dissolved. Set aside to cool.

2. When the mixture begins to set, fold it into the beaten egg whites, then beat until the mixture reaches consistency of soft marshmallow. Add the lemon juice and stir to blend. Use as cake frosting, then coat the frosted cake with the grated coconut.

makes enough thick frosting for filling, top and sides of a 3-layer, 9-inch cake

CC

CLAUDIA RODEN'S
ORANGE CAKE pareve
(ADAPTED FROM *THE BOOK OF JEWISH FOOD*)

2 thin-skinned juice oranges
1½ cups (½ pound) blanched almonds
1 cup sugar
6 large eggs, separated
Pareve unsalted margarine and matzoh meal for preparing cake pan
Confectioners' sugar, for decoration (optional)

1. Preheat the oven to 350°F.
2. Scrub the oranges well. Place the oranges in a covered pot with a few inches of water and cook over medium heat for about 1 hour, or until they are soft and may easily be pierced with a fork. Remove the oranges from the water and let cool. Cut open and remove the seeds.
3. In a food processor or by hand, mince the pulp and peel of the oranges very finely.
4. In a blender or food processor, grind the almonds with ½ cup sugar to the consistency of coarse flour. Transfer the mixture to a large bowl, adding the remaining ½ cup sugar and minced orange. Blend in the egg yolks.
5. In another bowl, beat the egg whites until stiff. Fold into the orange-nut mixture.
6. Grease a 10-inch springform cake pan with margarine and then dust with matzoh meal. Pour the cake mixture into the pan. Bake for 1 hour, or until the top is lightly browned and the cake feels firm (but not hard) to the touch.
7. Place the cake on a rack to cool. Run a knife around the side, release the springform and remove the ring. Let the cake cool completely before attempting to remove it from the bottom of the pan (or serve from the pan bottom).
8. Before serving, the cake may be dusted with confectioners' sugar, if desired. You may lay paper strips or shapes on cake, dust over them with sugar and then remove the papers to leave a pattern.

makes 8 to 10 servings

LS

MARGARETEN FAMILY'S PASSOVER CHEESECAKE dairy

For best flavor, refrigerate this overnight.

for the crust

1 small box (2¼ ounces) Passover egg kichel
½ cup sugar
1 teaspoon cinnamon
¼ cup melted unsalted butter

for the filling

¾ cup sugar
2 teaspoons potato starch
1 tablespoon matzoh cake meal
2 eggs
½ pound cream cheese, at room temperature
½ pound creamed cottage cheese
1½ cups sour cream
Juice and grated rind of 1 lemon
3 tablespoons grated orange rind

1. Preheat the oven to 400°F.

2. To make the crust, crush the kichel to fine crumbs, using a blender or a food processor if possible. In a bowl, combine with the sugar and cinnamon.

3. Stir in the melted butter, then press this mixture into the bottom and partway up the sides of an 8-inch springform pan.

4. To make the filling, in a small bowl, combine the sugar, potato starch and matzoh cake meal and set aside.

5. In another bowl, beat the eggs. Beat in the cream cheese until smooth. Force the cottage cheese through a sieve and add it, beating well. Add the sour cream, lemon juice and lemon and orange rinds.

6. Stir in the sugar and starch mixture. Pour the batter into the prepared pan. Bake for 5 minutes.

continued

7. Turn oven down to 325°F and bake 60 to 70 minutes longer, or until lightly browned on top. Remove from the oven and allow to cool completely. Refrigerate at least 1 hour before serving. The cake is better if made a day in advance and refrigerated overnight.

NOTE: If desired, cover the top of the cake with strawberry halves. In a saucepan, simmer ½ cup strained strawberry jam for 5 minutes and spoon the warm glaze over the berries.

makes 6 to 8 servings

FF

SPICED PRUNE TORTE pareve

for the cake

6 large eggs, separated
1 cup sugar
½ cup matzoh cake meal
¼ cup potato starch
1 teaspoon cinnamon
½ teaspoon nutmeg
¼ teaspoon cloves
1 teaspoon vanilla extract
¼ cup unsalted pareve margarine, melted

for the filling

1½ cups sugar
6 tablespoons water
3 large egg whites
1½ teaspoons vanilla extract
1 cup unsalted pareve margarine
½ teaspoon cinnamon
¼ teaspoon nutmeg
¼ teaspoon cloves
½ cup finely chopped, pitted, cooked prunes
6 whole cooked prunes for decoration (optional)

1. Preheat the oven to 350°F.
2. Line the bottoms of two 9-inch layer-cake pans with foil and grease well with margarine.
3. To make the cake, in a bowl, beat the egg whites until foamy. Slowly beat in ½ cup of the sugar, 1 tablespoon at a time. Beat until stiff but still shiny.
4. In another bowl, beat the yolks until thick and gradually beat in remaining sugar. In another bowl, combine the matzoh cake meal, potato starch and spices.
5. Fold the yolk mixture into the egg-white mixture and fold in dry ingredients. Fold in the vanilla and the margarine. Divide the batter between the two pans and bake about 25 minutes, or until cake springs back when lightly touched. Let cool in the pans.
6. To make the filling, combine the sugar and water in a saucepan, bring to a boil and cook to 240°F, using a candy thermometer, or until the soft-ball stage.

continued

7. In a bowl, beat the egg whites until stiff but not dry. Add the sugar syrup slowly, beating constantly. Add the vanilla. Cool thoroughly.

8. In another bowl, cream the margarine well. Add the egg-white mixture, 2 tablespoons at a time, beating well after each addition.

9. Reserve a scant cup of the plain filling for the top of cake. Fold the spices and chopped prunes into the remaining filling.

10. Split each cake layer into two. Stack 4 layers on a cake plate with some of the prune filling between each layer. Spread the reserved plain frosting over the top layer and decorate with whole prunes, if desired.

makes 10 servings

JH

CYNTHIA ZEGER'S CHOCOLATE CAKE pareve

A chocolate cake that Craig Claiborne deemed "exceptional."

Oil or pareve unsalted margarine for greasing pan
10 eggs, separated and at room temperature or slightly warmer
1 cup less 2 tablespoons sugar
6 ounces semisweet chocolate, melted slowly over a double boiler and cooled
2 cups finely chopped (not ground) walnuts

1. Preheat the oven to 350°F. Grease a 10-inch springform pan.
2. In a bowl, beat the egg yolks and sugar until very thick and lemon colored. Stir in the chocolate. Fold in the nuts.
3. In another bowl, beat the egg whites until stiff but not dry. Fold into the chocolate nut mixture. Turn into the pan and bake 1 hour, or until the center springs back when lightly touched with the fingertips. Cool in the pan.

makes 8 to 12 servings

CC

HANNA GOODMAN'S CHOCOLATE NUT TORTE *pareve*

(FROM *JEWISH COOKING AROUND THE WORLD*)

Apples are an unusual ingredient that gives this torte a special sweetness and texture.

>   6 large eggs, separated
>   1½ cups sugar
>   1 cup walnuts, chopped
>   4 ounces semisweet chocolate, grated
>   2 Delicious apples, peeled, cored and grated
>   ½ cup matzoh meal
>   Confectioners' sugar, for garnish (optional)

1. Preheat oven to 350°F.

2. In a bowl, beat the egg yolks with the sugar until lemon colored and thick enough to ribbon. Gently stir in the walnuts, chocolate, apples and matzoh meal.

3. In another bowl, beat the egg whites until they form stiff peaks but are not dry. Fold into the egg-yolk mixture, gently but thoroughly, using a rubber spatula.

4. Turn the mixture into a 9-inch springform pan and bake for 45 to 60 minutes, or until the cake springs back when pressed lightly with a finger. Cool in the pan before removing to a serving dish. If desired, serve sprinkled with confectioners' sugar.

makes 8 to 10 servings

MS

MAIDA HEATTER'S
CHOCOLATE WALNUT TORTE pareve
(ADAPTED FROM *MAIDA HEATTER'S GREAT CHOCOLATE DESSERTS*)

A rich chocolate sponge nut cake from an acclaimed baker.

> 12 large eggs, separated
> 1 cup sugar
> 8 ounces semisweet chocolate, melted
> 8 ounces walnuts, finely ground
> Pinch of salt
> Confectioners' sugar for decoration (optional)
> Melted semisweet chocolate for decoration (optional)

1. Preheat the oven to 350°F.
2. In a bowl, beat the egg yolks with ½ cup of the sugar until well blended, about 2 minutes, at high speed in an electric mixer. Beat in the chocolate and fold in half the nuts. Set aside.
3. In another bowl, beat the egg whites with the salt until very softly peaked, then gradually beat in the remaining sugar and continue beating until the egg whites hold firm peaks but are not dry.
4. Stir a little of the egg whites into the chocolate mixture, then gently fold in about half the remaining egg whites. Finally fold in the remaining nuts and the rest of the egg whites.
5. Spoon the mixture into an ungreased 10-inch tube pan. Bake 1 hour and 15 minutes.
6. Remove the cake from the oven and turn upside down on a rack or suspend, upside down, over the neck of a bottle until completely cooled. Use a knife with a thin, stiff blade to loosen the cake from the pan by running the knife carefully and closely along the sides of the pan. Invert the cake onto a serving plate. It may be dusted with confectioners' sugar or drizzled with a lacework of melted chocolate.

makes 6 to 8 servings

FF

BESSIE FEFFER'S SEVEN-LAYER CHOCOLATE CAKE pareve

A Passover variation of the popular seven-layer cake.

½ pound fine-quality semisweet chocolate, Elite brand if possible
1 tablespoon unsalted pareve margarine
8 ounces orange marmalade
2 large eggs
2 tablespoons brandy
1 cup white wine, preferably semisweet
8 matzohs, preferably round
Chopped walnuts

1. In the top of a double boiler, melt the chocolate, margarine and the marmalade over simmering water.

2. Add the eggs and beat with a wire whisk until the mixture is as thick as sour cream. Add the brandy and remove the pan from the heat.

3. Continue beating until the mixture again attains the consistency of sour cream.

4. Pour the wine into a large, shallow dish. Dip the matzohs, one at a time, in the wine just to moisten but not to soak. Place the moistened matzoh on a cake plate and coat with a layer of the chocolate mixture. Top with another moistened matzoh and more chocolate until all are used. Use the remaining chocolate to frost the sides. Decorate with nuts and let set at room temperature.

makes 6 to 8 servings

JH

EDDA SERVI MACHLIN'S
KING'S CAKE parve/dairy

Torta del Re

(ADAPTED FROM *THE CLASSIC CUISINE OF THE ITALIAN JEWS*)

2 tablespoons unsalted butter or unsalted pareve margarine
2 tablespoons matzoh meal
5 large eggs, separated
1 small pinch salt
1¼ cups sugar
2½ cups (10 ounces) blanched almonds, chopped fine
1 teaspoon vanilla extract
1 teaspoon almond extract
Grated rind of 1 lemon
Confectioners' sugar
Sliced or slivered almonds, toasted, for decoration (see Note, page 6)

1. Preheat the oven to 325°F.

2. Grease a 10-inch springform pan with butter or margarine and sprinkle with matzoh meal and set aside.

3. In a bowl, beat the egg whites with salt until stiff and dry.

4. In a larger bowl, beat the egg yolks until foamy, then gradually add the sugar and continue beating until the mixture is lemon colored. Gradually add the chopped almonds, then the extracts and lemon rind. You should have a very hard paste.

5. Mix a third of the beaten egg whites with almond mixture to make it softer. Carefully fold in remaining egg whites and pour into the prepared cake pan.

6. Place in center of the middle rack in the preheated oven and bake 1 hour without opening oven door. Turn off the heat; open the door and leave the cake in the oven for 10 to 15 minutes. Remove from the oven and place upside down on cooling rack.

7. When the cake is cool, remove from the pan and place upside down on a cake dish. Sprinkle the top generously with confectioners' sugar, using a sifter, and sprinkle with toasted almonds.

makes 8 to 10 servings

MB

COCONUT-ALMOND TORTE WITH SABRA LIQUEUR pareve/dairy

(FROM *THE JEWISH HOLIDAY KITCHEN*)

This torte tastes best one day after baking.

Vegetable oil for the pan
6 large eggs, separated
1 cup sugar (see Note)
1 cup blanched almonds, coarsely chopped
2 cups unsweetened, shredded coconut (see Note)
½ cup orange juice
¼ cup Sabra liqueur or orange liqueur
Grated bittersweet chocolate for decoration (optional)
1 pint strawberries (optional)
Whipped cream (optional)

1. Preheat the oven to 325°F and lightly grease a 10-inch springform pan.

2. In a large bowl, beat the egg whites until soft peaks form. Add ½ cup of the sugar and beat until stiff peaks form.

3. In a smaller bowl, beat the egg yolks with the remaining ½ cup of sugar until light and fluffy. Add the almonds and coconut and combine gently. Fold in the egg whites.

4. Place the cake batter into the pan and bake for 45 minutes, or until the crust is light brown on top and an inserted toothpick comes out clean. Remove from the oven and let sit in the pan for a few minutes. Prick the top of the torte all over with a toothpick or the prongs of a fork.

5. In a bowl, combine the orange juice and the liqueur, and pour over the torte while it is still in the pan. When the torte is completely cool, remove and, if desired, decorate with grated chocolate or strawberries. If desired, serve at dairy meals with whipped cream.

NOTE: If using sweetened coconut, reduce the sugar to ½ cup, adding ¼ cup to whites and ¼ cup to yolks.

makes 8 servings

JN

CAFÉ CROCODILE'S ORANGE-ALMOND FIG CAKE pareve/dairy

Andree Abramoff, owner of Café Crocodile in Manhattan, cherishes this recipe, which was her grandmother's. She serves it at her restaurant the first and second nights of Passover.

for the cake

10 large eggs, separated
1 cup sugar
1½ cups matzoh cake meal
1 teaspoon cinnamon
Zest of 1 orange
⅓ cup orange juice
½ teaspoon allspice
1 cup chopped almonds
10 dried Calimyrna figs, chopped
Vegetable oil for greasing the pan

for the syrup

¾ cup brown sugar
½ cup orange juice
½ cup (1 stick) unsalted butter or unsalted margarine
Orange slices for garnish

1. Preheat the oven to 350°F.
2. To make the cake, in a bowl, beat the yolks with the sugar until lemon colored. Add the cake meal, cinnamon, orange zest, orange juice, allspice and almonds.
3. In another bowl, beat the egg whites until stiff peaks form. Gently fold the whites into the cake mixture with a rubber spatula. Fold in the figs.
4. Grease a 10-inch tube pan with oil and pour the batter into the pan. Bake for 50 minutes.
5. Unmold the cake and let it cool.
6. To make the syrup, mix the brown sugar and orange juice in a saucepan. Bring to a boil over medium-high heat and cook about 5 minutes until the mixture starts to thicken slightly. Add the butter or margarine, and once melted, stir it into the syrup. To serve, pour most of the syrup over the cake, and pass the remainder on the side. Garnish with orange slices.

makes 10 servings

JN

HUNGARIAN HAZELNUT TORTE WITH HAZELNUT ICING pareve/dairy

(ADAPTED FROM ANDRE BALOG)

This festive iced nut torte has been in the Balog family for generations.

for the torte

Unsalted butter or pareve margarine for greasing pan
8 large eggs, separated
½ cup sugar
¼ cup orange juice
4 heaping tablespoons matzoh meal
4 heaping tablespoons ground hazelnuts

for the icing

¾ cup sugar
½ cup water
8 large egg yolks
1 cup (2 sticks) unsalted butter or pareve margarine, softened
½ cup ground toasted hazelnuts (see Note, page 6)
12 whole, shelled hazelnuts, for decoration

1. Preheat the oven to 350°F and grease a 9-inch springform pan well.

2. To make the torte, in a bowl, blend the egg yolks and sugar with an electric mixer until they are creamy yellow and smooth. Whisk in the orange juice, matzoh meal and ground hazelnuts. Set aside.

3. In another bowl, whip the egg whites until firm, then fold into the yolk mixture.

4. Put the mixture in the pan. Bake for 35 minutes.

5. While baking, make the icing. In a saucepan, boil the sugar in the water until dissolved. Continue boiling slowly over a low heat until the mixture reaches 238°F, the soft-ball stage on a candy thermometer. Alternatively, you can test the thickness of the syrup by dropping a small amount into a glass of cold water until it holds its shape.

6. In a bowl, beat the 8 additional egg yolks at medium speed until thickened, 3 to 4 minutes, and add the boiling sugar syrup a little at a time to the yolks while continuing to beat for 3 to 4 minutes, until light yellow. Beat for 2 to 3 more minutes until the mixture cools. Add the butter or margarine and beat at low speed for 5 more minutes until light and creamy. Add the ground hazelnuts and mix.

7. When torte is baked, allow it to cool completely, then slice it into 2 or 3 layers. Spread the hazelnut cream evenly on each layer and the top and sides. Decorate the top with whole hazelnuts.

makes 10 servings

JN

BARBARA TROPP'S PECAN-GINGER TORTE pareve

This torte is a featured dessert at the China Moon Cafe, chef Tropp's restaurant in San Francisco. It tastes best if baked a day ahead and wrapped airtight overnight. Serve it with seasonal berries. Or, at a dairy meal, top it with whipped cream or Barbara Tropp's fresh ginger ice cream, the recipe for which is in *The Modern Art of Chinese Cooking*.

4 ounces pecans, plus 18 perfect pecan halves
6 large eggs, separated
1 cup, minus 2 tablespoons, sugar
1 tablespoon fresh lemon juice
2 tablespoons fresh ginger juice squeezed from about ½ cup of very finely diced or food-processed pureed fresh ginger
Several twists white pepper (optional)
½ cup matzoh meal
½ teaspoon coarse kosher salt
1½ to 2 tablespoons finely minced crystallized ginger or finely minced glacéed apricots or thin rings of candied kumquats, for garnish (optional)

1. Lightly grease two 8- to 9-inch springform pans or two 9- to 10-inch tart pans with removable bottoms. Line the bottoms with greased paper. Preheat the oven to 350°F.

2. Toast the 4 ounces of pecans on a sheetpan for 15 minutes in the oven, turning them once midway. Let cool.

3. Mince the toasted pecans with a sharp knife or with an on-off food processor motion, until fine but dry.

4. In a bowl, beat the egg yolks until light. Add the sugar gradually, until the yolks turn very creamy and form ribbons on the beater.

5. Add the lemon juice, ginger juice and pepper, if desired. Beat to mix.

6. Add the minced pecans and matzoh meal. Beat until blended.

7. In a large bowl, beat the egg whites until they are blended. Add salt and continue whipping until the egg whites form firm peaks but are not dry. Lightly fold the egg whites into the nut mixture, until well blended.

8. Divide the mixture between the two prepared pans. Sprinkle the crystallized ginger, glacéed apricots or kumquats evenly over the top. Space eight pecan halves around the edges of each tart, putting a ninth in the center.

9. Bake in the middle or the bottom third of the oven for 40 to 45 minutes, or until a cake tester in the center of the cake comes out dry.

10. Let cool completely in pan. If time permits, wrap airtight and serve the following day.

makes 2 tortes

JN

MARGARETEN FAMILY'S WALNUT CAKE *pareve*

This cake is often served with Passover Chocolate Sauce spooned over it—an excellent complement to the nutty flavor.

½ cup matzoh cake meal
1 cup ground walnuts
10 large eggs, separated
Grated juice and rind of 1 lemon
Grated rind of 1 orange
Pinch of salt
1¼ cups sugar
Passover Chocolate Sauce (recipe follows) (optional)

1. Preheat oven to 350°F.
2. Mix the matzoh cake meal with the walnuts and set aside.
3. In a very large bowl, beat the egg yolks until thick and light. Stir in the lemon juice and rind and orange rind.
4. In another large bowl, beat the egg whites with salt until they begin to peak softly. Add sugar gradually and continue beating until stiff.
5. Fold the egg whites into the egg yolk mixture. Gently fold in the cake meal and nuts.
6. Spoon the batter into an ungreased 10-inch angel food cake pan. Bake for 45 minutes.
7. Remove the pan from the oven and turn it upside down (if necessary, hang it on the neck of a bottle). Allow the cake to cool completely in the pan. Remove from pan. If desired, spoon Passover Chocolate Sauce over the cake.

makes 12 to 16 servings

FF

PASSOVER CHOCOLATE SAUCE pareve

The addition of honey makes this chocolate sauce exceptionally rich. It is a special treat spooned over Margareten Family's Walnut Cake (page 302) and, of course, over ice cream or sorbet. Try it also as a dipping sauce for pieces of ripe, fresh fruit—particularly pineapple, orange segments, strawberries, pears and grapes.

1 cup unsweetened cocoa powder
¾ cup sugar
⅔ cup cold water
½ cup honey

1. In a saucepan, combine the cocoa and sugar.
2. Stir in the water with a whisk and simmer for 2 to 3 minutes.
3. Add the honey and simmer 3 minutes longer. Remove from the heat.

FF

CLAUDIA RODEN'S WALNUT CAKE WITH COFFEE FILLING pareve

(ADAPTED FROM *THE BOOK OF JEWISH FOOD*)

for the cake

6 large eggs, separated
½ cup sugar
1 cup walnut halves, coarsely ground
1 cup matzoh meal
¼ teaspoon vanilla extract
Unsalted pareve margarine and matzoh meal for preparing the cake pan
Confectioners' sugar and cinnamon to garnish
Haroseth (optional)
Coconut Jam (recipe follows) (optional)

for the filling

½ cup (1 stick) unsalted pareve margarine, at room temperature
½ cup confectioners' sugar
2 tablespoons instant coffee, dissolved in ¼ cup boiling water

1. Preheat oven to 375°F.
2. In a bowl, beat the egg yolks with the sugar until lemon colored. Add the walnuts. (Avoid grinding them too fine because they might be a little oily; the merit of the cake lies in distinguishing a nutty texture.) Add the matzoh meal and vanilla. Mix well.
3. In another bowl, beat the egg whites to stiff peaks. Fold them into the matzoh meal mixture.
4. Coat an 8-inch cake pan with a removable bottom, first with margarine and then with matzoh meal. Pour in batter and bake for 45 minutes. Cool on a rack, then turn out of the pan.
5. To prepare the filling, in a bowl, cream the margarine. Add the sugar and continue beating.
6. Add the coffee and continue beating. Allow mixture to cool to a good spreading consistency.
7. When cake has cooled, slice it in half horizontally with a serrated bread knife. Spread on the filling, replace the top and dust with confectioners' sugar and cinnamon.
8. Serve along with small dishes of haroseth and Coconut Jam, if desired.

makes 6 to 8 servings

LS

CLAUDIA RODEN'S COCONUT JAM

pareve
(ADAPTED FROM *THE BOOK OF JEWISH FOOD*)

This jam is best if made at least a day in advance and served in small portions for dessert or as an accompaniment to the Walnut Cake with Coffee Filling (page 304).

   1 pound (4½ cups, tightly packed) flaked unsweetened coconut
   2 tablespoons orange-blossom water or rose water (see Note)
   ¾ cup water, divided
   2 cups sugar
   1 tablespoon fresh lemon juice
   ½ cup unsalted or blanched pistachio nuts (about ½ pound in shells)
   ½ cup blanched almonds, chopped

   1. Place the coconut in a large bowl and sprinkle with flower water and then ¼ cup of the water, fluffing it with your fingers as you do so. Cover and leave overnight.

   2. In a heavy saucepan, combine the sugar, lemon juice and the remaining ½ cup of water. Simmer for about 5 minutes, or until the syrup thickens, stirring constantly. Add the soaked coconut to the syrup and bring to a boil again slowly, stirring constantly with a wooden spoon. Remove from heat as soon as it boils. (Overcooking will make coconut harden and become slightly yellow.) Allow to cool.

   3. Mix in the nuts and pour into a glass bowl. Serve the following day, or store in refrigerator in a tightly sealed sterilized jar for future use.

NOTE: Rose water and orange-blossom water, the distillation of petals boiled in water, are available at many gourmet stores and Middle Eastern markets.

   makes 4½ cups

   LS

CLAUDIA RODEN'S SPANISH WALNUT CAKE WITH SYRUP pareve/dairy

Tishpishti

(ADAPTED FROM *THE BOOK OF JEWISH FOOD*)

for the syrup

  2¼ cups sugar
  2 cups water
  1 tablespoon fresh lemon juice
  1 tablespoon rose water

for the cake

  5 large eggs, lightly beaten
  1¼ cups walnut halves, chopped
  ¾ cup ground almonds
  1 cup sugar
  Juice and grated zest of 1 orange
  2 teaspoons ground cinnamon
  Walnut oil, almond oil or butter for the pan

1. To make the syrup, in a saucepan, boil the sugar and the water with the lemon juice for 15 minutes. Stir in the rose water. Cool and refrigerate.

2. To make the cake, preheat the oven to 350°F. In a bowl, mix all the cake ingredients thoroughly. Line the bottom of a cake pan with foil or greaseproof paper. Brush the foil with oil or melted butter, pour in the cake mixture and bake for 1 hour until browned.

3. Immediately turn the cake out into a deep dish. Peel off the foil or paper, cut the cake into serving pieces and put them on plates. Lightly drizzle syrup over each piece, allowing them to absorb the syrup for 15 minutes, and serve.

  makes 8 to 10 servings

MO

LIZZIE GUBENKO'S INGBERLACH pareve

(FROM *THE INTERNATIONAL KOSHER COOKBOOK*)

2 cups honey
3 cups matzoh farfel
1 scant teaspoon ground ginger
1 teaspoon cinnamon
1 cup chopped walnuts

1. In a saucepan, bring the honey to a boil. Add the matzoh farfel and cook, stirring, for 15 minutes.
2. Add the ginger and cinnamon and continue cooking, if necessary, until the honey seems to leave the sides of the pan.
3. Have a large, moistened board available and spread the mixture onto the wet board with moistened wooden spoon, spatula or hands.
4. Sprinkle liberally with the nuts.
5. When cool, cut into squares and triangles.

makes 8 servings

RS

MIMI SHERATON'S PASSOVER HONEY NUT CANDY pareve

Noant

(FROM *FROM MY MOTHER'S KITCHEN*)

The contrasting scents and flavors of sweet honey, spicy ginger, and tangy orange rind and the crunch of walnuts make this candy one of the more memorable Passover treats. Do not attempt to make this on a rainy or very humid day, as it will not harden.

> 16 liquid ounces honey, preferably dark
> 1 tablespoon sugar
> ½ teaspoon ground ginger
> 1 pound shelled walnuts
> 1 tablespoon finely grated orange rind
> 1 tablespoon fresh lemon juice
> Light vegetable oil for platter

1. In a small, heavy-bottom saucepan, combine the honey and sugar and bring to a boil. Reduce the heat to low and stir until the sugar dissolves and the honey darkens slightly.

2. Add the ginger, nuts, rind and lemon juice. Stir over very low heat for 7 to 8 minutes, or until the nuts have absorbed some honey. Remove from the heat and stir for 1 to 2 minutes. Then, while still quite hot, pour onto a lightly oiled platter or cookie sheet. Spread to ½-inch thickness.

3. When the mixture cools and is fairly firm, cut into small squares. When cold and reasonably firm, separate into pieces. Store in a cool, dry place.

makes about 2 pounds of candy

MS

FRUIT OF THE VINE

By HOWARD G. GOLDBERG

Not very long ago, the choice of kosher wines in America used for Passover ranged from simple Manischewitz to Mogen David, both inexpensive. Today, the range is panoramic, and the prices are getting hefty: in 1998, for example, a complex California Cabernet Sauvignon produced under the Baron Herzog label sold for $40.

Kosher wine, like many other features of Jewish life everywhere, was profoundly influenced by the Six-Day War of 1967. Israel's seizure of Syria's Golan Heights led to the establishment of the Golan Heights Winery in 1983. And when red and white wines made from Heights grapes entered the United States around 1984, the Jewish community went into shock. For the first time in America, there were sophisticated kosher dry wines that you uncork!

Fifteen years later, the heavy, sweet, screw-top kiddush wines that shaped the American-Jewish palate still dominate Seder tables, but these days it's nostalgia, not necessity, that puts them there. These comfort wines, with names like Malaga Extra Heavy and Cream Niagara, are an American phenomenon. People remember drinking them when they were growing up; they are associated with shul, family, the holidays.

It wasn't always like this. A century ago, Jews from Western Europe equated dryness with kosher wines. But immigrants from Eastern Europe, where West European viticulture did not take hold, were reared on sweetened wines made from raisins, berries and other fruits. They carried this preference to the New World. In 1899, Samuel Schapiro, a winemaker and restaurateur on the Lower East Side of Manhattan, started making wine from Concord, an acidic American grape that needs sugaring for palatability. This grape and its pinkish-white counterpart, Catawba, still flourish in the Finger Lakes and

Lake Erie regions of upstate New York. For immigrants, wines like Schapiro Wine Cellars's—"The Wine You Can Almost Cut with a Knife" is still the company's motto—became the American Way.

But in the last fifteen years, complex dry varietal wines that derive from classic vinifera grapes grown in California, Israel, Europe and Chile have revolutionized tastes, even in Orthodox communities. These wines have become significantly competitive, both on regular and (the more expensive) reserve levels. They are perfect with meals of all kinds, holiday and otherwise. And they tend to range in price from $7 to $20, with a few ascending into the $30 bracket. This means that Jews are buying kosher Cabernet Sauvignon, Merlot, Pinot Noir, Petite Sirah, Zinfandel, Chardonnay, Sauvignon Blanc, Riesling, Gewürztraminer, Semillon and Chenin Blanc, and blends of these grapes. Do you still want semisweetness or sweetness, but stylishly formulated? Try kosher white Zinfandel. Looking for something for a supersnack? Pick up a late-harvest Riesling or Muscat.

Contrary to a popular impression, it isn't the grape or a rabbi's blessing that makes wine kosher. It's the enological process. A wine is kosher if it is made in accordance with Jewish dietary laws. First, the equipment must be used exclusively for kosher products or be sanitized properly before the button is pushed. Second, the grapes and wine can be handled only by Sabbath-observant Jews, from the crushing of the grapes until the sealing of the bottle; in this period, the product can be handled by non-Jews if the grape juice (called "must") or finished wine has been flash-pasteurized—that is, been made *mevushal*. (The jury is out on whether that process improves or impairs the wine.) Third, only natural materials are permitted: kosher yeast strains have been especially developed for fermentation; gelatin, sometimes used for clarifying nonkosher wine in barrels and tanks, must be replaced with a kosher alternative, such as egg whites.

Most kosher wines are also kosher for Passover, and notations authorizing Pesach use routinely appear on the front or back labels on bottles. The New York–based Union of Orthodox Jewish Congregations of America, whose kashruth-certification program is widely considered the most influential in this country, conveys this message by putting the letter P (for Passover) next to its symbol, a circled U. Extra rules govern the making of wine for Pesach. "Grain-based yeast cannot be used to ferment wines intended for Passover use," says Rabbi Yosef Eisen, a Union spokesman. "Nor can corn-based sweeteners be used."

The kosher wine revolution in America can be traced to the early 1970s, when the Royal Wine Corporation, known informally as Kedem, began importing dry French kosher wines. The first shipment, 1,000 cases, sold out in a week, but it took a number of years to develop broad distribution. Interest was heightened by the successes of Hagafen ("the vine" in Hebrew) Cellars, a winery established in the Napa Valley in 1979 by Ernie Weir, a graduate of the University of California at Davis's viticulture program. Today, the boutique produces nearly 10,000 cases of kosher wine a year. Then California-style wine originating in the Golan Heights began turning up in American stores, and the New Taste clicked into high gear. It has been fed partly by delicious wines carrying the Gan Eden (Garden of Eden) label made in the Green Valley of Sonoma County. The feisty owner, Craig Winchell, describes his product bluntly: "My Cabernets tend to be quite full flavored and robust. They are not for the meek." His winery was founded in 1985 and now makes on average 15,000 cases a year.

Today's market for made-in-America premium kosher wines is dominated by Brooklyn-based Royal Wine; it owns the California-based Baron Herzog and Weinstock labels, which have won numerous awards for excellence. But Royal, which is privately held by a New York Orthodox family, also covers other bases: it owns and aggressively pushes the Kedem label, which specializes in well-made traditionally sweet and semi-sweet wines that are typically sold at low prices. The Golan Heights Winery's formidable Yarden label denotes wines that are very tasty, age well and are therefore collectible and in international demand. The best reds are Cabernet Sauvignon and Merlot; the best whites are Chardonnay and Sauvignon Blanc. The Yarden brut and blanc de blancs sparkling wines can be excellent. The winery also produces pleasing wines under the Golan and Gamla labels that typically can be drunk early.

These wines share store shelves with other Israeli reds and whites that carry the Carmel label, made by the world's oldest kosher winery, founded in 1882. Carmel traces its origin to Baron Edmond de Rothschild's support of Jewish settlement in Palestine in the late 1800s. He sent the first batch of French rootstock and vines, which were planted in 1882 at Rishon le-Zion, nine miles south of Tel Aviv. Wine cellars were built at Rishon le-Zion and later at Zichron Yaakov, twelve miles south of Haifa. In 1896, the early Carmel wines, red and white, sweet and dry, were presented at an international industrial and cultural exposition in Berlin. (No prizes were given at the event.) A decade later, the vineyards and both wineries were deeded over to the growers, who formed the Société Cooperative Vigneronne des Grandes Caves.

Carmel's sweet wines had long been a byword in America, but a combination of years of poor quality and sudden competition posed by the Golan Heights Winery forced the firm to rethink every facet of its business and to spend millions of dollars on modernization. The result has been considerably improved premium wines, vintage dated like the Golan Heights Winery's bottlings, and sold at different prices. Those designated "Private Collection" are top of the line; the "Vineyard" grouping is second rank, and "Valley," third rank.

As for today's kosher French connection, an array of whites (Alsace, Chablis, Mâcon, Muscadet, Sancerre, Vouvray) and reds (Beaujolais, Bordeaux, Chinon, Côtes-du-Rhone, Minervois, Pomerol, Provence) are available. But they are uneven and must be carefully chosen, ideally with help from a knowledgeable salesperson. The same is true of a small range of Italian kosher selections, also reds and whites. For now, when in doubt, buy American or Israeli.

Howard G. Goldberg is a staff editor and writes about wine for *The New York Times*.

guide to bylines

AB	Andree Brooks
MB	Marian Burros
CC	Craig Claiborne
FF	Florence Fabricant
GF	Gail Forman
AH	Amanda Hesser
JH	Jean Hewitt
MH	Moira Hodgson
MS	Mimi Sheraton
BK	Barbara Kafka
DK	Dena Kleiman
EL	Elaine Louie
HN	Helen Nash
JN	Joan Nathan
MO	Molly O'Neill
LS	Lorna Sass
RS	Raymond Sokolov

sources

Angel, Gilda. *Sephardic Holiday Cooking: Recipes and Traditions*. Mount Vernon, NY: Decalogue Books, 1996.

Brooklyn Lubavitch Women's Cookbook Organization. *Spice and Spirit: The Complete Kosher Jewish Cookbook*, 1961.

Claiborne, Craig. *Craig Claiborne's Favorites from The New York Times*. Raleigh, NC: Quadrangle Books, 1975.

Claiborne, Craig. *The New York Times Cookbook*. New York: Harper & Row, 1990.

Claiborne, Craig. *The New New York Times Cookbook*. New York: Times Books, 1995.

Field, Carol. *Celebrating Italy*. New York: William Morrow and Company, 1990.

Frucht, Phyllis, ed. *The Kosher Gourmet*. Ladies Auxiliary of Temple Beth Israel, Maplewood, NJ, 1972.

Goldstein, Joyce. *Back to Square One*. New York: William Morrow and Company, 1992.

Goodman, Hanna. *Jewish Cooking Around the World*. Philadelphia: Jewish Publication Society, 1973.

Heatter, Maida. *Maida Heatter's Book of Great Chocolate Desserts*. New York: Random House, 1995.

Hewitt, Jean. *The New York Times Heritage Cookbook*. New York: G. P. Putnam's Sons, 1972.

Hewitt, Jean. *The New York Times Large Type Cookbook*. New York: Golden Press, 1968.

Iny, Daisy. *The Best of Baghdad Cooking*. New York: Saturday Review Press/E. P. Dutton, 1976.

Joyes, Claire. *Monet's Table: The Cooking Journals of Claude Monet*. New York: Simon & Schuster, 1990.

Kafka, Barbara. *The Microwave Gourmet*. New York: William Morrow and Company, 1987.

Kafka, Barbara. *Soup, A Way of Life*. New York: Artisan Books, 1998.

Levy, Faye. *The Low-Fat Jewish Cookbook*. New York: Clarkson N. Potter, 1997.

Machlin, Edda Servi. *The Classic Cuisine of the Italian Jews*. Croton, NY: Giro Press, 1992.

Meyer, Danny, and Michael Romano. *The Union Square Cafe Cookbook*, New York: Harper-Collins, 1994.

Nash, Helen. *Helen Nash's Kosher Kitchen*. New York: Random House, 1996.

Nathan, Joan. *Jewish Cooking in America*. New York: Alfred A. Knopf, 1994.

Nathan, Joan. *The Jewish Holiday Cookbook*. New York: Schocken Books, 1988.

O'Neill, Molly. *A Well-Seasoned Appetite*. New York: Penguin Books, 1995.

O'Neill, Molly. *The New York Cookbook*. New York: Workman Publishing Company, 1992.

O'Neill, Molly. *The Pleasure of Your Company*. New York: Viking, 1997.

Puck, Wolfgang. *Adventures in the Kitchen*. New York: Random House, 1991.

Roden, Claudia. *The Book of Jewish Food: An Odyssey from Samarkand to New York*. New York: Alfred A. Knopf, 1996.

Sheraton, Mimi. *From My Mother's Kitchen: Recipes and Reminiscences*. New York: HarperCollins, 1991.

Stavroulakis, Nicholas. *The Cookbook of the Jews of Greece*. Northvale, NJ: Jason Aronson, Inc., 1996.

Vongerichten, Jean-Georges and Mark Bittman. *Jean-Georges: Cooking at Home with a Four-Star Chef*. New York: Broadway Books, 1998.

Willinger, Faith. *Red, White & Greens*. New York: HarperCollins, 1996.

Yeshiva of Flatbush, Brooklyn, NY. *International Kosher Cookbook*, 1978.

PERMISSIONS AND ACKNOWLEDGMENTS

Special thanks to Marian Burros, Florence Fabricant, Moira Hodgson and Molly O'Neill for their many recipes from *The New York Times* that appear in this book.

My gratitude and appreciation to the following chefs, restaurateurs and cookbook writers for permission to reprint the following:

Andree Abramoff: Fish Dumplings in Turmeric Sauce (*Belehat Arouss*); Taglio Bianco Veal Roast; Artichokes, Sephardic Style; Café Crocodile's Orange-Almond Fig Cake.

Gilda Angel: Angel Family's Spinach Pudding (*Fritada de Espinaca*); Angel Family's Salmon in Rhubarb and Tomato Sauce; Angel Family's Leek Croquettes (*Keftes di Prasa*).

Larry Bain: Larry Bain's Grandmother's Haroseth.

Andre Balog: Chicken with Fresh Herbs and 40 Cloves of Garlic; Hungarian Hazelnut Torte with Hazelnut Icing.

Eva Capsouto: Sephardic-Style Macaroons.

Craig Claiborne: Salmon Pâté; Gravlax; Horseradish Sauce with Walnuts; Marion Siner Gordon's Beet and Horseradish Aspic; Quick Chicken Liver Pâté; Florence Aaron's Salmon and Egg Salad; Cabbage Salad with Ginger Dressing; Beef Broth; Cynthia Zeger's Carrot Soufflé Ring; Striped Bass with Sorrel; Chicken Sauté with Vinegar; Asparagus with Horseradish Sauce; Potato Pancakes (*Latkes*); Sweet Potato Salad; Macedoine of Fruit in Vermouth; Gingered Figs; Marion Siner Gordon's Coconut Cake with Apricot Glaze; Cynthia Zeger's Chocolate Cake.

Ivana Di Marco: Baked Bass.

Carol Field: Artichoke, Matzoh and Spinach Pie.

Joyce Goldstein: Pickled Salmon; Cornish Hens with Apricots, Tomatoes, Onions and Spices.

Hannah Goodman: Passover "Bagels"; Chocolate Nut Torte, reprinted by permission of the Jewish Publication Society.

Maida Heatter: Chocolate Walnut Torte.

Jean Hewitt: Gefilte Fish Soufflé; Passover Crispy Sticks; Chicken in Pomegranate-Walnut Sauce; Potato Kugel; Carrot Tsimmes; Spiced Prune Torte; Bessie Feffer's Seven-Layer Chocolate Cake.

Daisy Iny: Iraqi Sweet and Sour Lamb with Okra (*Bamia*).

Claire Joyes: Apple Meringue, reprinted by permission of Simon & Schuster.

Barbara Kafka: Microwave Gefilte Fish; Microwave Chicken Soup; Vegetarian Borscht.

Faye Levy: Low-Fat Potato Latke "Muffins."

Lubavitch Women's Cookbook Organization: Cyrel Deitsch's Sweet Potato and Carrot Tsimmes.

Edda Servi Machlin: Haroseth Edda; Red Snapper Jewish Style (*Triglie all'Ebraica*); King's Cake (*Torta del Re*).

Helen Nash: Roast Chicken with Dried and Fresh Mushrooms.

Joan Nathan: Nathan Family's Haroseth Balls; Sour Cream and Mushroom Dip; Herring Salad with Beets, Potatoes and Apples; Eggplant Salad; Polish Roast Chicken; Almond Pudding; Matzoh-Apple Schalet (*Charlotte aux Pommes*); Mississippi Praline Macaroons; Coconut-Almond Torte with Sabra Liqueur.

Molly O'Neill: Cecile Ratner's Russian Cabbage Soup; Teresa Thompson's Mushroom Consommé; Romaine and Walnut Salad; Roasted Vegetable Broth; Seared Striped Bass with Roasted Shallot and Garlic Puree and Caramelized Leeks; Lemon Roasted Chicken; Beet Crisps; Spinach with Garlic and Lemon; Prunes Poached in Red Wine; Malvina Kinard's Coffee Macaroon Crème.

Paul Prudhomme: Veal Roast with Mango Sauce.

Wolfgang Puck: Gefilte Fish; Moroccan Carrot Salad; Braised Moroccan-Style Lamb with Almonds, Prunes and Dried Apricots; Potato-Onion Latke.

Claudia Roden: Roden Family's Egyptian Haroseth; Peppers Stuffed with Cheese (*Pipiruchkas Reyenadas de Keso*); Turkish Eggplant Flan (*Almodrote de Berengena*); Spinach Fritada; Matzoh-Meat Pie; Orange Cake; Walnut Cake with Coffee Filling; Coconut Jam; Spanish Walnut Cake with Syrup (*Tishpishti*).

Michael Romano: Union Square Cafe's Matzoh Meal Polenta; Union Square Cafe's Roast Lemon-Pepper Duck with Honey Lemon Sauce; Union Square Cafe Sautéed Mushrooms.

Anne Rosenzweig: Haroseth; Butternut Squash Ratatouille.

Lenard Rubin: Southwestern Blackened and Braised Brisket of Beef; Southwestern Tsimmes Stuffed in Anaheim Chiles.

Doris Schechter: Chocolate Macaroons.

Mimi Sheraton: Essay, "Blessings of Food and Family"; Ashkenazic Haroseth; Kalechla (Mock Gefilte Fish); Chopped Mushrooms, Eggs and Onions (Vegetarian Chopped Liver); Knaidlach (Matzoh Balls); Cold Beet Borscht; Matzohs; Matzoh Brei;

Matzoh Meal Pancakes; Breast of Veal with Matzoh Ball Stuffing; Passover Honey Nut Candy (*Noant*).

Nicholas Stavroulakis: Albondigas, reprinted by permission of the publisher, Jason Aronson Inc., Northvale, NJ © 1996.

Pierre Troisgros: Red Snapper with Eggplant and Tomato.

Barbara Tropp: Pecan-Ginger Torte.

Charlie Trotter: Carrot Consommé; Lamb Shanks Braised in Red Wine.

Jean-Georges Vongerichten: Beet Tartare; Baked Salmon with Basil Oil.

Alice Waters: Grated Carrots with Parsley and Garlic.

Faith Willinger: Whole Roast Asparagus, reprinted by permission of HarperCollins Publishers.

Barry Wine: Gefilte Fish Beggar's Purses; Vegetable-Matzoh "Salad"; Stringed-Beef; Spicy Tomato Sauce for Brisket; Tsimmes Terrine.

Yeshiva of Flatbush: Lizzie Gubenko's Ingberlach.

INDEX